The First Scientist

The First Scientist

A Life of Roger Bacon

BRIAN CLEGG

CARROLL & GRAF PUBLISHERS
New York

Carroll & Graf Publishers
An imprint of Avalon Publishing Group, Inc.
161 William Street
NY 10038-2607
www.carrollandgraf.com

First published in the UK by Constable
an imprint of Constable & Robinson Ltd 2003

First Carroll & Graf edition 2003

ISBN 0-7867-1116-7

Printed and bound in the EU

For David Ball (1955–2001), another *magister*

Contents

Illustrations

Acknowledgements

Many thanks to all those who have helped me bring this book into its final form. Specifically to Peter Cox, my agent, for his help in clarifying my ideas and selling the concept; to Vasko Kohlmeyer for many detailed thoughts on approach; to Nick Robinson, Jan Chamier, Carol O'Brien, and Pete Duncan at Constable & Robinson for their enthusiasm; and to Lizzie Hutchins and particularly John Woodruff for making the copy-editing process a revelation.

Preface

The year 1992 should have been remembered as the 700th anniversary of the death of a man who changed the world. Yet the occasion passed without note. Few know of the remarkable achievements of someone who, more than any other, can be said to have invented science. When I told a friend I was writing a book about the thirteenth-century scientist Roger Bacon, he was surprised. 'Surely,' he said, 'Bacon lived in Elizabethan times?' This astonishingly original thinker has been obscured by the shadow of his unrelated and, in some ways, inferior namesake, Francis Bacon. It is telling that the otherwise authoritative volume of *The Oxford History of England* that deals with the thirteenth century – all 829 pages of it – makes only a single passing reference to Roger Bacon.[1] Since Stewart Easton's scholarly biography of Bacon,[2] which was written in 1952, no attempt has been made to put his life into perspective in a generally accessible work. This is a terrible injustice.

Bacon's individual inspirations are remarkable enough. When Christopher Columbus wrote to Ferdinand and Isabella of Castille to win their support for his voyages of exploration, he unknowingly used Bacon's work to promote his cause. Columbus thought he was quoting the French Cardinal Pierre d'Ailly, but the section of d'Ailly's book he found so impressive was lifted word for word from the writings of Roger Bacon. Armando Cortesão, the respected Portuguese historian of map-making, comments that Bacon's work was 'exceptionally significant'[3] in moving away from the stylized

maps of his time to ones that used a true map projection, the first
such in over a thousand years.

Equally influential was Bacon's awareness of the importance of
mathematics to science. Where his namesake, the Elizabethan
wunderkind Francis Bacon, had little enthusiasm for mathematics,
Roger Bacon knew that it was the mainstay of scientific thought,
commenting, 'He who is ignorant of mathematics cannot know the
other sciences and the things of this world.'[4] The mathematician
John Wallis, writing to his colleague Gottfried Wilhelm von Leibniz
towards the end of the seventeenth century, believed that in stressing
the crucial importance of mathematics to natural philosophy –
which was then becoming clear with the advances being made in
mathematical physics – Bacon was some 400 years ahead of his
time.[5]

Bacon was equally prescient on calendar reform. In David Ewing
Duncan's recent book on the calendar, Bacon is labelled 'a lone
genius proclaiming the truth about time'.[6] Bacon's efforts to revise
the calendar, which by his time was ten days out of synchronization with reality, were unsuccessful in his own lifetime, but in
1582 Pope Gregory XIII commissioned a reform which adopted
the measures Bacon had suggested. Great Britain and its colonies,
America included, continued adrift in time until 1752.

John Dee, royal astrologer to Queen Elizabeth I, considered
Bacon an unparalleled authority on the calendar, calling him 'the
flower of whose worthy fame can never dye nor wither'.[7] Dee notes
that Paul of Middelburg, the scientist and bishop born in 1446 who
was to head a papal commission on calendar reform, made great
use of Bacon's work.

In optics, Bacon's writings were vital works of reference well into
the Renaissance. In 1614, for example, Professor Combach, a
philosopher at the University of Marburg, republished Bacon's
optical work, calling him a 'most eminent man'.[8] There is no doubt
that Bacon's optical theories would have been known to Newton,
Descartes, Huygens, and others who transformed the science of

light in the seventeenth century, even if they knew nothing of the man responsible for the work. Bacon's understanding and imagination enabled him to foresee and describe instruments such as telescopes and microscopes, as well as such flights of fantasy as horseless carriages and flying machines.

Yet despite all these remarkable contributions, and a host of smaller firsts, it was Bacon's development of the principle of experimental science that makes him so important. For thousands of years before Bacon, and as far ahead as Newton's time, it was normal practice to accept the word of authorities rather than to observe anew, frame hypotheses, and test them using scientific principles. But Bacon, like the modern scientists who followed him, rejected this 'natural philosophy'. He would not accept pure argument; everything should be subjected to experiment.

So why, given this wonderful portfolio of originality, is Bacon now overlooked or under-rated? Prime responsibility has to lie with twentieth-century historians of science and their distorted view of Bacon. Typical was Lynn Thorndike, who remarked in his *A History of Magic and Experimental Science* that, 'It has yet to be proved that [Bacon] made any definite original contribution to any specific science.'[9] Even Stewart Easton, who had a much more rounded view, refers to Bacon as an 'armchair scientist'.[10] How could this frankly insulting image have developed?

From shortly after his death, the facts about Bacon were covered in layer after layer of myth and confusion. Although his work was known and widely used, the man himself disappeared, to be replaced by a fantasy figure. This fictional Bacon was considered a conjuror and a charlatan — a great irony, considering the effort he had put into exposing the fraudulent basis of medieval magic. So strong was this image, though, that the translator of one of his works, writing in 1659, had to excuse his subject, saying that Bacon's name might prove an inconvenience, but once his actual words were understood, the reader would have a new perspective.[11]

Over time, as more and more of Bacon's books were translated from the original Latin, his importance began to be re-evaluated. In the Victorian age, when the wonders of science and technology were being extolled around the world, Bacon was hailed as a scientific prophet, a nineteenth-century man calling out from the Middle Ages. But this image was not to last for long. Twentieth-century scholars would not allow Bacon to be represented as a visionary ahead of his time. They had a point – Bacon was medieval through – and through. But in their enthusiasm to counter Victorian ideas, later historians also denied that Bacon had made any real contribution to science. Such was the fervour to disassociate from the values of the previous century that no one noticed the baby being thrown out with the bathwater.

In this book I intend to put Roger Bacon in his proper place. Not only was he one of the first to develop the concept of science itself, but also he showed how important an understanding of science is for everyone. If Bacon was an armchair scientist, it was in the same sense that Einstein, who hardly ever undertook an experiment in his whole life, was an armchair scientist. When the 800th anniversary of Bacon's birth comes around in 2020, the response should not be the half-hearted recognition of a few academics, but something more – much more. It's time for Roger Bacon to receive the true esteem he deserves as one of the fathers of the modern scientific world.

I

Dust Motes

In this way might a child appear a giant, and a man a
mountain . . . So also we might cause the Sun, Moon and
stars in appearance to descend here below . . .

Roger Bacon, *Opus majus*

In the early summer of 1292, in the Franciscan friary at Oxford,
an old man lay dying. His eyes searched the wall for the splash of
light that often fell from the thin slit window of his monastic cell.
There was nothing now, just the dark stonework. That morning he
had waited patiently for some light. Now it was only an hour before
the shadow of Oxford Castle, just up the hill from the friary, would
block the sun for the rest of the day. The waiting didn't bother
him. Waiting had become a natural part of life in the long years
he had spent locked away in a prison cell. But he was disappointed
not to have had the small comfort of a little light.

The old man stretched his fingers, miraculously free from rheu-
matics, so that even that year he had been able to write another
book, his last ever. It had been slow work. He was, after all, seventy-
two years old, twice the age the average peasant could expect to
reach – but then he was no average peasant. The sluggish responses
of his body were so frustrating for a mind that used to outrace the
wind. He thought back to his most glorious year, 1267, when he

had poured out a million words, scratched onto parchment with a quill pen. Yet even then, at his peak, his hands could never keep pace with the turmoil of ideas in his mind. For a few moments he slipped back to the days when he blazed with the fire of certainty, knowing that the pope himself was waiting for his message.

The rustling of a robe brought him back to the present. No one entered the cell, but he was conscious of a presence outside the door. He shouted as best he could, 'I repent of having given myself so much trouble to destroy ignorance!'

There was no response. And then, like the Holy Spirit made visible, came the light, cutting across the narrow cell and trans-figuring the dancing dust motes before striking the wall – the same sight that had once delighted him in the barn of his childhood home. He smiled, realizing that he had fooled no one, especially not himself, in his repentance. Closing his eyes, he began to pray, composing himself for the end.

◄o►

We can only surmise the exact details of the last days of Roger Bacon. All that is recorded is that he died at the friary in Oxford, probably in June 1292, and that one of his fellow friars is said to have heard those final words of repentance.[12] But it is hard to believe that he did not think back to his early years, to the Bacon home-stead on the outskirts of Ilchester in the county of Somerset.

From the few references Bacon makes to his family it would seem that they were prosperous, in all likelihood the local squires. We can speculate that their home would have been grand in compar-ison with anything nearby, but they were more gentleman farmers than aristocrats. Of all the buildings on a country estate like theirs, the great barn was most likely to have stuck in Roger's memory, to re-emerge many years later in his fevered daydreaming. If it were typical of its kind it would be stone-built and facing onto a cobbled courtyard like the house itself. The barn would have been a natural sanctum for a boy. The building was tall and dark, with narrow slits for windows. On a sunny day, great streamers of light would thread through the barn as if the very forces that held creation together were being made visible. It may have been in the barn's dim vastness that the young Roger fell in love with light's glory, developing a fascination with nature that would stay with him throughout his long lifetime. As he would later write, 'Light and colour have a special beauty beyond the other things that are brought to our senses.'[13]

–◄o►–

In reality, though, we don't even know for certain the year in which Bacon was born. Most encyclopedias give it as 1214, but this is no more than a guess, based on surprisingly scant information. There is a single reference that is used to pin down the date of his birth, and that is sufficiently vague to have several possible interpretations. In the *Opus tertium*, the third of his masterly summaries of science written for the pope, he noted:

> I have laboured diligently in sciences and languages, and forty years have passed since I first learned the alphabet. I have always been studious and for all but two of those forty years I have been in study.[14]

As we shall see, there is good evidence that the *Opus tertium* was written in 1267. Going back forty years from then takes us to 1227. But here comes a big leap of faith. If his time 'in study' (in the original Latin, *in studio*) starts with the date at which he went up to university, then it's reasonable to infer that in 1227 Bacon was thirteen years old. This was the typical age of matriculation at Oxford or Paris, hence the magic figure of 1214 for his birth – and that's as good as the factual link gets. But even if Bacon did matriculate at thirteen (the age wasn't mandatory), there is still some degree of doubt about what he really meant.

If Bacon was being literal about learning the alphabet, it may well have been his primary education that began forty years earlier. Perhaps, then, he was only seven in 1227, bringing forward his birth date to 1220.

Alternatively he could have been born *before* 1214. It depends on just what he meant by being 'in study'. Would this include the ten years when he may have been confined in a Paris convent for his dangerous ideas? If he had ignored this period in his comment, then we need to work back fifty years from 1267 to when Bacon began his education. If this were true, then instead of 1220 he might have been born as early as 1210.

Looking back at Bacon's words, it seems unlikely he would say 'forty years have passed since I first learned the alphabet' if this forty-year span had a ten-year gap in the middle of it. It seems more reasonable that 1227 was the key date, so what needs to be decided is whether this was when he started his primary education or when he went up to university. Which of these you prefer depends on whether you think Bacon was speaking figuratively (not an unusual thing for Bacon to do) when he refers to first learning the alphabet or being literal about getting to grips with his ABC. My own preference is for the literal approach. There is no real reason for Bacon to be obscure here, so let's make him a child of 1220.

—◇—

When he was growing up, Roger's world – the Bacon homestead, the well-tilled fields and the nearby town of Ilchester – was thriving in the economic stability of the 1220s. Yet the boy's first few years had brought him close to the turmoil of civil war and the all too real possibility of calamity.

When Roger was born, England was experiencing the aftermath of King John's reign. John Lackland he was called, because he was his father's fourth child and expected to inherit no land. Although he finally got his hands on the crown, John never rid himself of the image of powerlessness that went with his nickname. He was fated to be best remembered in folk tales as the king's evil younger brother whose scheming made life hard for Robin Hood while Richard the Lionheart was off bravely fighting in the Third Crusade. The truth of the matter is that John was too inept to succeed in getting up to mischief in Richard's absence. It's true that he did try to stir things up, but he was outmanoeuvred by the administrators Richard had left in charge. Until Richard died, on 6 April 1199, injured in a skirmish with the French king's troops, John could never escape from his brother's shadow.

Roger Bacon's family, staunch supporters of the monarchy that they were, must have waited in trepidation for John's first actions after he was crowned a month later at Westminster Abbey. His track record was anything but encouraging. The Bacons were right to be concerned – it took John just five years to lose Normandy, the last of the English possessions across the Channel, to the French king, Philip II. In his repeated attempts to win it back, John succeeded only in running through his available cash with alarming speed. This meant more taxes for families such as the Bacons to pay for a war they had no interest in being pursued.

Like most of the ruling class, the Bacons were of Norman stock. By now, 150 years after the conquest, they had acclimatized to life in England and no longer thought of themselves as incomers – they had even taken an Anglo-Saxon surname. 'Bacon' may have come from the Saxon *baccen*, meaning 'beech tree' (the use of 'bacon' to mean a type of pork came later). Alternatively it could have been derived from the Germanic personal name Bacco, implying a fighter. It was the second or third generation of invaders that had quietly adopted this local name to emphasize how much they belonged. The Bacons' hearts no longer lay across the English Channel, in the fertile fields of Normandy.

True, Roger had still been given a good Norman Christian name, a French variant of the noble Danish name Hrothgar, but it was a

popular name among the incomers, and it had already been angli-
cized, the soft French 'g' replaced by the unforgiving, Anglo-Saxon
pronunciation that almost made the first syllable rhyme with 'dog'.
But that was as much of the past as the Bacons wanted to cling to.
A stable England was more important to them than regaining an
old homeland that was beginning to seem very distant.

Frustrated by his continental failures, King John found himself
what he reckoned to be an easier target, and contested the pope's
choice for Archbishop of Canterbury, Stephen Langton. But yet
again he had misjudged. Pope Innocent III excommunicated John
in 1209 and followed this up by encouraging Philip of France to
launch an invasion. Unable to stand up to the combined might of
Rome and Paris, John had to give in, not only submitting to the
pope's choice of archbishop but actually surrendering England to
Rome. While the transfer of power was symbolic – John immediately received it back as a fiefdom – the message was plain. Like
most of the king's mistakes, this one was expensive for his subjects,
whose taxes were raised yet again to cover the annual tribute the
pope now levied. They were paying rent on their own country.

By 1215, the hierarchy of England had suffered enough of John's
ruinous political incompetence. The barons, a heavyweight aris-
tocracy largely descended from the invading Norman chieftains,
revolted, capturing London in May. A month later, on the banks
of the Thames at Runnymede, John gave way to all-round pressure
to ratify a charter that clarified the rights to be granted in compen-
sation for the barons' submission to their king. This great charter,
or Magna Carta, was to become the forerunner of all modern
constitutions. At first, however, the king showed little sign of
changing his ways, so the barons held on to London and invited
Louis, the French dauphin, to invade England. By the time John
died, in 1216, Louis and the barons held much of the south-east.
The country was under siege from a foreign power. There was every
chance that once again it would fall to an invasion from across the
Channel.

These were the unsettled times into which Roger Bacon was born. Yet, though the threat from the barons' revolt was real, once John was out of the way it didn't take long to untangle the mess he had left behind. The new king, Henry III, was only nine years old, but he had a very skilful regent council in the respected Earl Marshall William, the papal legate Nicholas, and the Bishop of Winchester, Peter des Roches. This triumvirate soon made sure that the wind was taken out of the rebels' sails by wholeheartedly supporting an updated version of the Magna Carta. By the end of 1217, Louis was gone and the country was settling down to stability.

For the middle ranks in the areas of the countryside that had not been overrun by the French, life was better than it had been for a long time. The economy was growing, fuelled by increasingly effective farming. To the well-off, the Bacons included, food was becoming less a simple means of staving off hunger, and more a source of pleasure as oil, wine, and spices began to arrive from overseas. For the first time in many years, life expectancy was on the increase. On average, in John's reign a man could hope to live until he was thirty-five, while a woman, with the extra risk of death in childbirth, had an average life expectancy of just thirty-one years.[15] The Bacons could expect perhaps twenty years more, and Roger himself would live into his seventies.

Altogether, things were looking good. Even the runaway inflation that the country was suffering proved a boon for the Bacon household. There is something that sounds remarkably modern about inflation. But as long as there has been currency, there has been the possibility that prices will rise and the value of the coins in your hand will drop. King John's heavy taxation wouldn't have helped, but the thirteenth-century inflation was also fuelled by demand from the Continent for the superb wool from the English sheep flocks. The more popular the wool and other English products, the easier it was for merchants to lever up the prices.

Inflation was good news for the mint near the Bacons' home at

Ilchester. As cash was worth less, more of it was needed to pay for everyday purchases. The production of coins went into overdrive: during King John's reign the amount of currency in circulation had more than doubled, to around £300,000.[16]

This was also good news for the Bacons. Rising prices were driving up the cash value of agricultural products, and landowners were doing very nicely for themselves. Traditionally, the landed gentry had rented their fields to tenants, but in such times of inflation the income from rent could not keep up with the decreasing value of the currency, while the price of crops stayed well ahead. So the Bacon family would have taken every opportunity to pull their land into 'demesne' – repossessing it and working it directly for the benefit of their own household.

The changes that were sweeping the countryside also led to the expansion of nearby Ilchester. The town had its roots in the Roman fort of Lindinis, and by the time of the Domesday Book in 1086 it had become Givelcestre, 'the fort on the river Givel', after the medieval name of the River Yeo. Already by Roger's day the 'G' had been dropped, and in the broad local accent the name sounded like 'eel-chester'. The town had become a bustling centre of commerce as shops and market stalls sprang up to cope with the excess produce of landowners such as the Bacons. The town was nicely located for trade – it lay near the border with Dorset and almost bridging the two counties. When the Warwickshire historian John Rous was writing about Bacon in the mid-1400s – the first reference we have to Roger's place of birth – he made the mistake of saying that Bacon was born at 'Ilchester in Dorset'.[17]

There is no direct evidence to back up Rous's claim that this is where Bacon was born. It is quite possible that Ilchester and Bisley in Gloucestershire, which has also laid claim to Bacon, both wanted to be his birthplace in the same way that medieval monasteries exploited the relics they owned, and on occasion even raiding other religious sites to increase their share of attractions. The financial draw of tourism is nothing new. Relics and rumour of the famous, especially anyone with a mystical reputation, drew in pilgrims and medieval tourists and their spending power.

In addition, the monasteries were not above fakery. All the evidence is, for example, that the supposed burial of King Arthur and Guinevere in the chancel of Glastonbury Abbey, where their 'grave' can still be seen today, was just such a medieval piece of fabricated tourist bait. It worked – Glastonbury's George and Pilgrim Inn stands proudly today much as it did in 1490, when Abbot Selwood presented it to the chamberlain of the abbey to accommodate the busy trade in pilgrims who flocked into the town. Could it have been that Ilchester and Bisley had a similar agenda?

As we have seen, Ilchester was a significant town, which in Bacon's time had its own mint that went on coining money until 1248. Bisley was (and is) much smaller. It certainly existed in Bacon's time, being listed, as was Ilchester, in the Domesday Book, but it has always been a quiet backwater. Of the two, Ilchester was the more likely to bend history for its own ends, having more to gain from attracting passing trade. Yet it was also more likely to have been home to a family as rich as the Bacons without preserving any reminders of their existence in the form of monuments or documents. In a place the size of Bisley the Bacon family would have been much more memorable. On balance, Ilchester seems the more likely of the two.

The town would have seemed an exotic and exciting place to the young Roger but, if his upbringing was typical of the time, the centre of his early life would have remained the Bacon homestead. As the family's wealth increased, they ploughed it into their home and their business. The main house and the principal barn were probably built of stone, with traditional single-level living quarters dominated by a great hall, an open space to rival the barn, with a single aisle of stone arches down one side. It would have been a dim and draughty place as window glass was the privilege of the very rich, but, with a roaring fire in the evening and tables for the Bacons' workers to gather round, it would have been warm and welcoming.

We can imagine that, until he was thirteen, Roger would have spent most of his time around the courtyard and roaming the estate, largely unsupervised. When he wasn't left to his own devices, he would have been given some basic tutoring, perhaps by the local priest, in reading, simple arithmetic and the essentials of Latin. This was for practical reasons. Roger was not the eldest son, so the inheritance from the family would never be his. The natural assumption would be that he would take up arms in the service of one of the barons, or possibly enter the priesthood – priests were in considerable demand at this time, as new churches were springing up across the land. Ideally, at least if he became a man-at-arms, he would wed a rich widow or a girl with a good dowry to give him a solid financial basis. A hundred years before, this would have been quite likely for a priest too, but Rome's new insistence that clerics stayed unmarried had finally won over the most reactionary of English parishes.

For landholders such as Bacon's father, the idea of Roger moving away from the countryside and becoming a full-time scholar would have been unthinkable. The land was such an integral part of life that to abandon it for some abstract concept of learning would simply not have been an option. When the sixteenth-century writer of *The Famous Historie of Fryer Bacon*, a collection of folk tales about Bacon, was describing how his life in the university began, he imagined that Roger would have met with stiff resistance from his father:

'Boy,' [his father] said, 'you are not going to be a priest. There's no reason why you should be any more learned than me. You can already use the almanac to see when it's best to sow wheat and barley and peas and beans. I can teach you when and where to sell grain and cattle, as I've got every detail of the fairs and markets fixed in my memory, just as Sir John, the priest, can say mass without reading it.

'Take this whip. I'm going to teach you how to use it, and it'll be much more profitable to you than wasting your time with Latin.'

Before Roger could reply, his father silenced him. 'Follow my counsel or by the mass you'll feel my hand in anger.'[18]

(The original, rather quirky language of *The Famous Historie* has been rendered into modern English here and in other quotations in this book – a sample of the original text is in Appendix I.) In the story Roger soon escaped and ran away, first to a convent (at the time, the term applied as much to a monastery or friary as a nunnery) and from there to university. It's easy to understand why the writer of *The Famous Historie* thought this might have happened – it would have been a real enough possibility for many families and in fact bears an uncanny resemblance to the real story of Isaac Newton, born in 1642, some fifty years after the *Historie* was written. Although Newton didn't run away, he was pressed by his mother to abandon his hopes for an academic future and to take over the farm. In part, he engineered his escape by repeatedly neglecting the duties he was given. Even when he did escape, his mother tried to keep Newton at home by underfunding him, forcing him to work his way through his early years at Cambridge.

Luckily for Roger, though, his was no archetypal country squire's family for whom the most intellectual challenge was deciding which beast to hunt next. Roger's father had a high regard for learning – we know that at least two of his sons became academics[19] and that Bacon senior was prepared to support them financially, and also that his parents were more than happy to encourage Roger in his pursuit of education.

At that time, local schools were springing up around the country to cope with the rising demand for clergymen, lawyers, and administrators, but there was only one seat of learning in the whole of England that had a truly international reputation – the University of Oxford. When Roger reached the age of thirteen it was decided to send him away to get the best education money could buy.

Money would certainly have come into it. Entrance to the university was decided not by examination, but by the ability to pay for board, food, and tuition. So, often it was more the boy's parents who decided on his career than the boy himself. This is obvious from a sample letter included in a formulary, a guide to writing letters and legal documents produced around the time Bacon was at Oxford.[20] It contains a model note from a mother to her son at the Oxford schools, telling him that he is studying there because *she* has dedicated him to God from birth. Yet Bacon's love of scholarship ran so deep that it seems likely he went to Oxford, not because of his parents' wishes but of his own volition.

If Bacon was born in 1220, he is likely to have gone up to Oxford around 1233. Unlike his fictional alter ego in *The Famous Historie*, Roger could travel to Oxford without having to run away or enter a convent. He was acting with his father's blessing. Even so, his life was about to be turned upside-down in the first of a series of upheavals that would bring him inexorably towards the invention of science. At the age of thirteen he was moving from a quiet country home to a rowdy environment in which learning and death went side by side. Roger Bacon had ceased to be a child. Now he was a scholar.

2

Scholar!

> To neglect knowledge is to neglect virtue; the intellect
> lightened by the flame of goodness cannot help but love it.
> Love is only born of knowledge. Reason is the guide of a
> right will. It is reason which leads us to salvation.
>
> Roger Bacon, *Opus tertium*

Roger Bacon's transformation into a scholar began neither with logic nor with rhetoric, but with a haircut. Although the university was open to any young man who had the money to pay, there was one unbreakable entry requirement: students had to take on minor orders in the Church. This made them a formal part of the ecclesiastical hierarchy, not ordained priests or deacons but nonetheless subject to Church law, and they would require a tonsure. This artificial bald spot, said to have its origins in the Roman custom of shaving the heads of slaves, demonstrated that the wearer was a slave to Christ.

Once in Oxford, the regular maintenance of his tonsure would be down to professionals. One of the first new businesses to open after the university was established had been a barber's shop to cope with the new influx of heads to be shaved.[21] Back home, Roger would have had a first, worrying encounter with his father's razor. Only when Roger had received his crown of uncomfortably bare skin was he ready to set off on his journey into a strange new world.

For Roger, just getting to Oxford would have been a major adventure. He would certainly have been nervous at the prospect. For all its commercial activity, Ilchester was still only a small town in a minor county, and though Roger came from a wealthy family he would still have been an inexperienced country lad. But everything we know about him reveals the iron determination that drove him to achieve.

The trip, by horse-drawn cart along rutted roads, would have taken several days. In all, Roger's journey covered more than 150 kilometres. Although we can't be certain about his route, one of the few major roads from the West Country would have taken him past the ruins of Stonehenge. The great stones, already in place for over 3,000 years, had been partly dismantled by the Romans and looked much as they do today. Writing eighty years before, Geoffrey of Monmouth had told of this 'dance of the giants' being uprooted from a mountain called Killaraus in Ireland and shipped across the sea by none other than Merlin himself.[22] In later years Roger would come to regard magic as pure fraud, but the thirteen-year-old may well have stared at these mystical stones in wonder.

After crossing Salisbury Plain, there would still have been a good half of the journey to go. From Andover the most likely route to have suitably spaced towns for stopovers would have taken them northwards, up to Newbury to ford the River Kennet, and then on across the green fields to Abingdon, crossing the narrow bridge over the River Ock. Now, at last, Oxford would have come into view. For the first time, Roger Bacon could see the town that would be his home for the next fifteen years.

As the cart rattled through the high gate in the town walls, it may have struck Roger that Oxford was very like Ilchester, only on a more generous scale. Instead of one market there were four, with stalls running down broad streets of packed earth to form a great cross of commerce. From the south gate, the cart and its passengers passed straight into the first of these bustling alleys of trade,

Fish Street (now St Aldate's), while ahead lay Great Bailey (Queen Street), Northgate Street (Cornmarket Street), and the High Street.

Stalls were arranged according to their wares, following a custom backed by royal charter. First came the sellers of firewood, then the fishmongers and the tanners, their stalls piled with leather from tiny offcuts to whole hides. Up by the north gate were the storage bins of the corn merchants, and off in the side-arms of the cross were the sellers of gloves and bread and dairy produce, the potters and the wood merchants, the butchers and the straw-sellers. Many of the houses and shops fronting onto the market had smart stone facings, but down the narrow side streets were low wattle and daub houses tightly crammed together. Above it all the church towers rose, while over to the west side of the town the heavy fortifications of the castle merged into the town walls.

Around him, Roger was faced with the mélange of the urban and the rural that made up medieval town life. Any open spaces were turned into vegetable gardens or housed animals. Pigs rooted in the roadside earth. The homely smells of the animals mixed with unfamiliar industrial stinks to form a pungent cocktail of odours. Work best kept well away from human noses, such as skinning and tanning, wasn't moved outside the Oxford town walls until the mid-1300s.[23]

When the cart finally stopped it was in front of one of the ordinary houses of the town. If Roger had expected to see grand university buildings, a sort of educational monastery, he would have been disappointed. The clusters of halls and colleges that would form the heart of both Oxford and Cambridge were still a hundred years away. It wasn't possible to *see* the university at all, because it wasn't a place – it had no physical presence other than the students and staff. Students lived in lodging houses, renting rooms from townsfolk. Newcomers such as Roger would usually share, two or three to a room, to keep down costs and to have some companionship in this strange new home (a situation not uncommon in the present day). Lectures took place in larger rented rooms around the town, where the hard benches and simple desks of the students were arranged in serried ranks before the master's dais.

Oxford's academic origins were surprisingly humble. No royal charter or papal decree started the ball rolling – instead, it was all begun by the simple commercial decision of a travelling schoolmaster. In 1095, Theobald of Étampes decided to settle in Oxford. He was to teach there for around thirty years. Never before had there been such a need for educated young men. Parish churches, monasteries, and convents were all spreading fast and needing literate staff. The ecclesiastics had to compete for employees with business, the law, and government, in which sectors there was a burgeoning requirement for administrators and legislators with a broad enough education to cope with the new structures of post-Domesday England.

To begin with, tuition at Oxford was very basic. The curriculum was little more than the three Rs and a straightforward introduction to Latin. Anyone requiring further education still had to travel to the Continent, to centres of learning such as Paris or Bologna, which had already been turning out literate alumni for a century. Now, inevitably, there was pressure to establish an English centre of higher learning, one that could be reached without having to make the hazardous journey across the Channel and across Europe.

Oxford was not the most obvious choice. There were many cathedral cities with well-established schools that could have formed the nucleus of a first-rate university, and for many years Oxford showed no sign of its future glory. Although other teachers followed in Theobald's footsteps, and Oxford was home to an unusually large collection of convents and monasteries for its size, there was little to suggest that this medium-sized settlement would become a significant seat of learning. As late as 1180, Northampton, which had a larger body of students, was expected to become the natural academic centre of the country.[24]

What probably turned Oxford's chances around were the lessons learned during the spasmodic civil war between King Stephen and the Empress Matilda that lasted until the middle of the twelfth century. Oxford proved to be of outstanding strategic significance, centrally located and standing on that essential artery, the Thames. Its position in the transport network soon made it the ideal place to establish ecclesiastical courts, and where the law was practised it was logical that the law should be taught. Growth of the schools followed naturally.

By Roger Bacon's day, Oxford's early focus on law had broadened to cover a wider curriculum. Oxford had taken on Paris, the greatest university of them all, and was winning acclaim for its teaching in the liberal arts and theology – the twin jewels in the academic crown. Once again, it was a conflict that had given Oxford the chance to expand. From the mid-1190s to 1204 there was a near-constant state of war between England and France over possession of Normandy, and it became unwise for Englishmen to remain in Paris. In fact, many of the foreign scholars who were already studying there were expelled. However, now there was an obvious centre back home where students and masters could congregate – Oxford.

Yet just as the Oxford schools were beginning to develop a sense of identity, the whole structure collapsed. When King John's ill-considered attempts to stand up to the Church resulted in his excommunication in 1209, teachers who were also priests feared that John might launch reprisals against churchmen. At the same time, many foreign students began to leave, conscious that England could be plunged into war with Rome. But nothing much happened in the months following the excommunication, and the masters of the Oxford schools had an opportunity to restore attendances. Instead, a murder triggered an exodus.

Three Oxford students had been sharing a house. Although the students were supposed to maintain a chaste life they had not taken a vow of chastity, and one of them had a mistress. One cold night in December 1209, his amorous passions turned to something altogether darker, and after a heated argument he killed his mistress and fled, leaving the house and Oxford far behind. The girl was local, and news of her killing brought an angry mob onto the streets. The mayor and officers of Oxford panicked. They decided that action was needed quickly if they were to keep control of the town. They swept into the house, seized the other two students who lodged there, and dragged them away to be hanged in front of the mob.

The masters of the Oxford schools were appalled. It wasn't that they considered themselves above the law, rather that they expected to be left to themselves to handle a crime in which one of their students was implicated. Because every student at Oxford was a cleric in the minor orders, students should be subject to the law enforcement of the Church, not that of the town. In protest, seventy masters departed from Oxford with remarkable swiftness, taking hundreds of students with them. Many of the deserters moved to the newer, then much smaller group of schools in the quieter and presumably safer East Anglian town of Cambridge.

With England's future hanging in the balance, not too much consideration was given to settling Oxford's dispute. Only after the king had submitted to the pope in 1213 was there an opportunity to restore the town's schools. The papal legate, Cardinal Nicholas, was sent to England to sort out the details of John's submission. He restored order in Oxford, and in 1214 set in place the structures that effectively established the university. He gave the Oxford schools a chancellor and drew up a binding charter with the town, which henceforth had to keep its legal hands off the masters and scholars.

The penalties for the town were detailed and financially crippling. Rents on lodgings provided by townspeople for the students were slashed to half their previous values for the next ten years. The town was obliged to provide 52 shillings a year – the cost of building a couple of typical houses – in perpetuity for the support of poor scholars. It also had to give a dinner for 100 of the poorest scholars each St Nicholas Day (6 December), probably the anniversary of the hanging. Those who took part in the killing of the two students were forced to do penance at their graves, while the few masters who had stayed on in Oxford were suspended from teaching for three years. The schools were granted corporate rights in a charter that the town was forced to renew each year. Technically, though Oxford was not referred to as a university until 1231, Nicholas made it such in all but name.

◄○►

By the time Roger Bacon arrived, the university had more than recovered from the exodus in 1209. It now consisted of different schools and the houses of the religious orders that had sprung up in the town, with faculties of arts, theology, law, and medicine. Although the university was organizationally separate from the religious houses, there was a lot of interplay between the two, with lecturers from the orders working in all the faculties. There were still grammar schools under the same administration, though they were never a true part of the university and eventually became totally separate.

The Oxford masters, as they had demonstrated in their exodus, enjoyed an independence from authority that gave the town a different atmosphere from the sometimes oppressive if still dominant Paris. This independence of character enabled the university to rise swiftly, so that by the end of the century there were acknowledged to be three great universities in the western world: Paris, Oxford, and Cambridge.

For Roger, the Oxford of 1233 would have combined excitement and fear. Although the university was an ecclesiastical establishment, it had an exhilarating energy that can only be described as rumbustious. The behaviour of students, even then, was the cause of much concern to their elders. In 1231 the king made special provisions for his sheriff to help the university authorities deal with riotous students, and for the dungeons of Oxford Castle to house troublemakers who needed time to cool off.

Unlike the relatively peaceful Ilchester, Oxford was no place to be out at night on your own. Once the gates were closed and the curfew bell rang, it was asking for trouble to walk the streets. Attacks leading to death in the gutter were commonplace, either through criminal assault or becoming caught up in the large-scale brawls that regularly broke out between townsfolk and members of the university. In their dress the scholars would not have been any different from the youths of the town, but the characteristic tonsure made sure that they stood out in a crowd. There was also fierce rivalry between northern and southern student factions.

The magnitude of the disturbances is made plain by a 1274 request by the mayor and bailiffs of the town addressed to the crown:

> We write to inform your lordships that last Saturday the northerners of the University of Oxford on one side and the Irish with their accomplices on the other [the southerners were often called Irish, as the southern province of Britain included Ireland] made an armed affray, so that some are dead and some grievously wounded. The Irish side, being at length depleted by its losses, has been driven out of the town; the said northerners remain in the town and continue to bear arms, by reason of which we are in fear of more serious harm.[25]

When the Sheriff of Oxford intervened on the king's behalf it became obvious that this had been no minor scuffle. Fifty of the students were accused of murder.

Another vivid incident dates back to when Bacon was an MA at Oxford. In 1238, the new papal legate, Otto, was visiting the town and staying at Osney Abbey to the south-west. A party of students and masters went out to greet him, but the pleasant formality went very wrong when the master cook of the abbey threw a pot of boiling water over an unfortunate Irish student who was begging at the abbey door. One of the other students then drew his bow and shot the cook dead (even on a social occasion, appropriate weaponry was needed for protection). The welcoming party turned into a seething mob, and the legate had to be smuggled to safety further down the Thames at Wallingford. There was a drastic clampdown on university freedoms, only lifted several months later once the regent masters, the ruling lecturers at the university, had performed an act of penance, walking barefoot through the streets of London to the legate's residence. Bacon was probably not a regent master and so would not have taken part in this degrading display of subservience. As for the students, they soon resumed their wild behaviour.

It now seems almost inhumane that Bacon should be thrown into this drunken, violent society at the age of thirteen. The view that children and adolescents needed a different type of care would not emerge until the fifteenth century, which saw the formation of the college system in the university to provide protection and a substitute for the guiding hand of the family home. In Bacon's day no distinction was made between a thirteen-year-old boy and an adult. Roger was as free to make mistakes and learn lessons, whether salutary or fatal, as any young adult. He would have to learn, and learn quickly.

—◦—

After the initial shock of the rowdy atmosphere, Bacon probably soon came to love his new environment. Compared with his schooling back home, this was heady stuff indeed. The core of his studies was formed by the *trivium* of grammar, logic, and rhetoric. Here Roger got his first taste of philosophy, which would prove to be his driving interest for perhaps the next twenty years. Later in his studies he would encounter the early precursor of science courses in the separate *quadrivium* – arithmetic, geometry, astronomy, and music. For the next eight years Bacon would become immersed in the joys of academic study, a sponge soaking up all he could hear but not yet ready to venture his own opinions.

In those eight years Bacon surfaced, if he surfaced at all, just once – as a minor character in the tale of a troubled king. The contemporary chronicler Matthew Paris relates that a well-known Dominican preacher, Robert Bacon (no relation, as far as we are aware), told King Henry III, who was holding a council at Oxford in 1233, that there was no hope of peace while two of Henry's favourites, Peter des Roches, the Bishop of Winchester, and Peter des Rievaulx, continued to manipulate power. Paris takes up the story:

> Then a certain clerk who was present at the court, Roger Bacon by name, a man of mirthful speech, said with a pleasant yet pointed wit: 'My lord king, what is it that is most hurtful and fearful to those that sail across the sea?'
>
> 'Those know it,' the king replied, 'who have much experience of the waters.'
>
> 'My lord,' said the clerk, 'I will tell you: stones and rocks,' meaning thereby Pierre de Roches [sic].[26]

It would be satisfying to think that Bacon was responsible for this advice to his king. Yet Bacon would only have been an inexperienced thirteen-year-old in 1233, not yet a master of arts. (Even if we take 1214 as the year of his birth, he would still not have received his MA by then.) He had no particular standing, no reason why he should find himself in a social situation in which he could exchange witticisms with the king. It is not impossible that this was our Roger, but Paris could well have embroidered the story.

Bacon's stay at Oxford would certainly have kept him there until after 1239. His was nothing like the typical three-year course followed by present-day undergraduates – after all, this was not only his further education but his secondary schooling as well. He would have stayed a minimum of eight years and probably remained at the university for longer. But discovering exactly what happened to him after that time requires some careful detective work.

If Bacon's academic career were like that of most of his contemporaries, he would have spent six years studying to complete his baccalaureate (becoming a Bachelor of Arts) and another two to get his MA. We are now so accustomed to seeing cabalistic initials after names that we don't give their original meaning a second thought. The 'M' in MA stood for *magister* – a master who was licensed to teach in a university. Once he had become a master, which would be around 1241, Bacon had to decide on his next course of action.

There were two clear options. Of the university faculties of the time, two dominated: arts and theology – arts because it was the largest subject and the foundation on which others were built, and theology because it was the ultimate, most important topic of study. To teach in the arts faculty, Bacon would only have to get some experience in discussion and dispute. To teach in theology, however, he would need to study for eight more years before he could become a Master of Theology, and then a further eight years before he could receive his doctorate. There is no evidence from Bacon's writing that he ever took the theology course, nor is he listed as a doctor by any of the universities of the day. Teaching the arts would have brought immediate satisfaction; theology required a much longer period of study. Bacon was a young man who throughout his life preferred practical application to abstruse theory. It seems likely that he chose the first option.

Surprisingly, the best confirmation we have that Bacon really did become a master in the Faculty of Arts is his later attitude towards theology. His writing on the subject, while interesting, was old-fashioned for the period. If his first real career move had been into the Faculty of Theology he would have picked up much more of contemporary thirteenth-century thinking. Whether he agreed with these fashionable opinions or dismissed them, had he become part of the theological mainstream he would have had a much more detailed knowledge of the latest developments than shows through in his writing. It seems likely, then, that he remained a master of arts.

Once he was established in the Oxford Faculty of Arts, Bacon could have stayed there for the rest of his career, pursuing his prime interest of philosophy, subsequently disappearing into the ranks of obscure medieval philosophers and remembered, if at all, by a handful of specialists. But something happened to expose him to a whole new world. In the early 1240s, Bacon moved to the University of Paris.

━◦━

Paris was home to the greatest university of the time, a seat of learning that enjoyed the special protection of the papacy. As would soon be the case at Oxford, it flourished thanks to the ubiquity of Latin as the language of academic discourse. Latin made it possible to have a single melting-pot where scholars from across the Western world could exchange ideas in an exhilarating atmosphere.

For Bacon, the move to Paris was promotion to the very top of the academic ladder. The timing was no accident. All of a sudden, he found that his expertise on Aristotle, one of his favourite topics of study at Oxford, was a desirable commodity in Paris. Since before Bacon's birth, several of Aristotle's books, particularly those on natural philosophy, the *Libri naturales* and *Metaphysics*, had been banned in Paris because the authorities felt that the views of the great Greek philosopher were dangerously close to heresy.

It may seem odd that Aristotle, who until 1209 had been accepted as a philosopher whose ideas in many ways prefigured Christian thought, should have been banned. But the exclusion was part of a sweeping condemnation of the theories of two men preaching a theology that was thought to be pure heresy, Amaury of Bennes and David of Dinant. Though any connection of their ideas with Aristotle was tenuous, they claimed Aristotle as an authority, and that was enough to push the Paris authorities into the ban. This move caused much grumbling in Parisian academic circles. Many scholars argued that it was ridiculous to attempt to study and teach natural philosophy without reference to some of the most important texts on the subject.

To fob off the moaning academics, in 1231 Pope Gregory IX used the standard politician's delaying tactic to avoid making a decision – he appointed a commission to look into the problem. In theory, his commissioners, William of Auxerre, Stephen of Provins, and Simon of Authie, would work through the disputed books and produce a set of revised editions, bowdlerizing Aristotle to make his works safe for students' eyes. However, there is no evidence that anything was ever done, and Gregory's choice of commissioners makes it likely that this was his intention all along. In less than a year, two of the three commissioners had died – the pope had hardly chosen a young, dynamic team to bring Aristotle back to Paris. His was a cynically calculated ploy.

Meanwhile, rival universities were making the most of this chink that had appeared in the Parisian intellectual armour. The little-known University of Toulouse announced that it was well worth making the southward trip for its lectures on Aristotle's *Libri naturales*. The crafty Toulouse masters produced a flyer, the earliest known example of such advertising still in existence, which pointed out in large letters that the *Libri naturales* was a book 'which has been prohibited in Paris'.[27] Oxford, far less under the pope's thumb, covered the full spectrum of Aristotle's writing and also benefited from the censorship in Paris.

As so often happens with censorship, the result of banning these books was not so much to suppress them, but rather to make them seem more attractive, to make people go out of their way to find just why they were so dangerous. By the mid-1240s Aristotle was even creeping back onto the Paris curriculum. But after more than thirty years of exclusion, Paris had a dearth of masters with the appropriate knowledge to pass on Aristotle's wisdom. It was this lack of local experience that now made Bacon and his expertise so attractive to the university authorities – and gave him the opportunity of a new and, as it happened, unpleasant travel experience.

By now Bacon would have been accustomed to the journey between Oxford and Ilchester, but getting to Paris was an undertaking on an altogether different scale. Not only were there the dangers of a long journey on lonely roads, with thieves likely to swoop on unprotected travellers, but there was also the English Channel to face. Bacon had probably never even seen the sea before, let alone set out across it on a boat that must have seemed perilously fragile, sailing over unpredictable, cold grey waters. There were no dedicated ferries; Roger would have made the crossing on a merchant ship carrying those desirable English fleeces to continental buyers. On such ships the passengers perched on bales or leaned weakly over the side, helpless with seasickness.

Although Bacon was now in a different country, much about the University of Paris would have struck him as familiar – it had been the model on which Oxford was formed. The language was the same – Latin was not only the logical choice at Paris, but you could be fined for not using it – and the habits of the students were no different from those of their counterparts at Oxford. Bacon would even have associated largely with other Englishmen, for the Faculty of Arts at Paris was divided into four 'nations' – three French and one English – to help make the administration of this, the world's biggest student grouping, more manageable.

Even so, Paris itself was doubtless a revelation, for it was built on a scale that Bacon could scarcely have imagined. From his lodgings, perhaps on the Left Bank of the Seine, where the English nation was located, he would have seen the immense bulk of the Cathedral of Notre Dame, a brand-new monument to the art of man and the glory of God. By then it was almost finished: the towers and the facing of the great transepts were still under construction, covered in a mass of wooden scaffolding that looked like a spider's web from a distance, but the great nave and choir rose from the Île de la Cité like a huge natural stone outcrop. All around, the feverish turmoil of the city streets made even the bustle of Oxford seem restrained.

Despite its size, though, some aspects of Paris would have been a disappointment. The great whaleback of Notre Dame rose out of streets that had hardly been touched since Roman times. The paving was broken and decayed, and on wet days the roads became quagmires of mud. Open sewers flowed down the middle of the streets, their filth often discharging directly onto the roadway. High-heeled boots were not so much a fashion statement in Paris as a necessity.

By now Bacon was a master rather than a student, but medieval masters were no stand-offish dons. There was much less of a social divide between the two groups than there is now. Whenever there was trouble in the streets, masters fought alongside students. And despite the six o'clock start to the lecturing day, the English nation of the Faculty of Arts that Bacon was joining was famed for its members' ability to carouse into the night, and for their huge appetites for food and drink. It was Oxford writ large.

The best guess for the exact date of Bacon's move to Paris is based on the great men he heard speaking at the university. He lists three key names – Alexander of Hales, William of Auvergne and John of Garland[28] – who were all active until at least 1245, so it seems reasonable to assume that he crossed the Channel in the early 1240s. A single piece of evidence does suggest that Roger arrived even earlier, though. One of his books is an untidy collection of thoughts on preventing ageing, called *De retardandis accidentium senectutis: cum aliis opusculis de rebus medicinalibus.*[29] The style is not as polished as it is in many of his other works, suggesting either that we have only the first draft or that it was an early piece of writing. Bacon claims that he was asked to write it by two 'wise men', one of whom was Philip, Chancellor of Paris.[30] Philip died in 1236, so this would seem to indicate that Bacon was already in Paris by then.

Few other facts back up this hypothesis. The earliest possible year that Bacon could have reached Paris had he headed straight there after his receiving his MA is 1235 – and this assumes the earlier

birth year of 1214. But that would have been too early for him to
be asked over to help reintroduce Aristotle (the ban was reinforced
in 1235), and at the time Bacon was still a fresh young *magister*. It
seems unlikely that the chancellor of Christendom's greatest university would have invited a young, complete unknown to write a book
about ageing for him. If Bacon was indeed born in 1220 he could
not have moved to Paris before 1241. Also, although some scholars
put this book at the start of Bacon's life, many others consider it a
late work, Philip's name being used to give it spurious authority.[31]

◄○►

If Chancellor Philip was an unlikely contact for Bacon, Paris was
certainly to bring one new association that would shape his future.
It was there that Bacon met a mysterious figure who would open
his eyes to the fascinating possibilities of science. This was Peter of
Maricourt, often referred to as Peter Peregrinus, probably because
he had been on a lengthy journey (a 'peregrination'), a pilgrimage
or perhaps one of the crusades.

   Peter is a sketchy figure, dimly portrayed by indirect references.
Even his origins are uncertain, though there was a village called
Mehariscourt near the Abbey of Corbie in Picardy, where legend
suggests Peter came from. Only one of his works survives, an impressive treatise on the nature of magnets, *De magnete*. Yet we do know
that he had a powerful effect on Bacon, because Bacon tells us so
himself.

   From the way he writes about Peter, Bacon obviously developed
a huge admiration for the man. They were very different people.
Although Roger was fascinated by the idea of experimentation and
developed concepts that made science possible, he was mostly a
theorist, whereas Peter Peregrinus was an experimenter through
and through. It is easy to get the feeling from Bacon's writing that
Peter induced in him the same sort of wistful admiration that a
chaste writer of romances might feel for the exploits of a Casanova.

Bacon calls Peter a 'master of experiment' and writes of him in the *Opus tertium*:

> He gains knowledge of matters of nature, medicine, and alchemy through experiment, and all that is in the heaven and in the earth beneath . . . Moreover, he has considered the experiments and the fortune-telling of the old witches, and their spells and those of all magicians. And so too the illusions and wiles of all conjurors; and this so that nothing may escape him which ought to be known, and that he may perceive how far to reprove all that is false and magical.[32]

Bacon clearly learned much from Peter. Later, inspired by Peter's example, he would write very astutely about the fraud that lies behind magic. But most of all, he was impressed by Peter's love of experiment. Later on he comments that Peter could live royally if he wanted to,

> But because . . . he would be hindered from the bulk of the experiments in which lie his chief delight, he neglects all honours and riches, especially since he will be able, when he wishes, to reach riches by his own wisdom.[33]

This mysterious Frenchman clearly had a huge impact on Roger. He was looking at nature in a way that was completely different from the viewpoints of any of the Greek philosophers Bacon had spent so much time studying. When he left Oxford, Bacon thought himself a philosopher, pure and simple. But in his lectures in Paris he had concentrated mostly on natural philosophy, works of speculation on how the world functioned. Witnessing the power of experiment through seeing Peter in action convinced him that here was a field that was grossly undervalued. It was a wonderful opportunity to carve his own niche, to make himself an authority. Only Paris was perhaps not the right place to do it.

If Roger were really to immerse himself in natural philosophy, he needed three things: funding, which would make it attractive to be closer to his family, as getting cash sent any distance was a highly risky business at the time, and simply communicating from Paris to England could take months; time, which he could ill afford to spend while giving lectures in Paris; and the company of like-minded individuals. Peter had proved an inspiration, but even he was not enough to provide the breadth of expertise that Bacon wanted. He needed access to the best theorists in natural philosophy, and, thanks to the Parisian ban on Aristotle, they were to be found back in Oxford.

Accordingly, after a relatively short time in Paris – perhaps as little as five years – Bacon returned to England. Sparked by Peter's experimental genius, he had a new mission in life. And, as if to underline the rightness of his move, he had recently discovered a secret book that seemed to support his new way of thinking. This book claimed that knowledge of nature, the knowledge that Bacon had so assiduously acquired and now wished to expand, was an essential requirement for the success of princes and powers. The book was *Secretum secretorum*, 'The Secret of Secrets'.

3

The Secret of Secrets

> So Aristotle might have been all the more ignorant of the
> deeper secrets of nature. And wise men are now ignorant of
> many things which the common crowd of students will
> understand in the future.
>
> Roger Bacon, *De mirabile potestate artis et naturae*

The short mysterious book called *Secretum secretorum*, 'The Secret of Secrets', proved irresistible to Roger Bacon. He would later edit his own version of it, adding copious notes to each page so that his readers would not overlook any of the wisdom it contained. The book appeared to be a letter from Aristotle to Alexander the Great, the famed general and king of Macedonia who had been Aristotle's pupil as a boy. It was an exciting blend of practical advice and mysticism, a combination that very much appealed to Bacon.

The *Secretum secretorum* belonged to a class of medieval literature known as 'mirrors of princes'. The genre emerged in Persia in the eighth century and soon became extremely popular in the Islamic world. Such books offered guidance to rulers, an undertaking that could prove very risky if done in a more direct form. In later medieval times there would emerge the court jester, an individual who could criticize the monarch and get away with it from behind the mask of humour. The authors of works like the *Secretum secretorum* had no such privilege to protect them, and instead opted for a mild fraud: they claimed that their books were the work of some famous sage from times past. That way, the author was safe from retribution if the advice didn't go down well, and if it did, the book would assume a spurious air of authority.

For the *Secretum secretorum*, Aristotle was selected as an impressive alias by the unknown author, who was almost certainly an Arab writer living no more than two centuries before Bacon himself.[34] But like his colleagues, Bacon was convinced of the book's classical origins and was strongly swayed by its arguments. A new translation published by the scholar Philip of Tripoli around 1243 is likely to be the text that Bacon first came across.

The *Secretum secretorum* demonstrated the powerful practical benefits of a knowledge of nature. It showed that the natural sciences were not just a matter of philosophical wonder, but also provided a pathway to success in overcoming military and civil problems. What's more, the book implied that a knowledge of art and nature was an essential part of understanding God.

'Art' in Bacon's time meant not just paintings and sculpture but anything made by the hand of man, so the *Secretum* was giving its blessing to invention and to science. This opened Roger's eyes to an alternative route to the recognition that he craved. At the time, theology was by far the most important subject to study. By taking the line that an understanding of art and nature was required before effective theology could be developed, he had a very effective means of undermining the theologians whose opinions and skills he was always swift to criticize.

The *Secretum* also portrays the idea of a universal knowledge of nature and art that Bacon was to make his own. In one of its more mystical sections, it tells how the sons of Seth (the son of Adam) were once the holders of all knowledge, which was subsequently lost and was only partially rebuilt by the ancient Greeks, the Arabs, and now the Christian academics. The book persuaded Bacon that the greatest goal for any searcher after truth was to regain this universal understanding.

With an inspirational lead from the *Secretum*, the experimental experience he had gained with Peter Peregrinus, and his understanding of the works of Aristotle and his contemporaries newly honed by his teaching in Paris, Bacon was set on a new career. Once back at Oxford, he set about studying science with a new vigour – or, rather, he set about studying natural philosophy. The distinction between natural philosophy and science is crucial, because it was Bacon who would steer away from the traditional approach and lay the foundations of what we would now regard as science.

The traditional approach, which had been used from the time of the ancient Greeks, was to take what was observed and analyse it by pure thought and dispute; there was no concept of testing out different hypotheses. Bacon would eventually introduce four crucial features to transform this approach into a completely new method. For the moment, though, he wholeheartedly threw himself into the study of natural philosophy.

This was to take up far more than time alone. As Bacon became drawn into the fascinating complexities of natural philosophy he began to make a serious dent in his family's undoubted wealth. He later wrote in the *Opus tertium*:

> During the twenty years in which I have laboured specially in the study of wisdom, after abandoning the usual methods, I have spent more than £2,000 on secret books and various experiments, and languages and instruments and mathematical tables etc.[35]

This is a staggering amount of money. In the thirteenth century, an unskilled labourer might earn a penny for a long day's labour in the fields. In the pre-decimal days of 240 pence to the pound, this amounted to one pound ten shillings (£1.50) for a whole year's toil. Bacon's expenditure was the equivalent of paying the wages of fifty men for a lifetime. For highly skilled craftsmen, things were a little better. For example, towards the end of the thirteenth century the masons crafting the exquisitely decorated Exeter Cathedral each went home after a year's work with a total of four pounds, seventeen shillings and tuppence-halfpenny (£4.86). A substantial house would cost in the region of two to three pounds to build, while 30 acres (12 hectares) of land would cost perhaps five shillings (25p) a year to rent. By comparison, each single year Bacon spent twenty times a mason's wages or enough to rent 400 farms.

It's true that anything connected with books was expensive in times when each manuscript had to be laboriously hand-copied. There is also a possibility that Bacon was referring to French pounds, worth only a third of their sterling equivalent. Even if that were so, his research expenditure could have bought him 500 houses or paid the annual wage bill of nearly a thousand workers. In modern terms, Bacon's family would have parted with more than £10 million sterling. To put the figure of £2,000 into a different perspective, the *entire* crown revenue in 1217 was £35,000.[36]

As this sum would suggest, he was pursuing his aim of understanding art and nature with the zeal of a fanatic, literally at all costs. The vibrant life of the young university that he had once so enjoyed and that was now all around him he practically ignored. He allowed nothing to distract him from what had started as an interest and was now an obsession. He later remarked that those around him were surprised that he didn't work himself into the ground. His remaining close friends seemed unable to stop him. By now his work had become so important to him that they were being left behind – and in later years, in need of more finance for more research, Roger was to find that he had left his friendships untended just a little too long.

At Oxford, Bacon now single-mindedly explored all that was known about the workings of nature. He read the surviving ancient texts that described classical inventions, real and imagined, and, inspired by what he had found, began to speculate about new possibilities. Today, if you were to ask people to identify an inventor who seemed ahead of his time, they would be likely to point to Leonardo da Vinci. Yet some 300 years earlier Roger Bacon had already envisaged many of the devices that Leonardo was to describe and draw.

In his letter *De mirabile potestate artis et natura* ('On the Marvellous Power of Art and Nature'), Bacon set out a veritable catalogue of wonders. Because of his constant concern to separate the realities of nature and the fictions of magic, he began by establishing a very clear context for these inventions. These are 'marvels wrought through the agency of Art and of Nature . . . In these there is no magic whatsoever because, as has been said, all magical power is inferior to these works and incompetent to achieve them.'

Bacon then launched into an incredible list of modern concepts. He made the extraordinary claim that these devices had been constructed in antiquity and in his own time. He claimed to be 'acquainted with them explicitly, except with the instrument of flying which I have not seen. And I know no one who has seen it. But I know a wise man who has thought out the artifice.'

There seems a remarkable honesty in the way he admits to not having seen the flying machine. Yet it is widely thought that throughout the letter Roger was in fact describing ideas of his own devising, none of which had ever become physical reality. It is just possible, though, that some of these remarkable inventions had been made real by Peter Peregrinus.[37]

So what was in Bacon's collection of medieval mechanical wonders?

It is possible that great ships and sea-going vessels shall be made which can be guided by one man and will move with greater swiftness than if they were full of oarsmen.[38]

Ships and boats were, of course, nothing new. Prehistoric people built simple rafts consisting of logs bound together in a flat structure, or hollowed out a tree in the form of a dugout canoe. The Romans had turned the fighting ship into a sophisticated weapon of warfare. Yet the two means of motive power available to shipbuilders had not changed over all the years of construction. To make a boat move through the water took the effort of men pulling on oars or the force of the wind on its sails. It wasn't until the end of the nineteenth century, 600 years after Bacon's death, that a steam engine could be made small and light enough to fit into a ship's hull. Even then the requirement that a 'great ship' should be guided by 'only one man' would not be realized until the advent of computerized control systems in the late twentieth century.

It is possible that a car shall be made which will move with inestimable speed, and the motion will be without the help of any living creature. Such, it is thought, were the *currus falcati* which the ancients used in combat.

Like the self-propelled ship, Bacon's horseless carriage required the steam engine to make it possible, but it was truly brought into existence in 1885 when Karl Benz and Gottlieb Daimler independently came up with cars that did indeed move 'without the help of any living creature' thanks to an early petrol engine. Yet the propulsion alone wasn't Bacon's only original idea. For many, a horseless carriage would simply replace a horse with a mechanical equivalent, travelling at a familiar walking pace. But Bacon's carriage was going to 'move with inestimable speed' – exactly how we might imagine a medieval observer would regard a modern vehicle.

Interestingly, Bacon seems to have arrived at this concept as a result of a misunderstanding. He thought that self-propelled cars were possible because he assumed that something similar had previously existed, in the shape of the mythical *currus falcati*. These vehicles were rumoured to pull themselves, but this must have been propaganda rather than fact – *currus falcati* are thought to have been perfectly ordinary chariots.

In coming up with an idea as a result of a misunderstanding, Bacon made himself an early entry in a list of illustrious but confused inventors. When the French king Louis XVI saw the Montgolfier brothers' hot-air balloon in 1783, he was so impressed that he ordered his scientific officer, Jacques Alexandre César Charles, to develop one for him. Charles had not seen the Montgolfiers' balloon, and the king was unable to describe how it worked. Starting from scratch, Charles reasoned incorrectly that the Montgolfiers must have used the newly discovered gas hydrogen, as this was lighter than air, and so invented the gas balloon.

It is possible that a device for flying shall be made such that a man sitting in the middle of it and turning a crank shall cause artificial wings to beat the air after the manner of a bird's flight.

The flying machine, which Bacon owns up to not having seen for himself, is the only machine where the principle described is not a practical one. Many attempts would later be made to construct flying machines with wings that beat like those of a bird, but such endeavours were doomed to failure because the effort required to lift the bulk of a person far exceeds the amount of energy that could ever be put into the wings. Birds only manage to become airborne because they are extremely light for their bulk and have a remarkable amount of power in their musculature. Toy-sized craft that use the flapping principle (ornithopters) have been made, but the principle does not scale up to full-size aircraft.

The most basic form of workable airborne device, the kite, had been around since the fifth century BC, but it was Bacon who gave a hint of the principle on which the modern fixed-winged aeroplane functions, pointing out that air should be able to support it in the same way that water supports a boat. Leonardo da Vinci was to revisit Bacon's concept of an ornithopter, but he also devised a helicopter-like mechanism and, most significantly, a glider. The first practical glider was made by the English inventor George

Cayley, who also drew up plans for a fixed-winged powered aircraft in 1799, but it was not until 17 December 1903 that American bicycle-makers Wilbur and Orville Wright built and flew the first piloted powered flying machine, and brought Bacon's idea to life.

> Similarly it is possible to construct a small-sized instrument for elevating and depressing great weights, a device which is most useful in certain exigencies. For a man may ascend and descend and may deliver himself and his companions from peril of prison by means of a device of small weight and of a height of three fingers and a breadth of four.
>
> It is possible also easily to make an instrument by which a single man may violently pull a thousand men toward himself despite the opposition, or other things which are tractable.

While Bacon is not explicit about his subject here, he seems to be describing a pulley system where the effort applied is magnified by the pulleys. Simple machines for amplifying force – pulleys, levers and screws – had been common since ancient times, but the form Bacon describes would not be available until it became possible to construct complex precision pulley blocks, perhaps 500 years later. For good measure, he throws in the concept of a lift, a device that would not become reality until the nineteenth century.

> It is possible also that devices can be made whereby, without bodily danger, a man may walk on the bottom of the sea or of a river. Alexander used these to observe the secrets of the sea, as Ethicus the astronomer relates.

This was probably the least original of Bacon's machines. For around 1,600 years, practical means had sought to make it possible for a human being to survive under water. As Bacon points out, Alexander the Great was said to have tried out a primitive form of diving bell, and Aristotle mentions similar devices. However, it

wasn't until the eighteenth century, when there was a better understanding of atmospheric pressure, that practical diving bells began
to be produced.

Bacon's collection of wonders was amazing. In one short burst
in a letter to an acquaintance he listed self-powered ships, the horseless carriage, the flying machine, something that sounds like a pulley
system, and a diving suit or diving bell, most of which would not
become practical for another 600 years. Compare this with the work
of the fêted twentieth-century science-fiction writer Sir Arthur C.
Clarke, author of *2001: A Space Odyssey*, who is usually cited as the
leading example of technological foresight. In an article published
in *Wireless World* in 1945, he predicted the use of communications
satellites around twenty years before they became reality.[39] There is
no doubt that this excellent writer had an unusually precise ability
to speculate on the future of technology, but Bacon puts even Clarke
into the shade.

Of course, Bacon was not alone in describing marvellous inventions. Classical romances describe all manner of impossible
constructs, but they were presented as magical devices. In the
mythology of ancient Greece, for example, Hephaestus, the smith
of the gods, was said to have constructed a magically powered man
of brass called Talus, who guarded the island of Crete. This remarkable creation may have indirectly inspired one of the totally fictional
legends that by Elizabethan times had been constructed around
Roger Bacon. Bacon was said to have built a head out of brass, so
cleverly constructed that it could speak. It was not based on scientific principles, however, being powered by exposure to 'the
continual fume of the six hottest simples' (a 'simple' was an extract
from a single plant). This was just the sort of magical fantasy that
Roger was so scathing about.

By contrast, the inventions he discussed were set squarely in the
field of science and engineering. Remember his remark that these
are 'marvels wrought through the agency of Art and of Nature . . .
In these there is no magic whatsoever.' There was nothing obscure

about them either. Compared with the cryptic and veiled predictions of a Nostradamus, Bacon's work was clear futurology, not requiring the sort of after-the-event interpretation that is so often applied to prophesy. Bacon is not indulging in fantasy, but describing what he believed human ingenuity could construct. Roger Charles, the nineteenth-century Victorian biographer, writes of this list that 'it is a dazzling picture and one to confound modern science, which believes itself born yesterday.' We are so used to the developments of the last hundred years that perhaps it takes a Victorian view to appreciate how remarkable were the concepts set out in Bacon's letter.

◄o►

Once he was in full flow, Bacon did not stop with mere mechanical devices. Optics had always been a subject that fascinated him, and here too his inventive mind could see all sorts of possibilities. He began with the idea of using mirrors and lenses so that 'one appears as many, one man an army' – an effect suggested could be used in war so that 'infinite terror may be cast upon a whole city or upon an army so that it will go entirely to pieces'. Whether such an illusion could ever have fooled anyone is another matter; however, he then went on to describe optical devices that would come into use hundreds of years later, where 'lenses are contrived so that the most distant objects appear near at hand and vice versa':

> We may read the smallest letters at an incredible distance, we may see objects however small they may be, and we may cause the stars to appear wherever we wish. So, it is thought, Julius Caesar spied into Gaul from the seashore and by optical devices learned the position and arrangement of the camps and towns of Brittany.

Bacon's incorrect assumption that Julius Caesar had used telescopes did not make his concept any less remarkable. After all, Bacon was the foremost expert on optics of his day. He understood as few had done before how the primitive lenses and mirrors then in existence bent light rays. Others, da Vinci included, would follow him in referring to the possibility of making telescopes and microscopes, but the first known examples would not be made until 300 years later. It was in the late sixteenth century that the Digges father-and-son team may have first demonstrated a telescope,[40] and around 1590 when another family partnership, Hans and Zacharias Janssen, constructed a microscope.

With the telescope and microscope under his belt, Bacon went on to imagine using the power of the basilisk, a non-existent creature that was then thought to kill as a result of emanations in its sight:

> Devices may be built to send forth poisonous and infectious emanations and influences wherever a man may wish. Aristotle taught this to Alexander, so that by casting the poison of the basilisk over the walls of a city which held out against his army he conveyed the poison into the city itself.

If this sounds much more vague and mystical than a piece of modern technology, bear in mind that Bacon assumed that the basilisk was a real creature, with a natural if quite amazing way of imposing death through sight (sight was then assumed to be a flow of light emanating from the eyes). He goes on to describe channelling this deadly light using lenses:

> But of sublimer powers is that device by which rays of light are led into any place that we wish and are brought together by refractions and reflections in such fashion that anything is burned which is placed there. And these burning glasses function in both directions, as certain authors teach in their books.

Bacon went on to describe orrery-like instruments that were working models of the heavens. Such devices would not see daylight

until the seventeenth century. The orrery is sometimes confused
with the much older astrolabe, but that was a two-dimensional (if
sometimes beautiful) instrument of metal circles used to observe
the sky, the precursor of the sextant, and dates back to the ancient
Greeks. Bacon's description is so precise that it is tempting to wonder
if his one-time colleague Peter Peregrinus had devised such a
machine, perhaps inspired by Bacon's work on geographical and
celestial locations:

> The great power of mathematics can build a spherical instru-
> ment, like the artifice of Ptolemy in *Almagest*, in which all heavenly
> bodies are described veraciously as regards longitude and lati-
> tude, but to make them move naturally in their diurnal move-
> ment is not within the power of mathematics. A faithful and
> magnificent experimenter might aspire to construct an instru-
> ment of such materials and of such an arrangement that it would
> move naturally in the diurnal motion of the heavens . . . In the
> presence of such an instrument all other apparatus of the Astrol-
> ogers, whether the product of wisdom or mere vulgar equip-
> ment, would cease to count any more. The treasure of a king
> would scarcely merit comparison with it.

Bacon suggests that the device could be made to move directly by
the action of the heavens, just as other physical phenomena, from
comets to the tides, are driven by external forces. While there is no
suggestion that Bacon had in mind a working mechanism, the idea
of driving an 'engine' by gravity was to return in instruments as
common as the humble cuckoo clock. The cuckoo clock is kept in
motion by the weights that hang below, which exert a force through
the action of gravity, just as the tides are produced by the gravitational pull of the Moon.

Finally, and in great depth, Bacon explored the manufacture of
gunpowder. Others had described the inflammable nature of black
powder, and various highly flammable compounds had been in use

in warfare since Greek fire, a gelatinous petroleum-based mixture, had been developed in the seventh century AD to attack ships at sea. But Bacon was the first to put across the explosive force of gunpowder:

> For the sound of thunder may be artificially produced in the air with greater resulting horror than if it had been produced by natural causes. A moderate amount of proper material, of the size of the thumb, will make a horrible sound and violent coruscation. Such material may be used in a variety of ways, as, for instance, in a case similar to that in which a whole army and city were destroyed by means of the strategy of Gideon, who, with broken jugs and torches, and with fire leaping forth with ineffable thunder, routed the army of the Midianites with three hundred men.

There were limits to Bacon's vision. He did not conceive of the ability of gunpowder to blast a projectile, a discovery that would change the face of weaponry for ever. Even so, his was the first real insight into the military value of black powder and the wider capabilities of science to make a difference to everyday life.

—◦—

With Bacon's list of inventions in front of us, it is worth exploring a little further his assertion that he had seen most of the mechanical devices himself. We know from Bacon's own account that Peter Peregrinus was a great experimenter who was prepared to try out things that others would simply not consider.[41] It is not inconceivable that Peter was capable of putting together models that really did propel themselves as Bacon describes, perhaps using weights and pulleys to power them.

Also, Bacon himself would certainly have been able to experiment with pulleys and levers. And though he does not state explicitly in the letter that he had constructed the optical devices that are mentioned, we do know that he carried out many experiments with mirrors, prisms and lenses, as he describes in the *Opus majus*:

> The wonders of refracted vision are still greater; for it is easily shown by the rules stated above [demonstrating the workings of lenses] that very large objects can be made to appear small, and the reverse, and very distant objects will seem very close at hand, and conversely. For we can so shape transparent bodies, and arrange them in such a way with respect to our sight and objects of vision, that the rays will be refracted and bent in any direction that we desire, and under any angle we wish we shall see the object near or at a distance.
>
> Thus from an incredible distance we might read the smallest letters and number grains of dust and sand owing to the magnitude of the angle under which we viewed them . . . [42]

With his particular expertise in this field, it seems quite possible that he may not only have described the microscope and telescope but also built primitive versions during his twenty years of research.

If so, why was it another 400 years before these devices were put to practical use? Even in Bacon's day, a telescope would have had obvious military benefits, and Bacon was clearly aware of this potential in his reference to Julius Caesar spying on Gaul. Also, an ever-present motivation in his work was the desire to give the Church more strength to stand up to its enemies. If he could have presented Christianity with an unparalleled surveillance tool, why did he not do so? If he had built a telescope, why was it not pressed into use immediately?

Although this is pure speculation on my part, I think it quite possible that Bacon had constructed a simple telescope by around the late 1240s. Given his fascination with optics and the experience of experimentation he had gained while working with Peter Peregrinus, it is hard to believe that he never used two lenses to form a simple telescope. The lenses available then were very crude, giving a misty, distorted image, yet it would take little more than two such lenses and a tube of leather to make a workable instrument. However fuzzy the view, it would show things more distant than the naked eye could see, and that would have been enough to prove the telescope's worth.

But if Bacon did make a simple device, he was never to get the opportunity to show it off outside his immediate circle of friends. His life was to undergo another drastic change, and any of his belongings, including anything he had invented, would probably have been left with his family – who were to lose everything in the turmoil of civil war. If Bacon's precious devices had been stored at the family home, they would have been destroyed. And there would be good reasons why Bacon would never re-create such instruments later on.

For the moment, though, he was to about take a bizarre leap into the unknown. He was about to surrender voluntarily everything that he held dear.

4
The Order

Men used to wonder before I became a friar how I
managed to stay alive, owing to my excessive labours.
And yet I was as studious after as before; but I did not work
as hard, since it was unnecessary owing to the exercise
of wisdom.

Roger Bacon, *Opus tertium*

Roger Bacon was a man driven, capable of spending the equivalent of £10 million on his research and experiments. He was an independent thinker; he had incredibly strong ideas and passions; he liked to have things his own way. He put his work ahead of anything else. Yet suddenly, in his early thirties, he threw up his entire way of life to become a Franciscan friar.

This was no small decision. It meant surrendering all his worldly possessions. More significantly, Bacon could not do this without abandoning the whole direction of his life and work. In modern terms we would probably describe Bacon's enormous step as a mid-life crisis (though it was made at an age when many of his contemporaries were already dead).

Bacon may have begun to worry about the direction his life was taking. Even so, there are good indications that he became a Franciscan friar for entirely practical reasons rather than purely as a result of self-analysis. We have seen that once he returned to England he worked his way through the exorbitant sum of £2,000. That must have happened before he joined the Franciscans, for when he became a friar he would have given up all his personal wealth. We can well imagine that his family had finally decided that enough was enough, and withdrawn their financial support. If so, Bacon might have seen in the Franciscan Order an alternative source of funding.

Also, his opinions, which he later put into writing in *Compendium studii philosophiae*,[43] would by then be making him unpopular in some circles. He was never slow to criticize other academics, which would not have won him many friends. What's more, as he pressed forward into new areas of investigation he was in danger of gaining a reputation as a dabbler in the black arts. The Franciscans may have had a harsh routine, but they were well known for protecting their own. They lacked the estates and privileges of the monastic orders, so they were seen as less of a political threat by the Church authorities, and they had begun to win high positions in the universities and the ecclesiastical hierarchy. Bacon was joining a club that would make his standing in the eyes of the universities more secure. But the protection of the Order did not come without a price – and Bacon was to pay that price in full.

It is easy to have a stereotyped image of the cloistered life – ancient orders following long-established rules; timeless peace in ageless, hallowed buildings. But to apply this picture to Bacon's time would be grossly anachronistic. The Order of the Friars Minor, the Franciscans, literally 'the little brothers' ('friar' being a corruption of the Latin *frater*), had not been formally constituted until 1223. Roger Bacon was older than the Order itself. This may well have been part of the Franciscans' appeal to him. This was no hidebound organization, but a new and vibrant development in the Church. Those in control were still finding their feet, and the Order wasn't quite certain where it was going, but it had risen from nothing to become a formidable force in the Church in a matter of a few years. The small beginnings St Francis of Assisi had made in 1208 were now sending out large ripples.[44]

St Francis was a remarkable man. Properly Giovanni Francesco Bernadone, he was born in 1182 into a well-off merchant family in Assisi, a town in the rolling Umbrian hills of central Italy. For years he led the carefree life of a young man with plenty of money and few responsibilities. He was out to enjoy every minute. But local political rivalry brewed up into a skirmish between Assisi and the nearby city of Perugia. Francis was captured, and while in prison he suffered a near-fatal illness that brought his mortality home to him. When he returned to Assisi, still only twenty-three, he began to work among the local lepers and helped restore some of the local churches that had fallen into disrepair.

Francis's father did not like the change in his son and took legal action to disinherit him. Francis ignored the threat and continued to care for the poor and the sick. By 1208 he had gathered around him twelve disciples, and together they went out into the world with the humble intention of spreading the word of God and doing good among the poor. Francis died in 1226, but the movement he had started took on an immediate momentum.

Unlike the older orders of monks who hid themselves away in contemplation, the Franciscans took an interest in all of creation and were always looking for practical ways to help their fellow men. In return all they asked was sustenance – they were a mendicant order, technically beggars reliant on the gifts of others to support their work. In their simple grey robes – they were soon given the nickname 'the grey friars' – they became a common sight across Europe.

Initially, like St Francis himself, the Franciscans took the model of Christ's words to his apostles in St Matthew's gospel very directly. Jesus had said (Matthew 10:7–13):

> . . . proclaim the message 'The kingdom of Heaven is upon you.' Heal the sick, raise the dead, cleanse lepers, cast out devils. You received without cost; give without charge.

Provide no gold, silver or copper to fill your purse, no pack
for the road, no second coat, no shoes, no stick; the worker earns
his keep.

When you come to a town or village, look for some worthy
person in it, and make your home there until you leave. Wish
the house peace as you enter it, so that, if it is worthy, your peace
descend on it; if it is not worthy, your peace can come back to
you.

This was exactly what Francis expected his followers to do – not
to stay in any one place too long, but to move around, spreading
the word, doing good deeds and living where they could. Francis
urged them, if they needed any long-term lodgings, to build simple
cottages of mud-plaster and wood, enough to provide shelter but
nothing more.

The friars set out with every intention to follow this way of life.
But they found that in practice it was very difficult to do good
without being rewarded. Their movement was popular. It didn't
just appeal to those who joined the Order, or even those who were
helped by the friars. The great and the good rather approved of
these clerics who had none of the interest in power that seemed to
be a tiresome preoccupation with the rest of the Church hierarchy.
These were gentle churchmen who knew their place. So before long,
benefactors were providing buildings to help the Order in its good
works, without regard for the friars own views on such permanent
establishments.

This tendency to be generous went to the very top of the social
structure. Henry III made nearly a hundred grants to the two earliest
friaries in Oxford – those of the Franciscans and the Dominicans.
These were often in the form of permissions, such as the right to
take timber from the nearby royal forest of Shotover, a real benefit
when building work was under way. Later, in 1289, Edward I was
to start a tradition of handing over 50 marks (around £35) a year
to the Franciscan friary.

The friary was not grand by the standards of the great monasteries, but it was already a sizeable structure when Bacon arrived. Originally based in the parish of St Ebbe by the town's south gate, the site had rapidly expanded so that it now extended out through the town walls between the south gate and the castle at the west. The most striking part of the structure was the church. The thirteenth century was a time of wonderful inventiveness in church building. The French gothic style with its high pointed arches was beginning to dominate the skylines of Europe, and the master masons of the day continually attempted to outdo one another with new and more dramatic ideas.

In a monastery church, the public nave was usually secondary to the monks' part of the building, the choir. At the Franciscan friary, though, the masons had given a great deal of thought to the Order's desire not to lead a secluded existence. The church, still under construction when Bacon arrived, had an unusual shape. Since it was the ability to get the word to the people that mattered, there was not one nave but two, forming a T shape along with the third arm of the choir. This doubled the size of the congregation that could be accommodated. The revolutionary design idea never caught on elsewhere, but somehow characterized the Oxford friars' view on life.

In one respect, though, the friary was like a monastery: it was a tight collection of buildings for working, eating, and sleeping as well as a place of prayer and preaching. Next to the church was a cloister, a covered walkway opening onto a central courtyard for ambulation and contemplation. It was common practice for Franciscans to have their dormitories above the cloister to make double use of the space. In Bacon's day there would have been between fifty and seventy friars in the house, engaged in praying, teaching and learning, and ministering to the people.

From the start, Bacon would have found that he had less freedom than when he had been pursuing his private studies or lecturing at the universities. Although friars weren't expected to undertake the punishing schedule of services adhered to by monks in enclosed orders, they still attended church several times a day unless their work kept them away, and also had menial tasks to perform. There were no servants, and everyone was expected to do their bit.

In joining the Order, Bacon had given up much, but had hoped to gain even more. Spiritually, he was well aligned with the friars. His simple, practical faith fitted well with theirs – both St Francis and Roger Bacon believed that action was more important than words alone. Bacon now also had the Order as a buffer between him and the enemies that his opinions might have brought him. But the most important benefit of being a Franciscan would, he hoped, be a closer exposure to the wisdom of some of the world's greatest natural philosophers.

◄○►

Life at the Oxford friary was geared to a pursuit of knowledge. The friary was unusual: Franciscan houses were usually only temporary resting places, but members of the Order based in Oxford might stay there all their lives. The emphasis on study fitted well with the Franciscans' interest in nature. It would become common for Franciscans to take part in voyages of discovery (several accompanied Columbus, for example) and to explore the possibilities that opened up as natural philosophy began its long transition into science. The friars' approach to study always had a practical side, which appealed hugely to Bacon, who was as easily frustrated by a lack of clear use for his science as he was by an impractical faith.

Indeed, the friary, even more than the university, should have been an ideal place for Roger to carry his studies forward. Books, such a rare commodity in the outside world, were an essential part of friary life. Copying books, a high art and a painfully slow one, had always been a particular skill of the religious orders, but the Franciscans and their brother friars the Dominicans, or black friars, went further. Each friary had its own library, and despite not being allowed personal property, a friar was able to retain copies of books that were necessary to his studies for the whole of his life. On his death, his books would be shared out among the libraries where they were most in demand. A later chancellor of the university, Richard Fitzralph, complained bitterly that the friars 'hoarded books'.[45] There would not have been a separate library building at the friary, though, and the books were probably kept at one end of the dormitory. Most friars slept communally, though there were individual cells for the sick which were sometimes used for concentrated study when the communal space was too busy.

The friaries also had catalogues of books and subjects, and even an early form of inter-library loan system whereby a book could be requested and sent from one friary to another. To make sure that the stocks were maintained, the Franciscans were forbidden to sell any book on theology, philosophy, grammar, or logic unless the friary already owned two copies. This was a necessary rule, as selling books must have been highly tempting even to some of the more dedicated members of the Order – a single volume could raise enough money to finance very many charitable works.

Not only could the Oxford Franciscans offer an unparalleled library, but they also included in their number some of the top natural philosophers, including Robert Grosseteste, who was one of Bacon's personal heroes. It's fair to say that Grosseteste was the first real Oxford star. The fame of his teaching spread not only through England but also to all the continental universities. He was the chancellor of the university from 1215 to 1221 and continued to be chief lecturer to the Franciscans in Oxford until he left to become Bishop of Lincoln in 1235.[46]

Although Roger's enthusiastic praise for Grosseteste made many early historians think that he learned science at the feet of this great man, the dates make this highly unlikely. Grosseteste moved to Lincoln well before Bacon seems to have shown any interest in science. However, there is little doubt that before he joined the

Order Bacon had read and reread Grosseteste's work and felt a spiritual sympathy with this one-time lecturer to the Franciscans. If Robert Grosseteste had found the Franciscan Order to be his spiritual home, then why should not Bacon find his niche there also? The two men shared one great love, a passion that was unequalled ✓ in any of their contemporaries. Grosseteste had shown an interest in experiment that was unusual for the time, but it was not this that gave Bacon such enthusiasm for the man and his work. The cords that bound Bacon to Grosseteste were the insubstantial rays of light.

—◀○▶—

Light had always been a powerful metaphor for the Christian Church. Jesus described himself as 'the light of the world', and in the Bible light is often synonymous with knowledge. But for Grosseteste, light was something more. He wrote that it was of 'a nobler and more excellent essence than all the forms that come after it' – meaning that everything was derived from light.[47] He believed that it was the means by which God had created matter.

Grosseteste never got too far with the practical physics of light – the closest he came was an inadequate explanation of the workings of the rainbow and an understanding that light obeyed geometrical rules in its motion. However, he obviously considered it to lie at the heart of creation, and this sense of importance was imparted through his writing and became part of his legacy to Bacon at Oxford.

It is impossible to read Bacon's work without being made aware to what degree light was his pet subject. He was to perform more experiments in the field of optics than in any other. In his great work, the *Opus majus*, he comments:

> If the consideration just mentioned [mathematics] is noble and pleasing, the one in hand is far nobler and more pleasing, since we take especial delight in vision, and light and colour have a

special beauty beyond the other things that are brought to our senses, and not only does beauty shine forth but also [optics and light] bring benefits and answer a great need.[48]

As always for Bacon, the true glory of a science is its usefulness, but here his strictly practical nature is tempered by a sense of wonder. The original translation, sometimes a little obscure, has been rendered into modern English here, and in other quotes from Bacon's work, but this fascination comes shining through. He goes on:

It is possible that some other science may be more useful, but no other science has so much sweetness and beauty of utility. Therefore it is the flower of the whole of philosophy and through it, and not without it, can the other sciences be known.[49]

Although many other feelings come across in Bacon's scientific works, here, I would suggest, is the fundamental, overriding one that lies behind his single-mindedness. It is often overlooked because Bacon found it easy to allow his frustration to pour out in criticism, so querulous negativity can appear to be a dominant characteristic. But here we see a different man, as delighted as a child by the beauty of light. It is the 'sweetness' of science and its 'beauty of utility' that always pushed Bacon on. Every great scientist since has shared this same passion.

Bacon's trip through the wonders of light began not with the workings of mirrors and lenses, but in the human head. It would seem madness today to begin a book on optics with a chapter entitled 'Concerning the internal faculties of the sensitive soul, which are imagination and the common sense', but this is what Bacon did. Modern textbooks plunge into wave theory or photons. Bacon started not with light, but with the human response to light.

We can see this as natural if we consider how Bacon would have thought about light. For him, science was not knowledge for its own

sake: it was knowledge accumulated with a specific use in mind.
He was enthusiastic about light not just for its fascination but for
its utility for man. Here he compares it to the other senses:

> Our experience of things here in the Earth we owe to vision,
> because a blind man can have no experience worthy of the name
> concerning this world. Hearing causes us to believe because we
> believe our teachers, but we cannot try out what we learn except
> through vision. If, moreover, we should adduce taste and touch
> and smell, we assume a knowledge belonging to beasts.[50]

The inner view, the human response, was also fundamental because
in medieval times some of the more bizarre of the ancient views
on light had yet to be overthrown. Empedocles, the deviser of the
four elements of earth, air, fire and water that were still accepted
without question in Bacon's day, described light as fire (it had to
be fire, as it could hardly have been earth, air, or water), flooding
out from the eye to illuminate the objects in the field of view.
Although later Greek philosophers introduced a role for the Sun,
which was now held to act as a sort of catalyst for vision (otherwise we should have been able to see in the dark), they maintained
that the primary source of light was the eye.

The most logical 'proof' that light originated from the eye came
from the ancient Greek philosopher Euclid, best known for his
contributions to geometry, who lived and worked around 300 BC.
So little is known about the man that there is even some doubt
about his physical existence. It was not uncommon for works of a
classical school to be ascribed to the head of the school, and –
more recently, we know that groups have taken this one step further
and published under an assumed name – a twentieth-century team
of mathematicians, for example, would produce a series of papers
under the name 'Bourbaki' – and some historians have suspected
that Euclid was, in fact, a team rather than an individual.[51] This
famed philosopher (whatever his make-up), is said to have imagined

looking for a needle that had been dropped on the ground. As he searched, even though he was looking in the right general direction, he couldn't see the needle. Then all of a sudden it sprang into view. Euclid reasoned that light from the Sun must always be hitting the needle and reaching the eye, so if that were the only light, we ought to be able to see the needle immediately. So sight, he argued, was dependent on the sunlight's interaction with a ray that shone from the eye, and that ray needed a conscious focus on the object.

This theory of light had not gone unchallenged. The Arab scientist Alhazen (properly Abu Ali al-Hasan ibn al-Haytham), who was born 250 years before Bacon in what is now Iraq, argued impressively that the eye merely responded to an external source of light.[52] Like Bacon, Alhazen could not resist the more practical approach of dealing with the 'how' as well as the 'why' of the world's workings. His practicality was almost his undoing. Soon famous in the Islamic world as an unequalled problem-solver, he was invited to Cairo by the king, al-Hakim. The king needed help with the Nile. The great river was a lifeline for Egypt, but its regular flooding was also a curse. Al-Hakim commanded Alhazen to devise a means of controlling its flow.

The young Alhazen soon found that taming such a potent force was beyond him. Yet if he admitted defeat he was in danger of losing his life. He could not tell the king that he had failed, nor would it be safe to run away, as the king's influence stretched far beyond the bounds of the country. There was only one alternative to suicide or a painful execution – he faked insanity and was locked away as a madman until the king died, years later.

Despite these lost years, Alhazen was the most advanced of all the Arab natural philosophers, not only translating and commenting on the work of the ancients but adding much of his own. He made careful observations of how different-shaped mirrors reflected light. He struggled to understand how materials like glass, water, and air changed a beam of light's path as it passed through. And he piled up argument after argument to show that light travelled directly

from a source (like the Sun) and eventually to be detected by the
eye, which was nothing more than a passive receptor.

Bacon had read translations of Alhazen's books, but decided that
his Arab predecessor had showed only that light could not depend
on the eye alone. Instead, Bacon believed that something emitted
by the eye 'changes the medium and ennobles it, and renders it
analogous to vision, and so prepares the passage of the light rays
from the visible object'.[53]

Since Bacon was considering light from an internal viewpoint,
he began by describing the brain and the linkage of the eye to the
optic nerve, something that it would be easy to assume was not
known about in his day. In fact it had probably first been discovered by Alcmeon of Croton, a Greek philosopher, who is believed
to have practised dissection in the fifth century BC.[54] Bacon's main
source seems to have been the eleventh-century Carthaginian
medical writer Constantinus Africanus, who also had dissected the
eye. Of course, Bacon and his contemporaries had no idea *how* a
nerve worked, but they had observed the presence of the nerves
linking the eyeball to the brain, and rightly deduced that this was
the means by which the phenomenon of sight travelled into our
consciousness. Bacon describes the nerves in some detail:

> But the two nerves, as we have stated, from the two directions
> right and left, meet, according to all authorities, and after meeting
> are divided . . . The nerve that comes from the right goes to the
> left eye and the one from the left to the right eye, so that there
> is a direct extension of the nerves from their origin to the eyes.[55]

There is no evidence that Bacon had direct experience of human
dissection. His description of the eye and the brain is remarkably
detailed, taking us through not only the optic nerve but also the
make-up of the eye, including the retina and other components,
but makes it clear he is passing on the observations of others.
Without any knowledge of the use of electrical impulses to transfer

information from the eye to the brain, Bacon assumed (reasonably enough) that the nerves act as conduits for the visual imagery that the brain would eventually 'see'.

He spent a little time describing the 'common sense', a term that has come to mean something so different that we forget its origins. The idea was that the 'common' (that is, shared) sense was where the inputs of all the other senses came together. Bacon tells us that the common sense 'judges concerning each particular sensation. For the judgement is not complete in regard to what is seen before the form comes to the common sense . . .'[56]

Happy that he had described how the brain coped with vision, Bacon proceeded to describe the structure of the eye at great length, commenting dryly that the earlier writer Constantinus 'teaches us to examine the heads of large animals when they are killed, but not in the summer or in the heat'.[57] Having then explained how the action of the eye interacts with the emissions from the object that is seen, he went on to explore the workings of mirrors and lenses, of reflection and refraction, using diagrams that are surprisingly reminiscent of the ones many of us faced at school.

One whole chapter[58] covers the mechanisms of a phenomenon everyone is aware of from childhood, but that still confuses many today – why stars twinkle. The arguments Bacon puts forward are surprisingly comprehensive. It might be that stars twinkle but planets don't because the planets are much closer than the stars (true). Some stars may twinkle more than others because they are brighter (not true – if anything, the low level of light, causing activation and de-activation of the rods in the eye, would contribute more to twinkling). He also suggests that it might be connected with tremors in the eye muscles when the observer tries to focus on a more distant object (false, but entertaining) and that it influenced by interruptions to vision and motion of the air (unclear, unsettled air can certainly lend fuzziness to the view).

Bacon's study of optics was detailed. Clearly this was a subject that delighted and intrigued him, but his observations went far beyond describing the paths of light rays when bouncing off mirrors and passing through lenses. Light was to lead him into something much more startling.

—◄o►—

In both his great work, *Opus majus*, and in *De multiplicatione specierum*,[59] a more specialist treatise written at around the same time, Bacon made an attempt to penetrate to the very heart of reality. The title of the treatise translates as 'On the Multiplication of Species'. It seems at first sight that this should be not a theory of light and matter, but some precursor of the work of Charles Darwin. However, Bacon had something very different in mind from the biological concept of a species as a grouping of similar organisms. In fact, Bacon's theory of species was the quantum theory of its day. This does not imply that it bears any resemblance to modern theory, or is some early predecessor, rather that, just like quantum electrodynamics, developed by Richard Feynman and his colleagues in the twentieth century, Bacon's propagation of species is an attempt to explain how light travels through space and interacts with matter.

In order to explain everything that was then known about the natural world, Bacon proposed that there must be something intangible, continuously pouring from every physical object, flowing out in all directions and responsible for all actions at a distance, such as sight, the heat of a fire, or the magnetism that had fascinated his friend Peter Peregrinus. Bacon thought that substance itself was a special kind of force, and that this force generated omnipresent rays which he called 'species'. Species were Bacon's nearest equivalent to our photons, the tiny, discrete units of light that lie at the heart of modern quantum physics. They were what has been described as a 'universal causal agent' – the insubstantial 'something' that makes events happen.

In developing the concept of species, Bacon was very dependent on the work of another of the great Arab natural philosophers, ✓ al-Kindi, though Bacon would go much further. Born at Kufa, now in Iraq, in AD 800, a descendant of the royal Kindah tribe from southern Arabia, as a young man Abu Yusuf Yaqub ibn Ishaq al-Sabbah al-Kindi moved to Baghdad, where he soon became well known for his scholarship.[60] A combination of skill and political awareness brought him to the attention of the Caliph al-Ma'mun, who was setting up in Baghdad a new centre of learning called the House of Wisdom, where the long-forgotten works of Greek philosophers were being translated into Arabic and the lost ideas of the ancient world given a fresh gloss.

Like Bacon, al-Kindi was a polymath, making significant contributions to medicine, alchemy, physics, and mathematics in his seventy-three years. He was the first physician to consider the effect of dosage on patients. Rather than prescribing an unmeasured quantity of a remedy, as had been the norm, he worked systematically through different dosages, noting which was most effective. He also was suspicious of the accepted wisdom in alchemy. No matter how much he attempted it, he was unable to convert base (ordinary) metals to precious metals or to transform any chemical element into another. Rather than question his own ability, he began to think that these standard alchemical procedures were more wishful thinking than scientific principles.

Al-Kindi wrote a book on optics in which he went beyond the physics of light to describe a more universal phenomenon.[61] He believed that there was a network of rays spraying out in all directions from every point in the universe and conveying power to surrounding objects. Robert Grosseteste had largely supported this theory, and grafted onto it Euclid's geometrical idea that light should travel in straight lines. With Grosseteste's variant of al-Kindi's theory, Bacon was ready to adopt these 'rays' as his 'species'.

Bacon thought that light itself was a species, but a very special kind because it was visible. This made it an unparalleled window onto the workings of creation. When he studied optics and performed experiments with light, he felt that he was manipulating the fundamental stuff of reality.

The *Opus majus* and a smaller work on burning glasses, *De speculis comburentibus*,[62] are full of carefully drawn diagrams showing Bacon's meticulous investigations into the behaviour of light. Having taken the Classical Greek idea that sight depends on light flowing from the eye and explained it using species, it was logical for him to suggest that light itself was a species flowing from the light source – the Sun or a lamp – but he imagined the eyes emitting a different form of species, the enabling ray that changes 'the medium and ennobles it, and renders it analogous to vision', making it ready for the light from the source to pass through to its destination.

In short, Bacon was saying that the species produced by the eye changed the substance that the light was passing through, opening up a pathway along which the species of light itself would flow. Although this principle turned out to be incorrect as the mechanism for vision, it provided a logical explanation which supported the theories that had been built on Empedocles' original idea of light emanating from the eye. Bacon's great concept was more than just a mechanism for sight, however. It also was a way of accounting for the underlying mechanisms of physics. It explained how matter interacted with matter and how light interacted with matter.

Although it has to be stressed that Bacon had no idea that light could act like a wave, there is also a strong similarity between the way his species multiply and the way that a wave works. The 'multiplication' part of the theory describes how a species gets from the source to the recipient. It doesn't fly through the air like a bullet. Instead, the source generates a species. This species then generates another species in its action on the intermediate medium. This species generates a further species, and so on across the distance spanned.

This 'multiplication' provides an explanation of an otherwise difficult concept – how one thing can act on another from a distance. It also explains how light seems to get weaker as its source gets farther away. As the species are multiplying out in all directions, they are effectively dividing, losing their original strength.

But the most interesting feature of Bacon's multiplication of species is the similarity between this theory and the operation of a wave. Think about what a wave is. Imagine the ripple of a wave passing across the surface of a smooth sheet of water. The water itself doesn't go anywhere, it just bobs up and down. It is the energy of the wave that passes across the water's surface. It's rather like a chain of people passing buckets: movement of the people represents the movement of the water, and the movement of the buckets represents the transfer of the energy. All it takes to turn this picture into Bacon's species is that, rather than passing buckets, each person empties the substance being moved into the next bucket along. This is the action of generating a new species, rippling along a chain like a wave passing through the water.

When the Dutch scientist Christiaan Huygens developed the first effective wave theory of light in the 1670s, he remarked that waves spread not by shooting out in straight lines but by each particle in the medium through which the wave is travelling pushing on all the particles around it.[63] He broke down each wave into tiny 'wavelets', each spreading out from adjacent points in the intervening medium. There is a surprising similarity between Huygens' propagation of wavelets and Bacon's multiplication of species.

The multiplication of species was intended to explain practically all of physics. For example, Bacon used exactly the same approach to explain the workings of the tides. It was already known that the Moon was responsible for the tides – in fact, Bacon ascribes the knowledge to the Arab philosopher Albumazar. More properly known as Abu-Mashar Jafar ibn Muhammad, this ninth-century astrologer is now best remembered for a theory that the world was created when the seven planets then known were in conjunction in the constellation Aries, and that the world would end with a similar conjunction in Pisces.

Bacon doesn't mention Albumazar's astrologically predicted

apocalypse, but he homes in on the linkage between tides and the Moon. He points out that Albumazar had merely noted the connection between the two without attempting any explanation. Bacon's means of tying the tides in with his theories is ingenious, even though he misses the more direct and straightforward approach of gravity. Bacon's Moon, low in the sky, can only hit the sea with rays (species) at shallow angles. This means, he argues, that the rays can only 'raise vapours' from the depths of the sea. These vapours, 'like swelling bottles', cause the sea to be driven from its channels and overflow. When the Moon is more nearly overhead, its forces 'draw forth vapours to the air and consume them' – in other words, when the Moon is higher, it evaporates the surface of the sea and so won't have the same effect. The tide recedes. Bacon is careful to point out that whereas what he is describing works similarly to the way heat will boil vapours off substances, it isn't actually the same thing – it's just a convenient way of describing it, an analogy for what is really happening.

When he came to deal with another gravitational effect, the pull of the Earth itself, Bacon achieved a similar mix of remarkable insight and unfortunate but understandable misdirection. Although the workings of gravity were not to be described in detail for another 400 years, when Newton came along, Bacon was aware that something – some influence (that we now call gravity) – made objects fall to the ground, specifically towards the centre of the Earth.

Bacon imagined a long bar, hanging in the air, lying horizontally, at a tangent to the Earth's curvature. The centre of the bar is closer to the Earth than are the ends of the bar (if you aren't sure about this, picture the bar as a million kilometres long). This means, Bacon decided, that the centre of the bar moves naturally towards the centre of the Earth, but the ends of the bar, instead of heading as they should towards the centre, move straight downwards – they are put under a strain by the conflict between the desire to head for the centre of the Earth and the rigidity of the bar.

Bacon was right about the strain, though without Newton's

insight he wasn't aware that the force would become weaker as the ends of the bar got farther from the Earth. This picture was made more vivid 700 years later, when the science-fiction writer Isaac Asimov used this exact same effect to set up one of the worst puns in the history of speculative fiction. He imagined a spacecraft passing too close to a black hole. Here the forces of gravity are immensely stronger than those of the Earth, so the spaceship is torn apart as the centre is ripped away from the two ends. After the disaster, only a piece of tattered debris remains floating in space a star mangled spanner.

While Bacon's idea of the bending bar was surprisingly good, he didn't do so well in his deduction from it, though what he came up with is quite ingenious. He pointed out that when something is put under stress it generates heat, perhaps thinking of how a piece of metal warms up if you bend it back and forth. As a falling object would be placed under stress by the variation in gravity, he reasoned, this explains why a falling object tends to warm up. In fact, the heating is caused by the resistance of the air as the object falls through it, and any effect from gravity would be incredibly tiny. Wrong as it was, Bacon's hypothesis was still impressively thought out.

◄○►

The subtlety of Bacon's theory makes it tempting to assume that he also dreamed up that other fundamental concept, the theory of the atom. In fact, Bacon was more than happy with the prevalent idea of his day, that fundamental building blocks of all matter were the four basic elements — earth, air, fire, and water. It's not that Bacon had never heard of atoms. Two philosophers of the fourth century BC, Leucippus and Democritus, had put forward the concept that everything was made up of tiny indivisible particles, which they were to call 'atoms'. This theory was seen as an interesting but implausible alternative to the four elements all the way down to Isaac Newton's time, and Bacon was not only aware of it but took time to disprove it. In the *Opus majus* he makes it clear that he holds the theory in particular distaste, commenting that as a result of it, 'Aristotle and all students of nature have been more hindered than by any other error.'[64]

It is to geometry that Bacon turns for his disproof, in a beautifully simple piece of reasoning that unfortunately overlooks one essential fact. He imagines a square made up of atoms, something like the diagram.

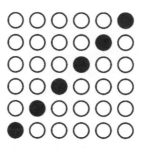

He then considers an atom to be a fixed size, effectively a unit of measurement. This square is 6 atoms high by 6 atoms wide. This means that the diagonal of the square should be just under 8.5 atoms long. But how can this be? You can't have a fraction of an atom (the word comes from the Greek for 'can't be cut') and, as can be seen from the picture, the diagonal is in fact only 6 atoms long. In my illustration this is perfectly understandable, as the gap between the atoms is larger along the diagonal than on a horizontal or vertical line. But in Bacon's mental picture the atoms were so infinitely tiny that they pressed against one another. Because there were no gaps, the atomic structure did not make mathematical sense.

Bacon's assumption that atoms were in effect points with no gaps between them seemed necessary to explain the solidity of matter. Today we are used to the idea that 'solid' matter in fact contains plenty of nothing, but in Bacon's time this view was simply not acceptable, so atoms could not be admitted into Bacon's world-view.

Even so, Bacon's concept of species was a noble attempt to produce a fundamental theory of physics. It was as comprehensive as any other theory until twentieth-century quantum physicists turned the scientific world upside-down.

◄o►

Bacon's theories of light and matter were a significant advance on those of Robert Grosseteste, who, as we have seen, had left Oxford before Bacon developed any real interest in science. But there was another Franciscan whom Bacon certainly did meet and who could perhaps have helped with his work.

Adam Marsh, or de Marisco as he is sometimes known, was certainly a superb scholar. He was Grosseteste's favourite pupil, inheriting his master's papers after Grosseteste's death in 1253 and succeeding him as lecturer to the Franciscans, a position he would still have held in Bacon's time. Bacon is quite effusive about Marsh's abilities in natural philosophy,[65] but from his writings it seems that Marsh was much more of a theologian and political savant than a scientist. Why, then, does Bacon talk of him in this way? One possible reason is that Adam Marsh was instrumental in Bacon's joining the Franciscan Order. Marsh might have been more of a natural politician than a natural philosopher, but following in the footsteps of the great Grosseteste he would have been aware of the importance of natural philosophy. Once he had come to appreciate Bacon's enthusiasm for the subject, it would seem natural that he should encourage Bacon to enter the Order so that he could continue the claim that the Franciscans provided the natural home for the study of science.

Bacon's shortage of cash, his need for protection, and his desire to take on board the novel religious aims and moral strength of the Order may well have been reinforced by a desire to discuss the sciences with individuals like Adam Marsh. However, his experiences within the friary would soon make him question whether he had made the right decision. Before long he would find that his scientific inquiries were to be curtailed. The Franciscan authorities were about to show him that being a friar demanded absolute obedience.

5
Time and the Antichrist

*My superiors and my brothers, disciplining me with hunger,
kept me under close guard and would not permit anyone to
come to me, fearing that my writings would be divulged to
others than to the chief pontiff and themselves.*

Roger Bacon, *Opus minus*

In 1251, before Bacon entered the friary and when he was still experiencing the heady delights of unconstrained research, he made a
return trip to Paris. Oxford was by far the best place to study and
discuss natural philosophy, but he knew there was nowhere better
than the back streets of Paris for hunting out a rare book or a tricky
mathematical table that had eluded him. Accustomed though he
now was to the hazards of such a journey, he could never have
anticipated that by entering the French capital he would be putting
his life in extreme danger.

In the *Opus majus* Roger comments calmly that he 'saw with [his]
own eyes' the march of the Pastoreaux rebels through Paris.[66] This
sounds like a mere distraction, an opportunity to watch a rural
pageant of sorts. In fact, it was the onslaught of a dangerous mob
of zealots on a mission to kill.

In the tradition of spontaneous action that can still erupt in
France, the Pastoreaux were mostly ordinary shepherds and other

rural peasants who rose up in protest against the religious practices of the day. Their objective, in so far as any mob can have one, was the release of the French king, Louis IX. Louis had been captured in 1250 during the Seventh Crusade, and had already been held for a year. The Pastoreaux were supposedly marching through France on their way to free Louis, but they never went anywhere near the Holy Land. Instead, they terrorized the ecclesiastical hierarchy of France.

It was said that many onlookers were amazed by the piety of these ordinary people; but equally surprising, and horrifying, was the ruthlessness with which they slaughtered their chosen enemies. Any clergyman, Jew, or member of a university who had the misfortune to cross their path was regarded as a fair target. If Bacon had had any sense, he would have kept his tonsure well covered when the Pastoreaux were rampaging through the city.

Before long, the Pastoreaux moved on from their original intention of saving Louis and assumed a more grandiose role: to save the world. They were convinced that the time of the Apocalypse, the end of the known world, was soon to come. It was to be followed by the thousand-year reign of Christ on Earth – the Millennium – but there would be resistance from the Antichrist and his agents: the clergy, the Jews, and the academics. With their sophistry, the clergy and academics had became the agents of hell. The Pastoreaux, on the other hand, considered themselves to be God's instrument in bringing the Millennium about. They were the poor who Jesus had named as the inheritors of Earth, who would now bring about God's kingdom.

Despite their humble origins, this remarkable group of peasants was in fact more than an unstructured rabble. They were led by a shadowy figure who claimed to have in his possession a document that had been handed down from the Virgin Mary. This manuscript was said to confer on the Pastoreaux the right to reclaim the Holy Land in readiness for the Apocalypse. This manuscript could be the object Bacon mentions when he describes what he saw:

I saw [the Pastoreaux leader] with my own eyes carrying openly in his hand something as though it was a sacred object, and in the way a man would carry relics, and he went with bare feet, and was always surrounded by a host of armed men, yet so dispersed in the fields that he could be seen by all who met him, making an ostentatious display of that which he carried in his hand.[67]

As they swept across France, the Pastoreaux formed their own Church, with a pontiff, cardinals, bishops, and clergy. It was as though they were trying to imitate the very organization they felt was obstructing the coming of Christ's thousand-year reign on Earth. In Paris and Orléans they were allowed remarkably free passage. The authorities were unprepared for such a powerful, near-spontaneous uprising and simply could do nothing to contain the Pastoreaux. With each week the rebels grew in strength. Before long they were considered not only a local threat, but an intolerable risk to the order of the country.

When Bacon was visiting Paris, the Pastoreaux were at the peak of their success: unstoppable, exciting, and extremely dangerous, although finally, according to contemporary chronicler Matthew Paris, they were destroyed 'like mad dogs'.[68] Bacon was not impressed with the Pastoreaux, suggesting that they were emissaries of 'the Tartars and Saracens'[69] – subversives guided by a foreign, infidel state. He would hardly have supported a movement that was anti-intellectual in the extreme and considered scholars like himself to be working against God. But one aspect of their beliefs would have struck a chord. Bacon too felt that the Antichrist was close on the heels of Christianity. Once he became a Franciscan, his very vocal opinions on this topic were going to land him in big trouble.

◄○►

Bacon had assumed that the Franciscan Order would provide a safe haven from which he could hold forth on matters of science. He could well have expected to retain a great deal of his independence. This may even have happened if Bacon had had a high enough profile and had been less abrasive. But there is no evidence that he enjoyed any fame outside his own specialist area, though he had been very public in his criticism of one Richard of Cornwall, a fellow academic and a severe disciplinarian. This Richard, said Bacon, was 'the most stupid author of these errors . . . the most renowned, who had the greatest reputation in that stupid crowd'.[70] Unfortunately for Bacon, in 1256 Richard took up the Franciscan Order's chief academic post in England, making him Bacon's superior several times removed.

Bacon was very naive when it came to personal relationships. Probably the closest he had been to anyone since he had left his family at the age of thirteen was Peter Peregrinus, and their shared fascination with experiment had left little room for misunderstanding. Bacon seemed to expect others to be prepared to take any remark he made, however scathing, as constructive criticism. If you called someone an idiot, he thought, they should be grateful and learn from it. But the world, particularly the medieval world, didn't work like that. It may have been a coincidence, but soon after Richard's appointment Bacon's academic career as a friar was cut short.

As often is the case with Bacon the circumstances are surrounded by a fog of conflicting reports, but he is thought to have been dispatched to the parent convent in Paris and ordered to undertake menial duties. He himself comments that his health broke down and he suffered from many infirmities,[71] and for the next ten years he had no contact with the outside world. But he also complains about the regime imposed on him in this period, saying, 'They forced me with unspeakable violence to obey their will.'[72] Anyone with strong opinions who enters an organization may well be forced to submit to a regime not to their liking. But it is certainly possible that Bacon's treatment was a calculated punishment, and that the 'infirmities' he claimed to be suffering from were the medieval equivalent of a modern politician stepping down 'to spend more time with the family'. Also, there is evidence that there was something more than Bacon's single-mindedness behind his punishment. In those early days of the Franciscans a bitter battle of words was raging over the way that the Order should conduct itself, a dispute that had echoes of that Pastoreaux march that Bacon had witnessed.

The friars were split into two informal opposing factions. One group, later to be called the spirituals, believed in following St Francis' rule to the letter. That included total poverty not just for members of the Order, but for the organization itself. The spirituals could not accept that a mendicant order, composed of friars who were supposed to live on alms, should own buildings, precious religious artefacts, and all the trappings of wealth. The other faction, the conventuals, believed that the Order as a body *could* own property. While the individual monks had nothing, according to the conventuals there could be little wrong in corporate wealth that reflected not their glory, but God's. This wasn't an easy argument to settle – there were no obvious rights and wrongs, and each side had a perfectly logical argument. Eventually this split would become so extreme that some of the spirituals would be branded as heretics.

From his writings on theology and his complaints about the Church hierarchy, it seems likely that Bacon sympathized with the spiritual wing, and though this faction was yet to be formally chastised at the time he was shipped off protesting to Paris, his viewpoint would already have become irritating to his fellow friars and, naturally, antagonized his superiors. His later comment to the pope (quoted at the head of this chapter), in which he complains of being disciplined and kept under close guard, seems to confirm this possibility. It's true that Bacon's personality predisposed him to suffer from a degree of paranoia, but they might still have been out to get him.

◄○►

In Bacon's time as a friar, one issue in particular was making the split between the spirituals and the conventuals more than just a difference of style. His fall from grace was a minor consequence of a particularly divisive theological and political battle that had ramifications far beyond the bounds of the Franciscan Order. This upheaval was to shake the whole Church. The struggle was based on a very similar vision to the one that drove the Pastoreaux, but this was no uprising of the common man. It originated in a struggle between the prophecies of a mystic and the political power of a saint – or at least, a saint-to-be.

The proto-saint's name was John of Fidanza, but he was universally known by the nickname given to him by St Francis of Assisi when he was still a boy, Bonaventura – literally 'good luck' or 'good fortune', and it was as St Bonaventure that he was canonized, in 1482. Bonaventura was much the same age as Bacon, born around 1217 in the Italian village of Bagnoregio, near Viterbo.[73] Also like Bacon, he spent some time at the University of Paris and later joined the Franciscans. But there the similarities between the two men ended. Bonaventura specialized in theology and lacked the background in the liberal arts and sciences that Bacon felt was essential to get a balanced picture. In 1257 Bonaventura was made Minister General of the Franciscan Order, the supreme authority of the Friars Minor.

The challenge to Bonaventura's direction of the Order came in the form of an extraordinary book. The author of this visionary work, called *The Everlasting Gospel*, was Joachim of Flora, an obscure mystic from Calabria in Spain who died around 1200. In the book he drew a parallel between the Christian Holy Trinity of Father, Son, and Holy Spirit with three ages in the development of human belief. The Father, the symbol of power and fear, was set alongside Old Testament times. The Son, the image of revealed wisdom, encompassed the New Testament times, including the lifetime of the Catholic Church. Finally, the Spirit had its equivalent in a third age of universal love, where there would be no institutions, even no further need for the Church. This period, the time of the eternal Gospel, would last until the end of the world. It was due to start in 1260 with a spiritual battle that would be spearheaded by an order of monks.

Bonaventura's predecessor as Minister General, John of Parma, had allowed another Franciscan, Gerard of St Borgo, to extend Joachim's predictions by announcing that it would be the Franciscans themselves who would make Joachim's vision come true. They, Gerard claimed, were the order of monks who would be responsible for ushering in the third age. (Technically the Franciscans weren't monks but friars, but the term 'friar' was not in use when *The Everlasting Gospel* was written, so Gerard felt that Joachim could be excused the mistake.)

Such predictions might seem harmless, but the Church hierarchy was concerned that, despite their apparent humility, the Franciscans were gaining too much power. To suggest that the Friars Minor alone would be the force to carry forward the flag of Christianity and to triumph against the Antichrist meant that Rome would be sidelined, and that could not be tolerated.

John of Parma was eventually forced to resign because he did not suppress the divisive *Everlasting Gospel*, though he did not suffer the same indignities as Gerard, who was incarcerated in a dungeon for the rest of his life. The direction of the Order was handed over to Bonaventura, who not only clamped down on anyone who showed any sympathy for Joachim's cause, but was soon to issue a swingeing edict that would strike at the very heart of Roger Bacon's life.

Bonaventura's new set of rules was set out in the Decree of the Chapter of Narbonne. It was an attempt to stamp out any divisions within the Order, and was enforced with the determination of a modern political party leader forcing a breakaway wing back into line. This constitution's wording was anything but conciliatory: 'We lay under a perpetual curse anyone who presumes by word or deed in any way to work for the division of our Order.'[74] The greater part of the decree imposed specific restrictions on the activities that friars could undertake. No documents were to be published without the permission of the most senior members of the Order – there would not be another Gerard of St Borgo – and books would now be strictly controlled. It would be an offence for a friar even to keep a book without explicit permission.

As far as Bonaventura was concerned, the very existence of the Order was at stake, and a significant public display of control was required to restore confidence. It wasn't just a matter of dealing with the followers of Joachim: the Franciscans had made themselves unpopular with the ordinary clergy. Parish priests found it irritating that the pope had granted the Franciscans permission to take on some of the paid jobs that the priests considered theirs by right. Receiving confession and presiding over the sacraments contributed significantly to a priest's income, but now the friars were doing it all with no expectation other than alms. Likewise, a funeral was always a good source of income, but many churchgoers now felt that the best place to be buried was in one of the graveyards of these humble servants of God. The irritating friars were in effect stealing cash from the pockets of ordinary churchmen, and they seemed to be getting everywhere. An infuriated priest would later comment that there was a 'fly and a friar falling in every dish'.[75] The resentment caused by this apparently unfair competition required Bonaventura to present a picture of total control to the ecclesiastical powers to ensure that the Franciscans' independence was not undermined.

In the eyes of his Order, Bacon's sin may have been to have followed Joachim too closely, or to have aligned himself with the spiritual wing, or it may be simply that he was regarded as too critical of authority. Whatever the reason, once the Decree of the Chapter of Narbonne was issued his fate was sealed. By then he had probably spent around four years in exile, hoping that he might soon be allowed to return to his real work. Once the decree was in place, though, his chances of ever writing again seemed slight.

For the next six years the turbulent energy that drove his interest in natural philosophy and his urge to communicate his wisdom had to be suppressed.

Although Bacon complained of the indignities he suffered at this time, and no doubt did not relish the menial tasks he would have been given, the biggest blow must have been the intellectual restrictions imposed by the decree. A man who had spent a fortune on books was now being told that he could not so much as read a book without explicit permission from a superior. Here was a man whose writing can only be called an outpouring – it is quite obvious from Bacon's masterworks that he was not a slow, careful writer, but rather allowed the words to rush out from his spirit – and yet he was being told that it was not acceptable to write without undergoing severe censorship from on high.

Bacon endured his exile of the mind for ten long years. But he managed to keep his intellect ticking over. The Franciscan authorities might be keeping him busy with activities that left little time for thought, but Bacon was not the sort of man who could be stopped from working by anything less than being chained up in solitary confinement. That too would come – but not yet. In the meantime, though his duties left him with little time of his own and his every action was carefully watched, he managed to find a pursuit which interested him and was entirely acceptable to his fellow friars. It offered him a chance to make use of his earlier studies of natural philosophy, and astronomy in particular, in a way that would benefit the whole Church. Bacon set out to untangle the calendar.

◄○►

Our measurement of time has always been dependent on astronomical cycles. The daily turning of the Earth, the Moon's monthly progress through its phases, and the Earth's annual circuit of the Sun are all responsible for elements of the calendar. Bacon knew this (though he would have said that the Sun travelled around the

Earth, as it appears to do), and made clear that time of day and the calendar were the responsibility of the astronomer:

> But no one can certify in regard to times except the astronomer
> . . . and if we consider this matter, we shall find in many ways
> how necessary astronomy is . . . For some of these calendars are
> lunar, some are solar and lunar, some have a fixed beginning as
> with the Jewish astronomers.[76]

It wasn't enough, though, to be aware of the bases of the various calendars. Bacon also knew that something had gone horribly wrong with the calendar of his day:

> I shall now introduce a subject . . . without which great peril and
> confusion cannot be avoided, although for long periods there has
> been manifold abuse in this matter. Since all this error proceeds
> from pure ignorance and negligence in its study, it is so much
> more contemptible in the sight of God and of holy men, and in
> the sight of all men as well as learned astronomers. But even
> ordinary computers [i.e. men who do calculations] are aware of
> the manifold error, and write in regard to it as well as do
> astronomers.

The calendar had gone astray. Reform was necessary, and Bacon, with his usual lack of subtlety, reckoned that Christianity was in danger of becoming a laughing stock:

> All people educated in computation and astronomy know it and
> deride the ignorance of the priests who maintain the actual state
> [of the calendar]. Unbelieving philosophers also, Arabs,
> Hebrews, and Greeks who live among Christians, as in Spain
> and Egypt and parts of the East and in many other regions of
> the world, abhor the folly shown by the Christians in their
> chronology and their celebrations.

In his otherwise excellent book on the development of the calendar, the writer David Ewing Duncan dedicates a chapter to Bacon entitled 'A lone genius proclaims the truth about time'.[77] While Duncan is not wrong in pointing out how in this matter Bacon stood above his contemporaries, he misunderstands the calendrical parts of the *Opus majus*, the great work that Bacon would eventually write in 1267, saying that Bacon addressed 'a strident missive' to Rome, 'an urgent appeal to set time right'. There is no doubt that Bacon believed the reform of the calendar to be important, and during his long days in the convent it probably did fill his thoughts for weeks at a time, but it is the subject of some 16 pages in the 800-page masterpiece he would eventually write. It is not given any particular precedence, either, being tucked away in a subsection on the role of mathematics. And it is difficult to see Bacon as Duncan's 'lone genius' when, according to Bacon himself, 'all people educated in computation and astronomy know it'. Even so, as a result of his spare-time work Bacon was suggesting with some force that the calendar needed an overhaul. So what had gone so terribly wrong with something that seems simple?

Bacon worked out that the calendar in use at the time made the year around 11 minutes longer than it was in reality. This trivial error, he reckoned, would mean that the calendar drifted farther away from the true progression of the seasons by a day every 125 or 130 years (he was very close – the actual figure is around 128 years). That doesn't sound a lot. But in the thirteenth century the calendar on which the days were ticked off had been established by Julius Caesar in 45 BC and had since shifted a good ten days from reality. As Bacon said, 'Since all things that are in the calendar are based on the length of the solar year, they of necessity must be untrustworthy, since they have a wrong basis.'

The original Roman calendar was a bizarre affair of ten months, spanning 304 days. These ten months were named Martis (after the god of war), Aprilis (seemingly an obscure reference to the best time for raising pigs), Maius (probably after a now-forgotten local goddess), Junius (for Juno, queen of the gods), and then, with supreme lack of imagination, Quintilis (fifth), Sextilis (sixth), September (seventh), October (eighth), November (ninth), and December (tenth). Soon after the calendar's inception, two more months, Januarius (after the god Janus) and Februarius (from the Latin word *februa*, festivals of purification) were tacked onto the year, bringing the total number of days to 355. It should have been 354 but even numbers were considered unlucky, so another day was arbitrarily added to make the length of the year an odd number.

This new year was a great improvement, but it still fell well short of matching reality. To cope with their year being around ten days too short, the Romans followed their Greek predecessors by adding in an extra day or month now and again to try to even things up. The result was a calendar that lurched backwards and forwards across astronomical reality depending on the efficiency with which priests performed calculations and on political decisions about when it was appropriate to add these extra days and months.

Such an arbitrary mechanism did not fit well with Julius Caesar's military precision. According to the historian Plutarch, writing about a hundred years afterwards, Caesar 'called in the best philosophers and mathematicians of his time' to take the calendar in hand. The team seems to have included the philosopher Sosigenes, who Caesar may have met while in Alexandria, and who may even have given the Roman emperor the original idea of reform.

The solution they settled on dated back to the Egyptian ruler Ptolemy III, but had been ignored in the Roman world. It established a year of 365¼ days by having three years in a row that were 365 days long, followed by a leap year that lasted 366 days. This wasn't enough, though, to bring things into line – the calendar had been allowed to drift away from reality for so long that the year 46 BC ended up 445 days long in order to restore the traditional date of the spring equinox (also called the vernal equinox), 25 March.

Caesar also changed the lengths of the months so that they alternated at 30 and 31 days, apart from the last month, February, which

ROGERIVS BACO,
Monachus in Anglia
Astrologiae Chemiae et Mathe,
seos peritissimus.
Nat. A. 1206.   Den. A. 1284.
Ex collectione Friderici Roth Scholtzii Norib.

Roger Bacon, taken from a copperplate after a contemporary engraving.

The George and Pilgrim Inn at Glastonbury, an early
example of cashing in on a medieval tourist attraction.

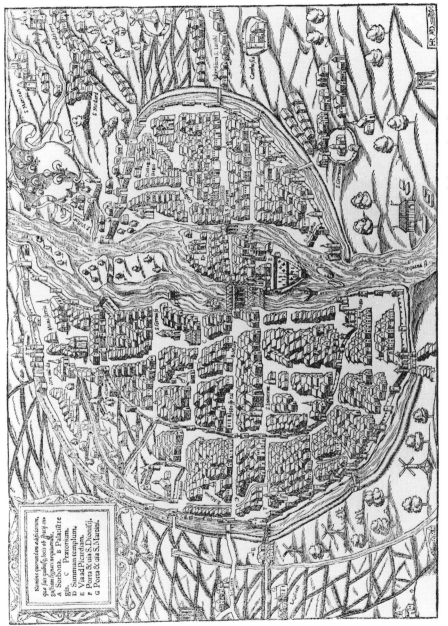

Paris in 1550, from *Cosmographia Universalis* giving an impression of the scale of Bacon's Paris.

Notre Dame, Paris, from *Les Curiositez de Paris* (1742).

Three major influences on Bacon:
St Francis, Bonaventura and Albertus Magnus.

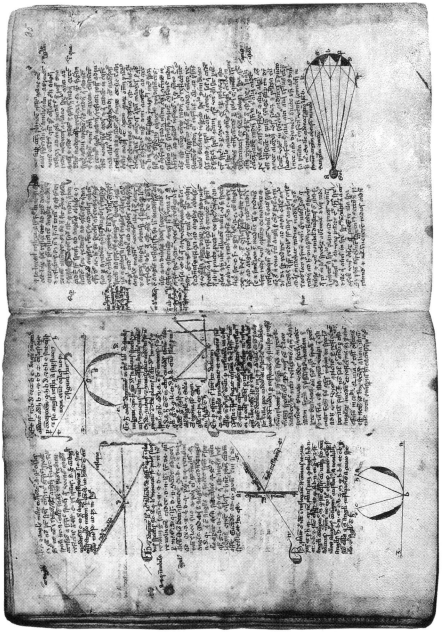

Optical diagrams from Bacon's *De multiplicatione specierum.*

King Louis IX setting off for the crusade.

Louis' great seal.

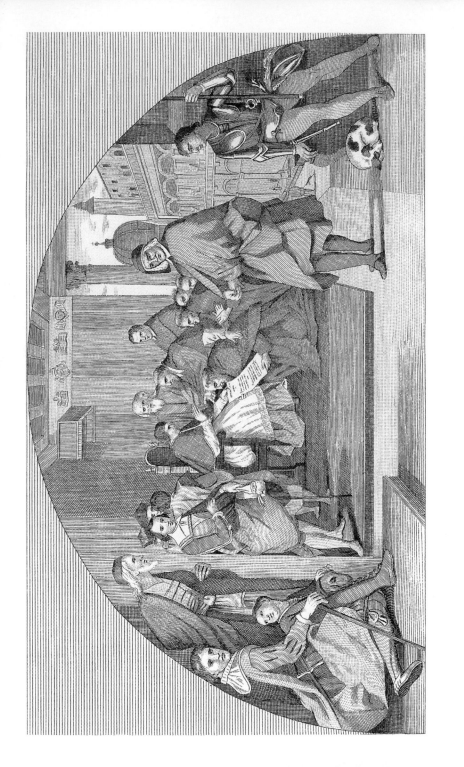

Pope Clement IV (Guy de Foulques) in Florence (8 June 1265) in the style of Bernardino Poccetti.

had 29 days in a normal year and 30 in a leap year. Unfortunately, he then shifted February from its end-marker position, fixing the beginning of the year as 1 January instead of 1 March. This brought the start of the year closer to the winter solstice, but made February no longer the obvious choice for the odd month out.

Beyond the minor changes of a day slipping back from February to January, and the renaming of Quintilis as Julius, after Caesar, and later Sextilis as Augustus, after his successor, the basic calendar as we know it had been established. It's a shame that Julius didn't decide to change the other numbered month names too, as his start of the year shift has left us with months nine to twelve labelled seven to ten. Yet, as Roger Bacon pointed out, even Caesar's calendar was an approximation. That year of 365.25 days was still 11 minutes away from the real year (as reckoned from one spring equinox to the next).

Does this really matter? What if the calendar does get several days out of synchronization with reality? Doesn't this really matter only in the extremely long term? Eventually, of course, the seasons would no longer correspond with the appropriate parts of the calendar, but it would take thousands of years for things to get really out of kilter. More worrying, though, for the Church was the timing of religious festivals.

As Bacon pointed out, there was an increasingly bad match between the religious calendar and reality. What was the point of considering Sunday a holy day if every 125–30 years the day that was treated as special shifted to a different point in the week? And what of the most important holy day of the year, Easter Day, the celebration of Christ's resurrection? This too had begun to be cele-brated on the wrong date thanks to the inaccuracies of the calendar.

As if the simple inaccuracy of dates were not enough, Bacon also found that this slippage would result in a particularly dramatic error as far as the calculation of the date of Easter was concerned. Despite the attempts of reformers who right up to the present day are still arguing for a fixed date for Easter, the timing of the festival is calculated by the same mechanism that is used to fix the date of the Jewish Passover, because the first Easter took place on the Sunday following the Passover. This means, roughly, that Easter occurs on the first Sunday after the first full moon that follows the spring equinox.

There are two equinoxes in a year, one in spring and one in autumn. An equinox (literally 'equal night') is the point where the Sun's apparent annual path around the sky crosses the celestial equator, making the day and night of the same length wherever you are in the world. The spring equinox falls exactly between midwinter and midsummer.

To simplify the calculation of Easter, the date of the spring equinox had been pinned down by the early Christians. According to Bacon, 'at the beginning of the Church' the spring equinox had been fixed at eight days before the Calends of April. Calends is the first of the month, one of the three key dates the Romans gave names to, setting all other dates as before or after one of these. (The other two named dates are the Ides, the middle of the month, either the 13th or the 15th; and the Nones, nine days before the Ides.) Bacon's 'eight days before the Calends of April' would seem to make the equinox 24 March.

However, Bacon also says that the Church later changed the date and 'now considers the equinox as fixed on the twelfth day before the Calends of April' – presumably 20 March. Bacon's account doesn't quite match the historical records of the Church. In AD 325 the ecclesiastical Council of Nicaea convened (at what is now the village of Iznik in modern Turkey) and set the equinox at 21 March, the date on which it fell in that year. But whichever date we use, the equinox was still fixed as a specific day in March in Bacon's time.

Given a fixed date for the equinox, all that was needed to work out the date of Easter was a table of the phases of the Moon. But, as Bacon had realized, there was a mismatch with reality. Along with the rest of the calendar, 21 March had been shifting. Because each day was 11 minutes too long, each year 21 March moved a little closer to 20 March. The equinox would move forward through the calendar at rate of around a day for every 128 years that passed. By around AD 450 it would have shifted to 20 March, by around 580 to 19 March, and so on. (Even in our modern calendar the equinoxes still shift dates because leap years provide uneven 'fixes', but they keep well within the limits of the Church festivals.) The spring equinox was an observed solar event, so Bacon knew that although the Church may have been ignoring the fact, its actual date would be common knowledge. In the thirteenth century the movements of the Sun still provided the principal means of timekeeping. As Bacon put it, 'Not only can the astronomer certify this fact, but any layman with the eye can perceive it by the falling of the solar ray now higher, now lower, on the wall or other object . . .'

Bacon reckoned that by 1361 the calendar would have dropped yet another day out of synchronization with the real world. Something needed to be done. He suggested that a day be missed out of the calendar every 125 years. Even so, he was cautious. First of all he guarded himself against accusations of disagreeing with a major council of the Church, saying, 'Without impairing the full authority of the Council of Nicaea, this cycle can be changed, because at that time there was no error.' In other words, they got it right at the time, and they didn't predict the need for change 'for the early Church did not have the advantage of astronomy'. That's not to say that astronomical ideas had moved on hugely since AD 325, but Bacon was acknowledging that those involved in the Council were either not aware of, or not taking advantage of, the astronomical knowledge of the day when they came to fix the date of the equinox. Bacon also is cautious about the figures he provides as 'No one has yet given us the true length of the year, with full proof, in which there was no room for doubt.'

Bacon makes his special plea for calendar reform in the *Opus majus*, addressed to the pope:

Therefore Your Reverence has the power to command it, and you will find men who will apply excellent remedies in this particular, and not only in the aforesaid defects, but in those of the whole calendar . . . If then this glorious work should be performed in Your Holiness's time, one of the greatest, best, and finest things ever attempted in the Church of God would be consummated.

His plea was to go unheeded. It was not until 1582 that Pope Gregory XIII's commission drew up a reformed calendar that instituted regular corrections to deal with the drift against astronomical reality. Although the new calendar vindicated Bacon's ideas, being almost exactly as he had suggested, he was given no recognition. What's more, this new scheme was accepted at the time only in the Catholic countries. Great Britain and its colonies, America included, continued to drift in time until 1752, while the Orthodox Christian countries did not adopt the Gregorian calendar until the twentieth century, the latest being Greece in 1924, six and a half centuries after an English friar had suggested that something was very wrong.

Despite being confined in the Paris convent, Roger Bacon had left his contemporaries behind in his bold attempts at reforming the calendar. But with his punishing schedule, the chance to communicate these ideas to the wider world must have seemed to him almost impossible. That he would get the chance to highlight his concerns about the calendar to the highest authorities – and to do much more for the future of science – he owed to the influence of one man, a man that Roger would never even meet.

6

Opus majus

Thus from an incredible distance we might read the smallest
letters, and number grains of dust and sand.

Roger Bacon, *Opus majus*

In the summer of 1266, Bacon was sent a letter. As soon as he
received it, his hands would have started to tremble. It wasn't the
surprise of being written to. Despite being confined in the convent,
he kept up a steady stream of correspondence. But this one letter
was so important that even Bacon, with all his cast-iron certainty,
would have been nervous about opening it. This single sheet of
parchment could be either his reprieve from exile or a ticket to
eternal condemnation.

Privacy was not highly regarded among the Franciscans, and it
would have been impossible for Bacon to keep the existence of this
letter a secret. The seal alone would have raised eyebrows and
prompted whispered comments throughout the convent. The letter
itself still exists. Although there is no record of Roger's reaction to
reading it, it is easy to imagine that triumph swiftly turned to despair.
His escape route from drudgery was booby-trapped. His passport
to freedom ended with a nightmare codicil.

◄o►

Around two years earlier, Bacon had discovered a potential saviour who might rescue him from his tedious exile. This man was Cardinal Guy Le Gros de Foulques (or Foulquois), sometimes known by the Italian version of his name, Guido Fulcodi.[78] It would be harder to find a greater contrast between two churchmen than between Bacon and de Foulques. Since boyhood, Bacon's life had been dedicated to the pursuit of knowledge. Although he longed for recognition as an academic authority, he had no political ambition – in fact, his distaste for politics was equalled only by his distrust of lawyers. Yet few had had more success in the law than Bacon's soon-to-be champion.

Guy was born in around 1195 at St Gilles in the French region of the Languedoc. In his boyhood, this beautiful mountainous province became a nightmare land of persecution. Local support for the dualistic Cathar heresy led to the first ever crusade against part of a Christian country. From 1209 onwards, cities were besieged and unrepentant Cathars burned.

This was no attempt at gentle persuasion. The crusaders, led by the half-English Simon de Montfort, tolerated no resistance. At Béziers, the first city the crusaders reached, de Montfort was determined to set an example in order to discourage resistance elsewhere. From within the city, now surrounded by a huge army, both the Viscount and the Bishop of Béziers attempted to negotiate with the attackers. De Montfort presented them with a list of 222 heretics. All they had to do was give up these offenders, they were told, and the attack would be stopped. The people of Béziers, Catholic and Cathar alike, refused. The result was horrific. The city walls were breached the next day and the crusaders swept in, destroying everything they could their lay their hands on. There was no attempt to identify the heretics or to save the young. Thousands of people were massacred. Contemporary sources put the number of dead anywhere between 30,000 and 100,000. Whatever the headcount, the slaughter was ferocious.

De Foulques, still a hot-blooded youngster, may well have had some sympathy with the heretics. His liege lord, Raymond Roger Trencavel de St Gilles, regarded the crusade as little more than an attempt by Paris to bring the autonomous Languedoc under French control. But de Foulques was already showing signs of becoming a canny politician and seems to have decided it was best to leave his native land to fend for itself while he pursued his career. The Languedoc fought bravely on during the thirty years of the crusade, but eventually the Cathars were wiped out.

De Foulques began to practise law and soon built up an impressive reputation. His legal success brought him into exalted circles, and it is likely that for a while he acted as private secretary to King Louis IX, the grandson of Philip II, who had joined the pope in initiating the crusade against de Foulques's homeland.

He married and had two daughters, but his wife died when he was in his fifties – an event that seems to have changed the course of his life. Perhaps the loss of someone so close made de Foulques look beyond worldly matters. Perhaps he was consciously following in the footsteps of his father, who entered a Carthusian monastery when Guy's mother died. Whatever the reason, he left the overtly political arena and entered the Church. This major shift of direction did not subdue de Foulques's ambition. In 1259 he was made Bishop of Narbonne, by 1261 he had been promoted to the influential post of Cardinal Bishop of Sabina, and in late 1263 he took on the tricky role of papal legate to England. It was then that de Foulques first heard of Roger Bacon.

By now Bacon would have lived through more than half of the ten years in which he was detained in the convent at Paris. Much of his time would have been taken up with the endless menial tasks that were part of friary life. Those who had incurred the displeasure of the Church hierarchy were deliberately allowed very little time for thought. Even so, Bacon had managed to work on the calendar, and he also claimed that he was sometimes allowed to instruct boys in mathematics, sciences, and languages, and to experiment with lenses. He also sent out a steady stream of requests for external

sponsors. He wanted someone to plead his cause, to arrange permission for him to return to Oxford and his life of study and teaching.
One of the people he wrote to was Cardinal de Foulques.

The message from Bacon was brought to de Foulques by one of
the clerks in his retinue, Raymond of Laon. Raymond managed
both to do Bacon an immense favour and to bring disaster upon
him in the same short conversation. Bacon comments in an unpublished fragment that the message he gave to Raymond (probably
only verbally) referred to 'writings which he was ready to compose,
but which were then not written'.[79] This was not the message the
cardinal received. Instead, he heard from Raymond that Bacon had
already produced a book that he would like the cardinal to see.
The seeds of confusion had been sown.

We don't have de Foulques's reply to Bacon, which seems to have
been some time in coming, but when it did arrive it caused Bacon
some consternation. The cardinal was, it seems, very interested in
the sciences and wanted to see Bacon's book. From the garbled
verbal message that the manuscript already existed, de Foulques
was expecting to receive the book by return. He did not even provide
any funding for its copying. And he gave Bacon no help with the
restrictions imposed by the Decree of Narbonne.

Bacon must have realized at once the impossibility of his task,
but he set about the practical steps that his limited powers allowed
him. He was all too aware that although he could not, as a friar,
hold any money of his own, to comply with the cardinal's request
he would require cash. He needed funds for buying books, tables,
and paper, and to employ copyists. The obvious place to turn was
his family, but as he explains:

> My parents and friends who supported the Lord King of England
> were ruined . . . I sent to England for money but have had no
> reply to this day because exiles and enemies of the King have
> occupied the land of my birth.[80]

In England, the relative stability of Bacon's early years had gradually broken down, and Henry III's initial good relations with his barons had soured. Some years before, in the mid-1250s, Henry had taken up the pope's offer of the Kingdom of Sicily as a realm for his second son Edmund (the territory consisted of most of present-day Italy south of the Papal States, plus the island of Sicily) – in exchange for a painfully huge settlement of 135,541 marks, then around £90,000. Henry couldn't find this amount by himself: he needed the help of his barons. But they weren't going to let him have his way without exacting a price of their own, and they saw an opportunity to shift the balance of power in the country. In a long session at Oxford they put together a proposed extension to the Magna Carta, the Provisions of Oxford.

One of the main changes the barons wanted was that the king's council should no longer be under his control but be elected by the barons themselves. It would be exaggerating to call this an early form of democracy, but it did build upon the Great Charter signed by King John's in checking the power of the monarchy. The Provisions of Oxford also had significantly more to say than the Magna Carta had about the rights of the common people.

However, there was squabbling over exactly what should go into the Provisions. As time went on, the pope gave up on Henry ever receiving the funds. Late in 1258 he let Sicily go elsewhere. Henry no longer had much reason for going along with the barons, but found that the Provisions of Oxford had too much backing for him to avoid giving at least token support to its proposals. By 1261, though, Henry was wriggling out from under the restrictions placed on him by the Provisions, and in 1263 the barons, led by Simon de Montfort, the Earl of Leicester (son of the Simon who had led the crusade against the Cathars) raised an impressive force and began to rampage across the country, seizing the properties of those who had supported the king against the Provisions. Their victims included Roger Bacon's family. The barons are unlikely to have set fire to the Bacon homestead and burnt it to the ground, but they would have handed it over to a loyal supporter of the baronial cause. If Bacon's family were lucky, they might have managed to stay alive and flee into the countryside. If not, they would have been killed.

By July 1263 the king had once more given way to the barons, but his acceptance was never more than a façade. One of his attempts to regain power brought the assistance of King Louis IX of France. Here was a marked difference between Henry and John: Henry knew how to get the influential French monarchy on his side. Louis wrote to the pope emphasizing Henry's difficulties. In response, the pope appointed Guy de Foulques to untangle the mess in England.

Although de Foulques was the pope's personal representative, the barons would not allow him into the country, and he had to operate from northern France. As the affair dragged on, with England unsettled by constant skirmishing and power struggles, de Foulques excommunicated the main upholders of the Provisions in an attempt to gain their submission. But it was only with the death of de Montfort, beheaded in a battle on the road between Kenilworth and Evesham on 4 August 1265, that the barons' control of the country slipped away.

Bacon said that his failure to get funding from his family was because of the barons' seizure of control, so it seems that his contact with de Foulques had taken place while the legate was attempting to bring peace to England. It says something for de Foulques's flexibility that in a period of such upheaval he was able to find the time to consider Bacon's request. Perhaps the friar's enthusiasm for science was a welcome distraction from painful affairs of state.

It is unlikely that Bacon was fully aware of de Foulques's role in the conflict. Locked away in the convent, he would have been only dimly aware of the affairs of his homeland. His main problem was the cardinal's expectation of a non-existent book. He must have wondered with what urgency his reply was expected and probably took every opportunity to ask any who might have contact with the cardinal's retinue to keep him up to date with de Foulques's business. It would have been quite a shock for him to hear in the December of 1264 that de Foulques had hurriedly left northern France.

De Foulques had been summoned by the conclave of cardinals meeting in Perugia (at the time, Rome was in dispute with the papacy), but it wasn't until his arrival that he was told why his presence was required. He discovered that a unanimous vote of the college had elected him to take over the Holy See, vacated by Pope Urban IV four months before. He was to be the next pope. De Foulques was totally unprepared for this turn of events and pleaded with the cardinals to let the burden go elsewhere, but they insisted, and the next year, 1265, he was crowned Pope Clement IV, a name he took because he was born on St Clement's Day, 22 February. Bacon's enthusiastic supporter was now the single most powerful person in the Church, if not the Western world.

With Guy de Foulques installed as pope, Bacon saw an opportunity to gain more practical support. First of all, he selected a new emissary. Instead of relying on one of de Foulques's retinue, he chose a trusted Englishman, Sir William Benecor, who acted as a courier between Henry III and the pope during the tribulations of the Barons War of 1263–7. Though we don't know for certain, it seems likely that there was a family acquaintance with Sir William who allowed Bacon to call on his services. The fact that the Bacon family had remained loyal to the king would put them in the same camp as Benecor – he could even have considered carrying Bacon's message to be the friar's due, considering the losses his family had suffered in the king's name.

Bacon did not forget the problems that had arisen the first time he tried to get help from de Foulques. This time he did not rely on word of mouth alone but sent 'a letter with verbal explanations'.[81] This letter was partly an apology that nothing had yet been done, and partly a request for financial assistance with the scientific studies that he felt would be of immediate benefit to de Foulques. We don't have Roger's letter, but from the reply he received he must have emphasized how his work was not just a matter of theoretical interest, but could be used to improve the state of the Church itself.

It wasn't that Bacon expected any special favours from de Foulques. Clement IV had shown from his earliest days that he would not stand the nepotism that had been rife in some earlier papal courts. Clement forbade his relatives to come to the court or to seek any financial advantages from their relationship. This edict even extended to his daughters. Suitors for their hands were curtly informed that the girls were 'children not of the pope but of Guido Grossus' (de Foulques was nicknamed 'le gros', but I can find nothing to suggest why: the obvious implication is that he was big, or possibly fat) and that their dowries would be nothing special. Whether this put off any potential suitors or whether it was their own choice, both daughters both ended up as nuns, taking the veil at the abbey of St Sauveur near Nîmes.

Finally, on 22 June 1266, from his residence in Viterbo on the slopes of Monte Cimino 65 kilometres north-west of Rome, Clement IV issued an instruction to Roger Bacon. This was the letter that Bacon had waited for so eagerly. In it Clement urged Bacon to send him 'writings and remedies for current conditions', but to use as much secrecy as possible and to carry out his action 'not withstanding any prohibitions of his Order'.[82]

This papal instruction was the best chance that Bacon had ever had. With the ultimate patron behind him he must have thought that he could not fail in his work. He set about writing the book that Clement thought he had already written, the book he refers to as his *Scriptum principale*, a trip through all of nature and art, his masterpiece-to-be. However, writing a work on this scale could not be undertaken without the right resources, and he needed the funds to make this possible. By this time the barons' hold on England was over; they were in disarray, and the danger to the king's old supporters had passed. But it was too late. Bacon's family was ruined. They could no longer fund his work.

Bear in mind that Bacon belonged to an Order that allowed its members no personal possessions and expected them to live by the goodwill of others. He had no dependable source of income. When he received the pope's instruction to produce the book he had no manuscript, no money, no parchment, no research materials, no permission from the Order to go ahead. Furthermore, he could not have attempted to raise funds without attracting the attention of the hierarchy of his Order. Yet revealing his intentions to the Order meant acknowledging two breaches of the Decree of Narbonne. This last restriction, though it sounds the most serious, was probably not too much of a problem in practice. Although the decree did prevent friars from writing books without the express permission of the Order, there is no evidence that the authorities would have objected to the production of a purely scientific book as long as it did not promote the heretical views of Joachim of Flora and his followers. But Bacon was already in disgrace and may have rightly suspected that some objection would be raised to his writing any book.

Bacon would also have been aware that to show the pope's letter to his superiors would prove that he had broken a second restriction. The decree also made it clear that friars were not to contact the pope without specific permission from the ecclesiastical hierarchy. While the papal seal would not have passed unnoticed, it was one thing to receive the letter, quite another to discuss it openly. What's more, the pope's instructions were to keep the work a secret. How could Bacon reveal his mandate in order to attract funding and obtain materials without breaking this injunction?

Stuck between a rock and a hard place, Bacon's only option was to show the letter to his superiors and risk any adverse consequences. Without permission he could not write the book, nor could he raise funds. It was a reasonable bet that the pope's authority would override the injunction against contacting the pontiff. As for secrecy, surely Bacon could not be expected to keep anything from his spiritual superiors? He may even have hoped that the

Franciscans would provide the funds and leave him to get on with the writing. Although he was obviously successful in getting permission, no cash seems to have accompanied it. Bacon had to dig up some finance from elsewhere.

His first attempt showed a distinct political naivety. He tells the pope that he 'solicited many great men', telling them that 'some business of yours had to be transacted in France'. To keep the injunction of secrecy he made sure that he did not 'say what it was that needed so much money.'[83] Not surprisingly, those great men, most of them previously unaware of Bacon's existence, gave him short shrift. The confidence trickster is not an invention of the modern era: then, as now, great men did not attain and retain positions of authority and power by responding to unsubtle demands for money from nonentities.

Bacon turned to his circle of friends. He seems to have been an uncomfortable acquaintance, as he tells the pope that he urged his friends to expend their all, to sell many things, and to mortgage the rest. Bearing in mind his background and situation, it would be surprising if Bacon had many friends left whom he could call upon in this way. It would seem likely that these were either university contacts or friends of his family. But it is equally likely that Bacon was embroidering the efforts he made in order to impress the man he was hoping would give encouragement and funding to his masterwork of science.

To persuade his friends to go along with his scheme, he assured them that he would send an expense account to the pope, so they would eventually get their money back. Hopefully, not too many of those he did manage to get to part with money did 'expend their all', because Bacon went on to say in the *Opus tertium* that he wasn't bothering with the expense account until he had a complete text to send to the pope – demonstrating impressive determination but a distinct lack of worldliness.

All these fundraising efforts raised around £60, a tiny sum in comparison with the expenditure of his earlier days. This relatively low level of funding, combined with the time pressure of sending something to a pope who expected a quick result, persuaded Bacon that he was faced with an impossible task. On the feast of the Epiphany in January 1267 he gave up on the attempt. Yet he had to do *something*. Persuading the pope of the importance of science to Christianity was the greatest opportunity he would ever have. So he opted instead to write a proposal, a brief document describing to the pontiff the advantages to the Church of having an appropriate work on science. The result was one of the most remarkable books ever written, the *Opus majus*.

—◄○►—

The *Opus majus* is an impressive tome: in the currently available translation it runs to 840 large pages. It is without doubt a masterpiece in its own right – it can be hard to remember that it was only ever intended as a humble proposal. Bacon calls it a *persuasio praeambula*, an introduction that was supposed to encourage the pope to authorize and fund Bacon's grander vision of a veritable library covering all aspects of natural science, with contributions from different experts as well as Bacon himself. He says at the start of the *Opus majus* that it is 'A plea that will win your support until my fuller and more definitive statement is complete.'[84]

The *Opus majus*, then, is a massive proposal for a different approach to natural philosophy. In it, Bacon identifies seven 'special' sciences. These seven are not exclusive – he also goes into such matters as grammar, geometry, music, and arithmetic, all of which play an important part in his overall picture, but the significance of his special sciences is that they were not being widely studied as part of the curriculum. Roger was highlighting the gaps in what was taught, areas where there was an urgent need for change.

The first of his seven sciences (though not as listed in the *Opus majus*) is perspective, but the meaning of this word has been modified considerably in the intervening years. In the *Opus majus*, *perspectiva* refers to the whole of the science we now call optics, which Bacon thought was sadly ignored by most of his contemporaries, with the noted exception of his favourite Franciscan, Robert Grosseteste.

The second topic is astronomy, which for Bacon was a combination of the traditional observations of the heavens, geography and astrology.

Next comes a section missing from surviving copies of the *Opus* that would be fascinating to see – the science of weights. It is likely that Bacon had in mind some aspects of mechanics as we now know it, but what he wrote remains a tantalizing unknown.

The fourth special science was alchemy (of which more later). The fifth was agriculture. Important though this is, it hardly seems worth labelling a special science, but by 'agriculture' Bacon meant much more than we would now assume – or, for that matter, than is suggested by the word's origins, from *agricola*, 'a farmer'. His definition of agriculture was much closer to what we would describe as part of biology, taking in the nature of plants and animals.

Next came medicine. The final entry in the list was Bacon's most original contribution: experimental science. This is not something we would now regard as a science in its own right, but Bacon had in mind a 'science of doing science', a meta-science that was the key to all of nature.

Although the *Opus majus* is remarkable, it was not all that Bacon completed in twelve months of frantic work. It is accompanied by two other preambles, the *Opus minus* and the *Opus tertium*, and a fourth document, *De multiplicatione specierum*.[85] This last book is a stand-alone piece and was probably intended as a first part of the final *Scriptum principale*. It's not unusual when trying to sell the concept of a book to include a sample as well as a proposal, and *De multiplicatione* may well have been that. But what was the point, having poured his all into the *Opus majus*, of producing two further preambles?

In medieval times any traveller was at risk of falling prey to murdering thieves. Bacon was well aware that if a manuscript turned up in the catch it would be discarded as worthless. He says in the two follow-up works that he was writing them as a back-up in case the *Opus majus* went missing on its way to the pope. They were presented as summaries of what was already a summary, condensations of his inspired but frankly overlong original proposal. Yet if providing a back-up were the only reason for the production of the two other works, surely it would have been easier just to have two copies made of the original?

It seems that the *Opus minus* and *Opus tertium* became separate works as a result of the process that brought the *Opus majus* into being. We have to remember the sheer time-consuming nature of producing a fair copy by hand of a book the size of the *Opus majus*, which amounted to around half a million words. It is likely that while it was being professionally copied, Bacon decided to provide a covering letter and a summary of what had become a major work in its own right. As he did so, he would have realized that in his haste there were some points he had missed out or treated too sketchily. Here was a chance to do something about it. Before long, that summary had become the *Opus minus*, another book in its own right.

The chances are the process now started all over again. The *Opus minus* wouldn't do as an introduction to the *Opus majus*: it also was too big. So Bacon began another summary. And again, new ideas flooded in. With the *Opus tertium* partly completed, he finally got the fair copy of the *Opus majus* back – but of course it was flawed. Rather than send it off in this state, he inserted some chunks from the *Opus tertium* and sent the main work back for a further copy to be made. (There is no definitive proof that this was the sequence of events, but detective work by the historian Stewart Easton on the different versions of the manuscripts makes it very likely.[86]) By the time the new *Opus majus* and the *Opus minus* had been copied, Bacon felt he had kept the pope waiting long enough. Rather than wait to have all three ready – or to substitute the *Opus tertium* for the *Opus minus* – he sent off the first two volumes.

In fact, given the time taken up by copying, he had produced the originals more quickly than anyone could reasonably have expected. It was one of the most remarkable single efforts of literary productivity imaginable. In a single year he had written around a million words, and that is not taking into account any redrafting he may have had to do. It would have taken most of his normal waking hours simply to write down all those words with a quill pen, never mind the references he would have had to assemble to pull it all together. Only by regularly working long into the night could he have achieved this remarkable feat.

Strangely enough, Bacon probably had the constraints of the Decree of Narbonne to thank for his ability to produce so much so quickly. Few have the chance to stand back from their work for years and let every aspect of it solidify in their mind, uninterrupted by the everyday need to make progress. There is an interesting parallel here in Isaac Newton, who was also forced to take time off – in his case leaving university for two years to escape the plague – and much of his later work is thought to have originated during this period of isolation.

In his ten years of exile, Bacon would have been able to go over in his mind all that he had learned so far. Not only did this enable him to pre-assemble much that he would later write, but it could have provided the opportunity to conceive of something new – to draw up an outline of modern science. By the time his three *persuasios* for the pope were complete, writing must have come as easily to him as breathing.

◄○►

The *Opus majus* began, most strangely to the modern eye, not with mathematics or physics or biology, but with the nature of error, philosophy, and the study of languages. Error is perhaps an understandable topic to get out of the way first. And any approach to science has to have an appropriate philosophical basis, even if it is unspoken. But why languages? Bacon put his case forcefully in the *Opus tertium*:

Knowledge of languages is the first gateway to wisdom, espe-cially for the Latins, who possess no theological or philosophical texts other than those composed in a foreign tongue. For that reason, everyone ought to know languages, needs to study them and understand their science. One cannot come to know them by natural means because they are dependent on persons' pleasure and they vary according to their will.[87]

By 'Latins', Bacon meant here those whose primary language of communication was Latin. He identified three reasons why it was important to understand languages and the three groupings into which those languages fell. Knowing other languages, he argued, was important for sciences both secular and divine (i.e. theology) because most of their source works were written in something other than Latin – particularly Hebrew, Greek, and Arabic, sometimes called the 'wisdom languages'. Bacon reserved some of his best invective for the quality of many of the translations into Latin avail-able at the time, encouraging scholars to go back to the original texts rather than relying on a dubious rendering of the original.

In the *Opus majus* his disdain for those who didn't appreciate the disadvantages of translation shines through:

it is impossible that the peculiar quality of one language should be preserved in [translation into] another. For even dialects of the same tongue vary among different sections, as is clear from the Gallic language, which is divided into many dialects amongst the Gauls, Picards, Normans, Burgundians, and others.

A fitting and intelligible expression in the dialect of the Picards is out of place among the Burgundians, nay among their nearer Gallic neighbours; how much more then will this be true as between different languages? Therefore an excellent piece of work in one language cannot be transferred into another as regards the peculiar quality that is possessed of the former.[88]

Language also had practical application 'in the Church of God and the commonwealth of the faithful'.[89] Here Bacon was making an unusually astute political observation. If you want to preach to the common folk, or to trade with foreigners, or to attempt to convert infidels, there is no point in trying to do so without learning the appropriate language. He was scathing of those who preached their Latin sermons parrot-fashion, not really understanding what they themselves were saying, and of those who went out to preach to foreigners without doing so in the listeners' mother tongue. As always, Bacon was interested in practical matters:

A knowledge of languages is very necessary for directing the commonwealth of the Latins [the western Christians] for three reasons. One is sharing the utilities necessary in commerce and in business, without which the Latins cannot exist, because medicines and all precious things are received from other nations, and hence arises great loss to the Latins, and fraud without limit is practised on them, because they are ignorant of foreign tongues, however much they talk through interpreters; for rarely do interpreters suffice for full understanding, and more rarely are they found to be faithful.

A second reason is the securing of justice. For countless injuries are done the Latins by people of other nations, the sufferers being the clergy as well as the laity, members of religious orders, and friars of the Dominicans and Franciscans who travel owing to the varied interests of the Latins. But owing to their ignorance of languages they cannot plead their cases before judges nor do they secure justice.

The third reason is the securing of peace among the princes of other nations and among the Latins that wars may cease. For when formal messages along with letters and documents are drawn up in the respective languages of both sides, very often matters which have been set on foot with great labour and expense come to nothing owing to ignorance of a foreign tongue. And not only is it harmful, but very embarrassing when among all the learned men of the Latins prelates and princes do not find a single one who knows how to interpret a letter of Arabic or Greek, nor to reply to a message, as is sometimes the case.

For example, I learned that Soldanus of Babylonia wrote to my lord, the present king of France, and there was not found in the whole learned body in Paris, nor in the whole kingdom of France, a man who knew how satisfactorily to explain a letter, nor to make the necessary reply to the message. And the lord king marvelled greatly at such dense ignorance, and he was very much displeased with the clergy because he found them so ignorant.[90]

Finally, Bacon said, a knowledge of language was useful in the service of the truth, in understanding matters of a speculative nature in philosophy and theology. In effect he was saying that it is useful to understand language itself, how it works, its idioms, the way we construct verbal models and use signs, in order to understand better what is being said.

The three classifications Bacon applied to language reflect the common aspects of usage at the time – the wisdom languages as a source of knowledge; Latin itself for communication among like-minded intellectuals; and the vulgar languages, the languages of the common herd, for preaching and business negotiation, though not for academic work as they had poor vocabularies.[91]

As with many of the subjects he studied, with language Bacon proved to be more the effective theoretician than the practical expert. (Despite the popular association with laboratories, many scientists are not good at experimentation – Einstein, for instance, confined himself to theory.) Bacon's ideas on linguistics were significantly better than his grasp of some of the tongues he studied.

He ruefully comments that his Spanish students found hilarious his bungled attempt to interpret a Spanish word that he had mistakenly assumed to be Arabic during an undergraduate lecture on Aristotle's *De plantis*.[92] (This botany book was actually written by one Nicholas of Damascus, the first-century BC Greek historian best known for his biography of Herod the Great, but at the time it was thought to be Aristotle's. There was quite a market in books allegedly written by the Classical philosophers but actually dating from the early medieval period.)

> For let one example suffice for many from the book on plants where he [Aristotle] says 'Belenum which is very harmful in Persia when transplanted to Jerusalem becomes edible.' This word is not the scientific one but colloquial Spanish. For *jusquiamus* or the seed of the cassilago is its name in Latin [what we now call henbane or *Hyoscyamus niger*, one of the nightshade family]. After being laughed at by my Spanish students, familiar as they were with the words of their own language, when I did not understand what I was reading, I at length learned from them the meaning of this word and of many more besides.[93]

Bacon went on to point out that when dealing with a scientific text it isn't enough for a translator to be well acquainted with the language. He also needs to have enough expertise in science to be able to make an effective translation.

According to Bacon there were two men who between them should have proved the ideal: Boethius, a philosopher from the late Roman period who 'had full mastery of the languages', and Robert Grosseteste, who 'alone [of the translators] knew the sciences'.[94] In fact, Bacon was being generous here to one of his great heroes. While Grosseteste certainly did know his science, he was not known as a translator and in fact relied heavily on others' translations of the classical authors. To be fair, though, towards the end of his teaching life Grosseteste came to realize just how important a clear understanding of the ancient languages was for all learning, and he made a serious effort to study them, particularly Greek.

Bacon's work on language showed his enthusiasm for keeping the practical alongside the theoretical. As well as the analysis of the significance of language in the *Opus majus*, he went on to write a number of short grammars. Although these books covered only a limited vocabulary, Bacon's Greek grammar was the first of its kind in the West to provide a systematic comparison of the structures of the Greek and Latin languages. Also, his insight into the nature of language itself was a real step forward.

Many of Bacon's ideas about the nature of language were esoteric, but a simple example shines out in the nature of signs, a concept Bacon covers in an unfinished chapter of the *Opus majus* sometimes called *De signis*, and one that also features in his last ever book, *Compendium studii theologiae* ('Collected Studies of Theology'). Think about what a sign is, in the most general sense of the term. It is a symbol, indicating the nature of an object or a concept. So, for instance, a sign saying 'bank' on the outside of a building identifies the nature of that building. If a sign is to work, there have to be two associations: there has to be a mind that recognizes the sign, and there has to be a link between the sign and the object it identifies. Bacon's views differed from those of his contemporaries over the priority of these two associations. Contemporary theologians such as the head of the Franciscan Order, Bonaventura, argued that the sign's link with the object came first, and only then could the intelligence interact with it as a sign. Bacon, however, believed that it was only the intellect's recognition of the sign that gave it a link to the object.

Each of these two propositions can be applied to the example of the bank. For Bonaventura the sign is always a sign, even if no one ever understands its function. For Bacon it is only potentially a sign until someone makes the connection. Intuitively, Bonaventura's view seems right. Surely a sign is a sign, whether or not it is consciously viewed? But in reality, the bank sign cannot exist without an intelligence first making the association. It is the intellectual development of the sign that comes first, followed by the association between the sign and the object. Bonaventura and his colleagues were giving words and images an absolute linkage with reality, where in fact intelligence is required to make the association. This may seem a small thing, but it is an excellent example of Bacon's ability to see beyond the accepted wisdom of his day.

We can see another of Bacon's insights in his argument for a better understanding of languages. He realized that it was too much to expect every scientist to be an expert linguist. He considered there to be three levels of linguistic competence: to be able to read and understand the rudiments of grammar, to be able to translate, and to be able to speak a second language as if it were your mother tongue. Only the first, he argued, was necessary for scholars. It was the accepted wisdom of the time that with good enough books it was possible to learn a language to perfection. Bacon disagreed. Only by direct contact and conversation with native speakers could a language be picked up completely. He might not have invented the language laboratory, but he certainly would have been enthusiastic about its use.

Something Bacon did come up with, though, and perhaps intended to include in the *Scriptum principale*, was the modern concept of a dictionary. After pointing out the need to understand the origins and meanings of a word in making a successful translation, he goes on to say:

> Nothing would be more useful than such a volume, if it furnished with all the words correctly written and properly pronounced, together with a trustworthy derivation and an accurate interpretation. But as it is we make countless mistakes in these four particulars . . .[95]

Bacon's four particulars – providing the spelling, pronunciation, derivation and meaning of a word – eventually became the mainstay of the true dictionary, though it was not until the eighteenth century that all his requirements were finally incorporated into a single work.

◄○►

From language, Bacon goes on in his *Opus majus* to a more likely foundation for the sciences: mathematics. But there is one part of his section on this subject that he considered just as much a part of language, forming a bridge between the two. This is music. That music should be considered a part of mathematics sounds a little puzzling, but Bacon uses the term 'mathematics' in a very broad sense. Music certainly has a mathematical construction, even if we are used to thinking of it more as an art, and fits reasonably comfortably in Bacon's classification. After all, the musical notes obey mathematical relationships in both pitch and duration, and some composers – notably Bach – have used mathematical principles, such as symmetry, in their compositions. But how is music related to the study of language?

For Roger, music encompassed the 'causes and reasons' of the phenomena that grammar describes. He says that music is to grammar as geometry is to carpentry. He considers it the theoretical foundation on which language itself is built. With a little consideration of the nature of sounds, this isn't such a strange picture. Vocal communication, the basis of language, is built around a series of sounds, timings, and intonations. When the main musical instrument is the human voice, as it was in Bacon's day, the linkage between music and language seems less strange.

Thankfully, Bacon's approach did not make it necessary for a scientist to be able to sing, but it did make an appreciation of the mechanics of music a useful vehicle for understanding some aspects of nature. Music, Bacon said, was the science of transient, discrete parts, a definition with implications that go far beyond the production of a tune.

He also linked music to rhetoric. At the time the 'science' of public speaking was part of a rigid trio of grammar, logic, and rhetoric. This trio, as we have seen, comprised the medieval liberal arts course, the *trivium*. Music was placed in the entirely separate *quadrivium*, along with arithmetic, geometry, and astronomy. To Bacon, the division seemed unnatural. At the time, rhetoric was based largely on the teachings of the Roman writer Cicero, who tied it strongly to logic, because his rhetoric was the sort of dry argument that might take place in a court. But Bacon, as ever favouring Aristotle, preferred to see a different side to rhetoric: the human, ethical persuasion that required good metre and rhythm and was aided by elegant prose – in short, the sort of speech-making that would benefit from an understanding of music.

–◄○►–

Once Bacon's precious manuscript was ready, it had to be taken to Pope Clement IV. Bacon entrusted this task to a young man by the name of John, whom he had taught for five or six years. It seems that John was his favourite pupil. Although John was probably no more than twenty, Bacon eulogizes over his abilities. It is possible, of course, that this was to explain why the young man was chosen for the important work of taking the books to the pope. But Bacon also uses John as an example of the benefits of his methods of teaching, which took a systematic approach to the whole of learning rather in contrast to the tedious learning by rote that was common at the time. What's more, Bacon says, John's speed of learning highlights the error of being too proud of having spent many years in study:

> Who, moreover, ventures to boast of his knowledge when the whole core of knowledge acquired by a man, however studious, through thirty or forty years with very heavy expense and labour, may be shown adequately by written and oral instruction to a

teachable boy in the course of one year or in less time? For I have proved this in the case of the boy present [i.e. John], who in the midst of great poverty and with little instruction by devoting scarcely a year to increasing his knowledge has so widened his field that all are surprised who know him . . .

Any educated person might listen with profit to this boy. No one [is] so learned, that this boy may not be indispensable in many ways. For although he has learned all that he knows by my counsel, direction, and help, and I have taught him much by the written and spoken word, nevertheless he surpasses me, old man though I am, in many ways, because he has been given better roots than I, from which he may expect flowers and wholesome fruits which I shall never attain.[96]

For Bacon, being an authority was a very dear desire, but nonetheless he was prepared to renounce such a position, and it is hard not to see in his words a particular pride in John. As a man who would never marry and never have children of his own, Bacon had obviously taken John to heart as the son he would never sire.

Exactly what Bacon sent in John's charge is not clear, but there was likely to be some form of covering letter (from which the unpublished text known as the Gasquet fragment quoted elsewhere in this book is thought to be taken[97]) accompanying the *Opus majus* and probably the *Opus minus*, along with the separate work *De multiplicatione specierum*. It is less likely that the *Opus tertium* was completed in time to be sent with them (and it may never have been sent off to the pope at all).

In his work, Bacon apologized profusely for the delay in responding to the pope's request. This seems surprising, as the pope's letter was written in the summer of 1266 and the *Opus* trilogy was probably completed in 1267. There seem to be only two possible reasons for this apology. Either Bacon was referring back to the pope's first letter, when Clement was the mere Cardinal de Foulques, or he suspected that the pope was still under the impression, given him by his clerk Raymond, that the book he was asking for already existed. It is also possible that Bacon felt a need to apologize because he had not managed to produce the actual masterpiece itself, but only a proposal, impressive though it was.

Tradition has it that after Bacon sent off his works to the pope, he returned to England. There is no firm evidence for this, but the fact that he was able to produce his massive works indicates that he must have been in a little more favour in the Order. Since he seems to have been moved to Paris under duress, it is quite likely that he did return to the friary at Oxford at this point. And with his sales pitch made, he could now start work on the real *Scriptum principale*.

All seemed to be going well. But two events would combine to throw his future into utter chaos – one external, one of his own making.

7

De profundis

In human affairs true mathematicians do not presume to
certain knowledge, but they consider how the body is
altered by the heavens, and when the body is changed the
mind is aroused, now to private actions and now to public
ones, yet in all matters is the freedom of the will preserved.

Roger Bacon, *Opus majus*

Day after day, sitting in chains in a dank cell, seeing no one, his
meagre ration pushed under the door by a guard who was never
glimpsed and who never made a sound. No one to speak to, no
one to hear his confession or to grant him absolution. For Roger
Bacon this was hell on Earth. The first verse of Psalm 130 would
have echoed through his mind time and again. Any member of the
Order would know the principal psalms by heart and this timeless
cry of anguish – *De profundis oro te*, 'Out of the deep do I cry unto
thee, O Lord' – must have seemed particularly apt for his situation. How had he come to this? How had he plunged from the
heights of being favoured by the pope to a life sentence that did
not even allow for release in death? Denied absolution, his sentence
would last for all eternity.

◄○►

With his main manuscripts on their way to Viterbo, Bacon would probably have spent a while bringing the last work, the *Opus tertium*, up to scratch in case it was needed later. He then had the luxury of time for thought. Probably for the first time in a year he was not desperately pouring his ideas into writing, not working to an impossible deadline. Even a man with Bacon's relentless drive would have appreciated a break. For just a few weeks the regular chores in the friary would have offered a simple release. No need to think, no need to write, just an opportunity to get on with things. Before long, though, the anticipation and the worry would kick in. Bacon had just placed his best efforts before the pope, the man he regarded as the ultimate arbiter on Earth.

All the evidence is, from the sheer volume of his outpourings in such a brief time, that Bacon was compelled to write. He may have been uncertain of how well the pope would receive the *Opus majus*, but he is unlikely to have waited for a response before getting on with his next task. Before long he would probably have begun to assemble some of the components for the great *Scriptum principale*.

We don't know what happened to the courier, John, on his journey, but we do know that he made it either to Viterbo, where the pope was based (Clement IV never entered Rome during his time as pope), or to Rome itself. A Vatican mathematician, a Polish philosopher named Erazmus Witelo who died in the late 1270s, makes it obvious in his writing that he has read the works that Bacon sent. But despite this, John's mission was to be a failure.

As Bacon began to pull together the first elements of his new work, he would have needed to contact the various friends who were holding manuscripts and notes for him. As the parchments began to arrive, so came rumours– whisperings that the pope was unwell. Then, on 29 November 1268, news began to spread across the Christian world with lightning speed. That day, Clement IV had died at his palace in Viterbo. As far as we know, he never even saw Bacon's magnificent *Opus majus*.

For Bacon, the death of the pope came as a hammer-blow. As

he pieced together the first fragments of his intended masterwork, a seething hatred began to boil inside him like some foul alchemical brew. For so long he had been mistreated, kept neatly out of the way in Paris. Now, when his great chance had arrived, fate had stolen it from him. There was frustration there in plenty: frustration that he could not get his message across, frustration that so many others with no real knowledge of science were able to attract the attention of the Church hierarchy as he had never seemed able to – and now that he had, the moment had been snatched away.

This frustration and anger flowed out into his writing. There was a new bitterness to his style. It was as if he could no longer concentrate on the careful logic of his philosophy and natural science until he had unburdened himself of his feelings. He produced a virulent book, supposedly the introduction to his masterpiece and innocently called *Compendium studii philosophiae* ('Collected Study of Philosophy') but in fact a rabid attack on almost every aspect of society and the Church.

Even before writing the *Compendium*, Bacon had shown that he was prepared to take on authority. In the second of his proposals for the pope, the *Opus minus*, he launched into an indignant tirade against corruption:

> One finds it in every town, in every village, in every camp; but at the same time there is corruption and a debasement of character that renders all efforts futile. Let us consider all ranks of society, and we shall find everywhere an infinite corruption, beginning with the highest level. For in the court of Rome, where formerly reigned, as it should, the wisdom of God Himself, the right of the laity now prevails, thanks to the constitution of the emperors – that right which is based on civil law and should regulate laymen only.
>
> So this Holy Seat is a prey to crime and falsehood, justice perishes there, peace there is violated, pride reigns there, avarice burns there, greed there corrupts morals, envy gnaws at all hearts,

and luxury there dishonours the whole papal court. And this is not enough: the vicar of God must be disowned by the indifference of his church, so that the world is left without guidance, with the result that for many years the Holy Seat remains empty, thanks to the efforts of jealousy and ambition!

The priests, in their turn – consider how eager they are to enrich themselves indifferent to the care of souls, busy in promoting their nephews, their friends according to the flesh, or even lawyers – whose councils overturn the world. As for those who pass their lives studying philosophy and theology, the priests cover them with contempt; they take from them all liberty and prevent them from acting for the salvation of souls. The monks, in their turn, are no better, and I exempt no Order.[98]

These are not the words of a man who was careful about what he said and to whom he said it. After all, Clement IV had been a lawyer. Bacon also seemed to be attacking his own Order for failing to live according to the precepts of its founder – and a casual reader might even have inferred a criticism of the pope himself. The only gap in the papacy longer than a few months in Bacon's lifetime was an interregnum of around two years between Celestine IV and Innocent IV's accession in 1243 – but perhaps Bacon is referring instead to the dispute between the authorities in Rome and the cardinals that was keeping the pope from Rome.

Bacon's remarks about the law reflected a change that was spreading across the Western world. As far as he was concerned, the law should be based on Christian moral philosophy, closely tied to theology. This had been the view of the Church at large, but there was a fly in the legal ointment – the rising influence of the University of Bologna. The study of Roman civil law had never totally died out in the north of Italy since the fall of the Roman Empire, and although Bologna did not have the academic clout of Paris, Oxford, or Cambridge, by the thirteenth century it had become central to the campaign to restore the Roman legal code.

If the Bolognese had been dealing with simple civil law, this might not have presented much of a challenge, but Roman law came as a complete philosophical package, dealing as it did with human problems and commerce, and excluding theology. This may seem perfectly logical now, but to Bacon and to many others in the Church, Roman law was an attempt to give greater weight to secular arguments than to sacred. If one truly believed in the teachings of the Church this did not make sense – and it certainly wasn't politically acceptable to the ecclesiastical hierarchy.

The Church rose to the challenge. In 1219, Pope Honorious III banned the study of civil law at Paris on the grounds that it threatened the study of theology. Yet the more politically astute members of the Church hierarchy could see that, sooner or later, the forces of change would prevail, and they resolved to avoid a future confrontation by incorporating Roman law into the Church's own legal code. This change of tack had much to do with the legal background of Bacon's late sponsor, Clement IV. Although the resulting ecclesiastical legal code, the canon law, was under the control of the Church, it was still based on Roman law and brought with it many of the values of the civil code. Despite its best intentions, the Church had succeeded in secularizing its legal operations.

Bacon's aversion to the law, then, was not a modern suspicion of lawyers as moneygrubbers and shysters. Instead, he saw the introduction of Roman law as putting the nature of moral philosophy at risk. In *Opus tertium* he wrote:

> More praise is gained in the Church of God by a civil jurist, though he may know nothing but the civil law and be utterly ignorant of canon law and theology, than by any master in theology and he is more quickly promoted to high ecclesiastical positions.[99]

Bacon's chief concern was to point to the immense dangers posed by secularization, but he was not above throwing in a xenophobic burst of patriotism. He notes in *Compendium studii philosophiae*:

> If clergymen and laymen are to be subject to the same law, at least let it be the law of England for the English, and of France for Frenchmen, and not the law of Lombardy.

(Bologna, from where the Roman law emanated, was then part of Lombardy.) The hatred of lawyers that pervades the *Compendium* is matched only by Bacon's obvious distaste for many contemporary theologians. There is no subtlety in his attack – it seems distinctly personal.

By now, Bacon may well have come to regret that he had chosen to teach in the Faculty of Arts in his early days at Oxford, rather than putting in those extra sixteen years that would have brought him a doctorate in theology and that seemed to be responsible for the praise heaped upon his rivals. To be considered an authority in the thirteenth century it was pretty well essential to be a doctor of divinity, even if the subject you were writing on was natural philosophy. And there is no doubt that Bacon longed to become an authority. In his day this was more than a descriptive word – it was a formal position. An authority was a person whose views defined the accepted position on a particular subject. Accordingly, some of Bacon's most vehement remarks were aimed at those who were already established authorities.

To make matters worse, it was common practice at the time to issue honorary 'wax degrees' to would-be theologians. Anyone who received a wax degree didn't have to work through to a Master of Arts, as Bacon had, before setting off on the theological route. Bacon, certain that an understanding of the sciences was essential for a full grasp of anything, theology included, was mortified by this practice. Again and again he railed at theologians who had gone into the subject too early without gaining an appropriate knowledge of art and nature.

Two English theologians in particular, Alexander of Hales and Richard of Cornwall, felt the weight of Bacon's opprobrium. Alexander was already dead, but it irritated Bacon that his opinions were still revered. Richard, still alive and well respected, was, as Bacon had already discovered, a dangerous enemy. Even these two, however, were spared some of the scorn Bacon poured on another, unnamed theologian who many now believe to have been Albertus Magnus, Bacon's German counterpart in the Dominican Order.

Like Bacon, Albertus studied natural philosophy and was later given an impressive popular title – *Doctor Universalis*, the universal doctor (Bacon would become known as *Doctor Mirabilis*, the miraculous doctor). Albertus' parallels with Bacon don't end with his title and his work. He was born in Lauingen in Bavaria around the year 1200, also into a wealthy family (in his case, the noble house of the Count of Bollstädt), and later joined one of the new mendicant orders, though he chose the Dominicans, the preaching friars. However, as Doctor of Theology at Paris, Albertus held an unrivalled position of authority that Bacon could only dream of – Bacon himself remarks that Albertus was put on a par with Aristotle by his contemporaries. Furthermore, he never fell out of favour with the Church, being eventually made a saint in 1931.

Albertus did not obtain a thorough grounding in the arts and sciences before becoming a doctor of divinity, something Bacon would always resent; even so, he was to make some distinctive contributions to medieval European science. He is often credited with the introduction of the Greek and Arabic works that would make it possible for European studies of nature to get off the ground. In fact, these had begun to filter through ever since the Christians reconquered Toledo in Spain in 1085 and obtained access to the Moorish libraries. Translations of Greek works via the Arabic and of original works by Arab writers had certainly begun by 1126, when the scholar Adelard of Bath published his first attempts.[100] However, Albertus helped the process along by making the translations widely available.

Bacon may have been aware of the contribution Albertus had made, but he was scathing about the man:

He is a man of infinite patience and has amassed great information, but his works have four faults. The first is boundless, puerile vanity; the second is ineffable falsity; the third is superfluity of bulk, and the fourth is his ignorance of the most useful and the most beautiful parts of philosophy.[101]

Apart from his thinly veiled jealousy of anyone who had received the doctorate that he had been unable to achieve, Bacon had two real problems with theologians such as Albertus. One was that they had often joined an order at early age, without experiencing the wider education of the schools. Bacon positively sneers when he comments that some of the students at Paris didn't think they had learned anything unless they had listened to the 'boys of the two Orders'.[102] His other complaint was that Albertus and other authorities would hold forth on any subject even though they lacked the knowledge of philosophy and science that Bacon knew was essential for a true understanding.

The better we understand Bacon's mind, the more obvious this viewpoint of his becomes. For him, experiment was the basis for testing scientific theories: the practical was necessary to prove the theoretical. So theology, inherently a theoretical science, relied on the practical sciences. Science enables us to know creation, which then helps us in our knowledge of the Creator. Bacon emphasizes this dependence in the *Opus majus*: 'I say, therefore, that one science is the mistress of the others, namely, theology, to which the remaining sciences are vitally necessary and without which [theology] cannot reach its end.'[103]

Valid though Bacon's views may have been, they did not go down well with senior theologians. He had already made himself unpopular by criticizing his fellows and their works, by studying aspects of science that were frowned upon, and by his support for the followers of Joachim of Flora. The bitterness he felt at missing out on his one great chance to have his opinions heard had now exploded in the vehement protest of his *Compendium*. It is not known whether the *Compendium* was ever published, but it is obvious that in writing it Bacon had gone too far.

What little we know about what happened next comes from a book called *The Chronicle of the 24 Generals*, kept to this day at Assisi. The generals in question were not military leaders but the supreme heads of the Franciscans, the Ministers General of the Order of St Francis. The *Chronicle* was written in 1370, a century after the events it describes. From its surprisingly well-preserved pages we learn that Bacon, 'a doctor of sacred theology', was condemned by the head of the Order, Jerome d'Ascoli, for 'suspected novelties'.

Jerome had replaced Bonaventura as Minister General when the saint-to-be died in 1274. More properly Girolamo Masci d'Ascoli, he had humble origins in Ascoli, a city in the central Marche region of Italy that lay within the Papal States. He entered the Franciscan Order at an early age, one of the 'boy friars' that Bacon had made it clear he had no time for, and rose rapidly to become Bonaventura's right-hand man. Later, as Nicholas IV, he became the first Franciscan pope.

The death of Bonaventura, instigator of the Decree of Narbonne, may have seemed good news to Bacon, but it soon became obvious that Jerome was even more ruthless than his predecessor when it came to preventing any potential schism in the Order. Despite 1260 having passed without the world coming to an end, the followers of Joachim of Flora, along with the other spirituals within the Order, still represented a challenge to the Minister General's control. D'Ascoli condemned a number of friars, who were held prisoner, probably at the convent at Ancona. There they would have been deprived of the sacrament even on their deathbed, kept in chains, and never allowed speak to anyone, even their jailers.

It is quite possible that Bacon, with his spiritual leanings, his infuriating manner, and his provocative writing, was one of those condemned, which would account for him being mentioned in the not entirely accurate *Chronicle of the 24 Generals*. Bacon certainly wasn't a doctor of sacred theology, but the fact that the *Chronicle* got one thing wrong doesn't necessarily make the whole entry on Bacon invalid. And whether or not Bacon openly supported the teaching of Joachim, he had certainly laid himself open to the crime of 'suspected novelties'. In fact, even without the bitter criticism that is so apparent in his *Compendium*, it is quite possible that some of his scientific studies would have been enough to lay him open to this mild-sounding but deadly accusation.

◄○►

Looking at Bacon's plight through modern eyes, it can be difficult to understand why his work was so disliked. We have seen that the man himself, like many other obsessives, could be abrasive and somewhat blinkered, but this hardly accounts for the weight of religious law that was brought to bear upon him. If his punishment was in part for his scientific views, his enthusiasm for personal inquiry rather than passive acceptance, it seems grossly unfair. How can it have been a crime to be curious?

The answer is to be found in the religious mood of the time, captured perfectly in the writings of St Augustine, one of the most powerful minds in the early Church, whose ideas were still held in respect in Bacon's day. Augustine was born in 354 in Tagaste, in modern Algeria. He was not without humour, famously remarking in his *Confessions* that he had prayed as a young man, 'Grant me chastity and continence, but not yet.'[104] But he also wrote, 'Nothing is to be accepted except on the authority of scripture, since that authority is greater than all the powers of the human mind.'[105] To be ignorant was not just bliss, but expressed a pious acceptance of the ultimate superiority of God.

A contemporary of Bacon's, Bishop Ambrose of Milan, adapted this guiding principle of Augustine's to the study of nature: 'To discuss the nature and position of the Earth does not help us in our hope of the life to come.'[106] Bacon's approach, as he made clear in the *Opus majus*, was that 'The result of all true philosophy is to arrive at a knowledge of the Creator through knowledge of the created world.'[107] Bacon was not dismissing the importance of scripture, or saying that the authorities were wrong, but pointing out that it should also be possible to gain knowledge of God by understanding his creation – the natural world itself. But in putting the power of investigation above the authority of scripture, he seemed in danger of putting man above God. Bacon must have been aware of what he was doing, and the reaction of the Church authorities should have come as no surprise to him. The light of the truth as he saw it must have been so blinding that he was prepared to risk anything to share it with others.

◄○►

Several elements of Bacon's science took him dangerously close to the line between acceptability and heresy. The detailed charges he faced (which are not recorded) may well have targeted his work on astrology, alchemy, and magic.

It may seem now that his support for astrology could well have given Bacon a bad name, but the medieval reasoning was quite different from any we might apply. Today, astrology is given short shrift by academics, but in Bacon's time the response would have been very different.

As we have already seen, Bacon divided astronomy into three categories. The first was celestial motion – what we would now regard as pure astronomy, factual information on the location and nature of the stars and the planets. The second was the application of celestial measurements to geography, in order to work out terrestrial positions; Bacon was one of the first in the medieval world to realize what an important guide the heavens were when attempting to produce accurate maps. The third component was astrology, which in Bacon's eye was no manipulation of the gullible by fraudsters, but a true science.

So, when Bacon applied to astrology exactly the same scientific

principles as he would to any other branch of knowledge, there
was no hint of magic in his approach. He was not suggesting that
astrological readings were the outcome of some supernatural influence, but rather a perfectly natural impact of environmental considerations on human feelings and behaviour. This is a point he
makes frequently and defensively, because his version of astrology
was not then universally popular. Some commentators of the time
felt that astrology was too close to divination. In the recent work
Roger Bacon and the Sciences, it is suggested there was a 'border dispute
between those who felt that it was down to natural philosophers to
observe what (if anything) was true in astrology and those who
expected the veracity of astrology to be decided by theologians'.[108]
But Bacon's careful scientific approach to the subject did have something in common with the position of established names of the
time, including Albertus Magnus and the great theologian Thomas
Aquinas.

In one of the notes Bacon wrote to accompany his newly edited
version of the *Secretum secretorum*, the supposed letter from Aristotle
to Alexander the Great that was such a favourite source of his, he
goes out of his way to make his own stance clear. His astrology is
no puppet-master, pulling the strings of human beings to follow a
pre-ordained destiny that denies the possibility of free will. Neither
is it a mechanism for predicting the future or describing what will
happen to us. It is simply an environmental influence, just as changes
in air and water around a territory can have an effect on the mood
of the inhabitants. (We now know that there is a link between the
amount of sunshine we are exposed to and our prevailing mood.
In some Scandinavian countries the absence of sunshine for long
periods of time is thought to be responsible for the unusually high
suicide rate. Bacon was describing a similar sort of effect.)

This picture of the stars and planets simply changing our moods
and inclinations is a little more logical than the sort of deterministic astrology that is still pumped out. The sort of astrology we are
now familiar with attributes a causal relationship between the

positions of the planets and events. Bacon's version merely allows the planets to influence the way we feel. We know that the Sun has a huge influence on the physical world, for example by generating our weather, keeping us warm and lit, and (with the Moon) producing the tides. It doesn't seem unreasonable, particularly given the medieval picture of the universe that put planets and stars much closer to the Earth than they are in reality, that they too should have been considered to have a direct impact on the way we feel and hence on how we act.

By saying that astrology merely has an influence on us, Bacon gets around the problem of losing free will. Free will was (and remains) a fundamental tenet of the Church. Without free will we cannot choose to do good or evil. To be able to sin, the Church argued, we *had* to have free will, otherwise the sin must have come from God – and to suggest that was heresy.

So Bacon saw nothing mystical whatsoever about astrology: it was simply the mechanical influence of the physical heavens on human temperament. The idea that a horoscope could predict something that was going to happen to you as an individual at a specific time was entirely off limits.

The mechanics of Bacon's astrology holds no great surprises for a modern practitioner. He used the Western form that had been devised by the ancient Greeks and was solidly established by the first century BC. Where Bacon differed from most of his contemporary astrologers was in using his favourite tool: experimental verification. This is now an essential component of any scientist's toolkit, but even today it is rarely applied to the fuzzy world of astrological prediction. Bacon would say that it is down to astrologers to prove or disprove just what was true in their deductions. He was also prepared to question the basis of astrology and ensure that his theory stood up to it – again, a good scientific approach.

Bacon provided a good example of his approach when faced with a classic argument against astrology – how could twins, who should have exactly the same astrological influences, differ so much in personality? He gave two reasons. In the first place, there was nothing in his astrology to say that twins couldn't be born with totally different personalities. Astrology would only allocate similar influences, just as twins might experience the same weather by being brought up together. He also points out in the *Opus majus* that any two points on the Earth, however close together, are at the focus of a different span of the heavens. Each point is the centre of a new horizon, and so

> . . . we see that two herbs grow out of the ground at the same time without anything in common, and for this reason twins in the womb of their mother receive a lot of difference in nature, so that afterwards they have different manners, and follow different arts and occupations through their lives.[109]

On its own, Bacon's astrology was not enough to get him into trouble. Some churchmen might have dismissed astrology out of hand, but many other respected men, some of whom would become saints, held views similar to Bacon's. Yet his fascination with astrology was joined by an equally strong inclination to investigate alchemy, and word was getting around that Bacon was dabbling in magic.

—◦—

Alchemy, a strange concoction of chemistry, mysticism, and confusion, had its roots more than 1,500 years before Bacon's time and would continue to influence scientific thought right down to the seventeenth century. The alchemist's concern was primarily how matter was made up, how to break it down into its fundamental constituents, and how to recombine the elements – earth, air, fire, and water – to make new substances. If an alchemist gained absolute control of the way the elements combined, he was thought to be capable of fulfilling two famed aspirations – turning base metal into gold and holding back the effects of old age. These quests are now so familiar that they are often held to be alchemy's *raison d'être*, but alchemy had the much broader aim of studying and manipulating the elements to get a better understanding of nature.

Alchemy had begun with the Greek philosophers' musings on the components of matter and had taken on a murky mysticism as Greek society came apart under pressure from Rome in the third century BC. But it was in the intellectual hotbed of Alexandria that the mystical mix of alchemy finally came together. Ever since Ptolemy I built the library at Alexandria towards the end of the fourth century BC, this Egyptian city had acted as a magnet for scholars from many different cultures. The mix of Greeks, Egyptians, Syrians, Jews, Persians, and others contributed to the development of the mystical ideas of alchemy, which, to give them more zest, were often attributed to religious and mythical figures – the Jewish leader Moses, the Greek god Hermes, the Egyptian goddess Isis, and a whole pantheon of other exotic figures.

While this mystical concoction was evolving, the technology of alchemy was being refined. As the application of heat seemed to be the best way of making elements combine and separate, a huge amount of effort was put into devising cycles of heating and cooling in the hope of achieving new combinations of the elements. It had been noticed that some parts of a substance would float away as air when heated, but if this air were cooled then the substances would re-form as liquids. This process, distillation, became an essential part of the alchemist's repertoire, as well as providing the basis for the production of strong liquor.

With the fall of Greece and the sacking of the library at Alexandria, what remained of alchemical knowledge, like all science, passed into the hands of Arab scientists. Where in other fields they would add hugely to the theories of the Greeks, in alchemy, if anything, Arab contributors added to the confusion. Although the four elements remained, the Arabs added two other materials, sulphur and mercury, which they regarded as special intermediate elements from which metals were believed to be formed. Exactly when the twin goals of transmuting metals and producing the elixir of life came to dominate alchemy is not clear, but it is likely that they were introduced in Alexandrian days and reinforced with the Arab adoption of the alchemical craft.

As far as Bacon was concerned, there were two types of alchemy. Theoretical alchemy (speculative alchemy) was concerned with the original concepts of how substances could be broken down into elements and how elements combined to make substances. This was the true parent of chemistry and, according to Bacon in his *Opus tertium*, was a discipline that was 'currently ignored', presumably in favour of applied alchemy (operative alchemy), which focused on the industrial and practical goals of transmuting metal on the one hand, and maintaining health and prolonging life on the other.

Bacon's alchemical picture was a threefold structure made up of elements, simple humours, and compound humours, each group split into four. At the base remained the four elements of earth, air, fire, and water. Everything was made of these four elements, typically using the intermediary building blocks of the humours. The four simple humours – blood, phlegm, choler (or bile), and melancholy (or black bile) – each contained all four elements, with a different element dominating: blood was primarily air, phlegm was controlled by water, choler was dominated by fire, and melancholy was mostly earth. Compound humours were to the simple as the simple humours were to the elements. Again each contained all four, but with one of the simple humours dominating the compound.

These simple and compound humours were of particular importance in one of the chief applications of alchemy – medicine. Bacon cites two specific medical applications of alchemy. The first was separating poisonous substances from natural medicines, leaving only the active ingredient (a common alchemical procedure was fractional distillation, splitting off different components of a mixture as each boiled away). The second involved prolonging human life by balancing the contributions of the four elements to produce perfect harmony. A balance was not achieved by having equal quantities of the four elements: for example, fire was much more active than the rest, and so less of it was needed. This balance was thought already to exist in gold, the perfect substance, but before it could be used medically the metal had to be treated alchemically to make it digestible.

Although Bacon was happy to write at some length on alchemy, there is no real evidence that he was much of a hands-on alchemist himself. His mysterious colleague in Paris, Peter Peregrinus, has all the hallmarks of a true alchemist, but Bacon was likely to be recording the findings of others rather than experimenting himself. There is certainly no evidence to back up the claim by the biographer Evalyn Westacott that 'Historians attribute to Bacon the discovery of phosphorus, manganese, bismuth, and the properties of antimony.'[110] Bacon was not an early chemist, as this seems to suggest, but he did regard alchemy as an important part of the scientific framework and hence opened himself up to accusations of sorties into magic and the black arts.

◄○►

We now tend to bracket any modern exponents of alchemy with those who still believe in the ability to wield magical forces, but for Bacon alchemy and magic were quite separate. Alchemy was a practical art, dependent on natural forces. Magic claimed to place supernatural forces at man's command and was generally worthless as far as he was concerned. So it is ironic that for several hundred years after his death Bacon would be considered a magician and a charlatan, when he himself was so hard on such people. In his letter *De mirabile potestate artis et naturae* ('On the Marvellous Power of Art and Nature') he makes it clear just what he thinks of such tricksters:

There are those who, by quickness of movement and by the appearance of the limbs, or by variations of the voice, or by the subtlety of instruments, or by shadows, or by playing on popular opinion, propound to mortals many wonders that do not have the truth of existence. This world is full of such people as is manifest – for jugglers deceive many by the quickness of the hand, and ventriloquists, by a variety of sounds in the belly and throat, and by mouth, produce human voices, at a distance or nearby as they wish, as if a spirit was talking in the manner of a human being. They also imitate the sounds of animals. Truly, the spurious and counterfeit causes, which are contrived with great deceit, show that the force is human and not spiritual. When inanimate things are moved rapidly in the shadow of dusk or of night, it is not truth but it is fraud and deceit.[III]

Bacon acknowledges the skills of open users of 'deception' such as jugglers and makes the leap of labelling as frauds those who claim to have actual powers but in fact only demonstrate worldly skills. Exactly the same argument is used by modern magicians who can duplicate the efforts of those who claim to possess extrasensory powers.

Bacon is at pains to distinguish between fraudulent gimmickry which purports to have magical power and serious knowledge which might be treated as if it were magic by the ignorant. He points out that:

> there are many elegant books which are devoted exclusively to magic, to symbols and characters, incantations, conjurations, sacrifices, and to things of that sort. Such for instance are the books *De officiis spirituum, De morte animae,* and *De arte notoria,* and an infinite number of others which contain none of the power of Art or Nature but only figments of the Magi. It must, however be taken into account that there are many books reputed to be magic which are not such but which contain the dignity of wisdom.

Should we still be in any doubt, he adds:

> Experience will teach us which books are suspicious and which
> are not; for if a book treats of the work of Nature or Art it is
> acceptable; if it doesn't it is to be left as suspicious and unworthy
> of the attention of a wise man.

Bacon's clear grasp of the fraudulent nature of most magic doesn't
mean that he dismissed the possibility of using natural forces for
good and evil. He pointed out the existence of psychosomatic cures
and placebos long before they were generally acknowledged by the
medical community. Bacon noted that a skilled doctor can use magic
symbols and characters, knowing them to be fictions, to cure,

> not because these characters and symbols are really efficacious
> in themselves but in order that the medicine may be taken more
> faithfully and with greater avidity and that the spirit of the patient
> shall be active and later shall settle and be glad, and that the
> active spirit shall be able to bring about many renovations in the
> body which properly appertains to it – so that by gladness and
> confidence it convalesces from infirmity to health.

Equally, he emphasizes the power of words, not because there is
any magical power in incantations and spells, but because the living
voice (and the accompanying vapours from the body) can have an
influence on other people.

Bacon also thought that vapours from the Moon can have an
effect on health. This is actually an example of what Bacon considered to be a perfectly natural phenomenon that we would have to
label as magic if it were to happen today. In the *Opus majus* he
describes a remarkable deadly lunar ray:

> For since we cannot avoid all impacts of species and forces of
> things evil and injurious to health, nor are we able always to

adapt our bodies to meet more fully the forces coming from things conducive to health, yet we should always be anxious to receive not the principal forces of harmful things, namely, those refracted and reflected in straight lines . . . And these considerations have place when a man is exposed to harmful celestial impressions, like the Sun in summer and the Moon at night, which exhaust our bodies. Hence many have died from not protecting themselves from the rays of the Moon. And especially this is true when a man is exposed to the rays of Saturn and of Mars, since these two induce much hurt and corruption in things, as experience teaches.[112]

Bear in mind that when Bacon refers to species, he is not thinking as we would of a type of animal or plant, but of what we would now call radiation (see Chapter 4).

In a telling section of the *Opus majus*, Bacon makes it clear why he is at such pains to emphasize the difference between magic and natural phenomena. Mathematics, the basis of science, was considered suspicious by many because two words were very similar: both were written *mathesis*, but one was pronounced 'matesis' and the other 'mathesis'. The first meant something like scientific knowledge, but the other was a type of divination, forming one of the five divisions of magic that Bacon defines as prescience, mathematics, charms, illusions, and fortune-telling.

This confusion would persist for hundreds of years. In Tudor times, 'calculating' was often used to mean employing magic, while in the seventeenth century the antiquarian John Aubrey (after whom a series of strange pits at Stonehenge, the Aubrey holes, are named) remarked that only a century earlier they had 'burned Mathematical books for Conjuring books'.[113]

Bacon's 'bad' mathematics was an extreme deterministic type of astrology that works on the principle that everything is written in the stars and must follow a predetermined path. As he says, having worked himself up into quite a frenzy, 'Philosophers universally condemn the madness of these false mathematicians.'[114] The false mathematicians, he feels, are not bad just because they subscribe to this deterministic astrology, but also because they attempt to use black magic to help bolster their power – they 'defile their studies in regard to the heavenly bodies by circles and figures and very silly characters and very foolish incantations'.[115] Bacon shows that he is no fool himself when it comes to how such people manage to keep a hold on their followers:

> Moreover, they have recourse to fraud in their acts, perpetrated by means of collusion, darkness, fraudulent instruments, or sleight of hand, in which they know there is deception, and they do many things to be wondered at by the foolish by these means, in which matters the influence of the heavens is not operative . . . they know in their hearts that their statements to others attributing influence to the heavens have no truth.

In the medieval world there was a much easier acceptance of the miraculous than is now the case, and people were often easy prey for tricksters. Magical symbols and inscriptions were also a source of wonder at a time when most people were illiterate. Bacon does not dismiss these out of hand, but explains his position in a very rational way. It was not uncommon for philosophers to hide some of their knowledge in secret forms (Bacon occasionally did this himself) to hide something from those deemed unworthy of knowing about it. He writes that these apparently irrational inscriptions:

> have been written by philosophers in their works about Nature and about Art for the purpose of hiding a secret from the unworthy, so that it should be as if it were wholly unknown – as the lodestone attracts iron for instance – and someone wishing to achieve his work under the eyes of the multitude might use magic symbols and characters to describe the force of attraction [in a concealed fashion].

So, says Bacon, 'many secrets of Nature and Art are esteemed magic by the untaught.'

His obvious acceptance of the necessity of keeping scientific knowledge secret from the masses comes as something of a surprise. But though Bacon had an indubitable urge to spread the knowledge of natural sciences outside academic circles, he did not believe in the universal availability of knowledge. In medieval times, the idea that knowledge in the wrong hands was dangerous was taken very seriously. That was why the Bible had not been translated into English and other national languages. It was felt that most people could cope with knowledge only if it were first filtered through an expert.

Bacon makes this very clear: 'I recall,' he says, 'that the secrets of nature are not to be committed to the skins of goats and of sheep that anyone may understand them.'[116] He quotes classical authors on the subject: 'It is stupid to offer lettuces to an ass since he is content with his thistles.'[117] And 'The man who divulges mysteries diminishes the majesty of things, and a secret loses its value if the common crowd knows about it.' Bacon was, after all, not really a man of the people. From wealthy beginnings he entered the heady intellectual circles of the universities of Paris and Oxford. He feels there is a definite dividing line between the common herd and the cognoscenti: 'In this discussion distinction ought to be made between the common rabble and the wise who are sharply set off from it.'

Bacon tells us that things believed by everyone (both the wise and the rabble), and the less obvious ideas that have been carefully examined by the wise, are true, but we must assume that the rest – the unsupported beliefs of the common herd – is false. He goes on to say that 'In commonly accepted ideas the crowd is in accord with the wise, but in the proper principles and conclusions of the arts and sciences it is discordant.' The rabble, Bacon believes, is too easily fooled by appearances and taken in by sophistry. 'Thus the crowd is in error in its opinions of proper and secret qualities, and so is divided from the wise.' Despite his argument against sophistry Bacon is guilty of it here, but he has to be understood in the context of his times rather than our own. The fact remains that he was unusual in that he wanted to make the facts of science available to everyone who could appreciate them, but what he meant by 'everyone who could appreciate them' was typical of his time.

This view had come down strongly from the early Church. When we look at the parables in the New Testament today, they seem to be simple stories used to illustrate Jesus' teaching. It's clear, though, that some early Christian writers, including St Mark, thought that the point of the parables was to wrap up the teaching and make it obscure, so that it would have its full impact only on those it was intended for – 'the wise', as Bacon called them. Mark's viewpoint comes across strongly in his gospel (Mark 4:10–12):

> And when he was alone, those who were about him with the twelve asked him concerning the parables. And he said to them, "To you have been given the secret of the kingdom of God, but for those outside everything is in parables; so that they may indeed see but not perceive, and may indeed hear but not understand . . .'

This idea as expressed by Mark, which some scholars think sprang up in the early Church rather than coming directly from Jesus, is reflected exactly in Bacon's opinion that:

> If by chance any magnificent truth falls to [the crowd's] notice, it seizes upon it and abuses it to the manifold disadvantage of persons and of the community. A man is crazy who writes a secret unless he conceals it from the crowd and leaves it so that it can be understood only by effort of the studious and wise. Accordingly the life of wise men is conducted after this principle, and secrets of wisdom are hidden by a variety of methods.

Here Bacon was drawing a clear distinction between people who could make sensible use of knowledge and those who could not.

In his opinion there were plenty who were nominally students of nature who really couldn't cope with the greater truths. He comments in the *Opus majus*:

> We see that such [a divide] is the case among professors of philosophy as well as in the truth of our faith. For the wise have always been divided from the multitude and have veiled the secrets of wisdom not only from the world at large but also from the rank and file of those devoting themselves to philosophy.

Bacon goes on in his letter on art and nature to describe seven different ways to obscure the truth from those who should not come across it, from simple misdirection to the use of codes and ciphers. It would be exaggerating to say that he invented any of these means of encryption or hiding a message, though. As early as the fifth century BC we have reports of clever techniques being used to conceal messages. In 480 BC, Xerxes, the king of the Persians, launched an attack on Greece. A sympathizer in Persia is said to have sent a secret message warning the Greeks of the attack by scraping the wax off the wooden tablets used as writing boards, painting a message on the wood, and then replacing the wax to produce an apparently blank tablet. When the Persians sailed on Athens, the Greeks were ready for them, drawing them into an ambush and wiping out much of the Persian fleet.

Although not original, Bacon's introduction to hiding the message from the masses does provide a good list of techniques. It begins with hiding the information 'under characters and symbols' – effectively by using jargon or representations as typically might be found in a modern scientific textbook. Although this approach isn't actually designed to limit the communication of information, the fact is that the reader doesn't have to read too many pages of a textbook on an unfamiliar scientific subject to become totally lost.

After characters and symbols comes the parabolic approach that Mark's gospel refers to. Bacon gives a specific example:

others in enigmatical and figurative expressions, as in the case where Aristotle says in his *Liber secretorum* 'O, Alexander, I wish to show you the greatest of secrets, and it behoves you to conceal this Arcanum and to perfect the proposed work of this stone of art which is no stone, which is in every man, and in every place, and in every time, and which is called the goal of all philosophers.' Such expressions are found in many books and sciences, and innumerable writings are obscured in this fashion, so that no one may understand them without his teacher.

Bacon is describing a special kind of jargon intended to obscure the message. In his example the writer is referring to the philosopher's stone, but uses indirect language to make it less clear. The text becomes, in effect, a code, a secret language known only to the teacher and to those students with whom the teacher has provided the key. It performs a similar function to an in-joke, providing an inner connection for the members of a group while excluding others in a way that is specifically designed to frustrate them.

Bacon goes on to consider more conventional ways of encrypting information. He points out that:

Others hide their secrets in a third manner by their method of writing, as by writing with consonants only, like the Hebrews, Chaldeans, Syrians, and Arabians, and as the Greeks do, for there is much among them which is obscured in this way.

This practice was probably originally intended as much a form of shorthand as a way of hiding away the text, but there certainly are examples, such as the Greek technique of writing the actual message in small marks above dummy characters (see Chapter 9) where the intention was to keep the contents secret.

Bacon's fourth and fifth techniques involve the substitution of different letters, either by using more than one alphabet as 'Ethicus the Astronomer hides his wisdom by writing Hebrew, Greek, and Latin letters in the same word' or by using a substitution of their own devising. In modern code-breaking, such encipherments are straightforward to crack. A simple letter-for-letter substitution, for example, is easy to decipher because we know how often different letters appear in a given language. Because, for instance, *e* is the commonest letter in English, we can guess that the most frequently occurring character in a simple substitution code probably represents the letter *e*. Bacon, though, without a knowledge of such frequency analysis, thought it a particularly tough challenge:

> . . . authors hide their secrets by means of special letters, devised by their own ingenuity and will, and different from those which are anywhere in use. This is a most serious impediment, and was used by Artephius in his book *De secretis naturae*.

Next in Bacon's cryptographic stockpile comes the production of a particular shape or diagram, where the positioning of the dots and lines conveys information as well as the characters themselves. Artephius, a twelfth-century mystic, is again quoted as using this technique:

> . . . actual letters are not used but other geomantic figures, which function as letters according to the arrangements of points and marks – and this method is also used by Artephius in his science.

Finally, Bacon makes a rather obscure suggestion:

> Seventhly, there is still a better way of obscuring which is comprehended in the *ars notaria*, which is the art of noting and writing with whatever brevity we wish and with whatever rapidity we desire – and by this mean many secrets are hidden in the books of the Latins.

It is possible that Bacon was imagining a truly magical means of concealment (the *ars notaria* was an infamous magic text of the time), but it is equally likely that he is referring here to true shorthand, where very short marks are used to denote words or even sentences. Without a standard approach, a personal shorthand can be a highly effective code.

◄o►

The rest of Bacon's letter goes on to describe several ways of mixing gunpowder. The first is certainly a good example of the sort of obscuring Bacon describes as his second method of concealment. It appears to be about the production of the 'philosopher's egg', one of the main goals of any alchemist, a substance that among other things was thought to effect the transmutation of ordinary metals into gold. In practice, though, the description is a concealed recipe for preparing the three constituents of gunpowder – saltpetre, sulphur, and carbon (charcoal). Chunks of text have clearly been thrown in with no purpose other than to obscure, and in fact Bacon even highlights this at the beginning of a particularly meaningless passage:

> Understand this if you can; for without a doubt there will be a composition from the elements and so there will be a part of the stone which is not a stone, which is in every man and which you will find in its proper place in every season of the year. Then you take oil which is like a salve or a viscous cheese not to be broken asunder at the first thrust.

While some of the jargon here was meaningful to an alchemist – so that, for instance 'the stone which is not a stone' was a common way of referring to the philosopher's egg or philosopher's stone – the whole section makes no real contribution to the recipe. Some interpreters, notably one Lieutenant-Colonel H. W. L. Hime,[118] have suggested that this portion of the manuscript makes use of the so-called Argyle cipher, where key words are surrounded by meaningless text and can be picked out by using a special piece of paper with holes cut out in the appropriate places. Hime provides a possible solution, picking out some of the words in the text. But with no key provided for the uninitiated reader the approach is so open that it would be possible to totally reverse the meaning by picking out different words. An interpretation of such a code with no guidance on the structure can never be certain.

Each of the other concealed descriptions of gunpowder is in turn slightly less obscure, and the third seems to come closest to a formula – simply substituting obscure terms like 'bones of Adam and of the Calx' for the actual components of the mixture. The letter finishes with what may be a fourth formula, this time absolutely literal in approach, but using an anagram or some other encoding to conceal the key information. It reads:

> However of saltpetre LVRV VO PO VIR CAN VTRI and of sulphur: and so you will make thunder and lightning, and so you will make the artifice. But you must take note whether I am speaking in an enigma or according to the truth.

As is the way with anagrams, with a certain amount of ingenuity several appropriate solutions can be deduced. At least one interpreter, working from a version in which the hand-copied text reads LURU MOPE CAN UBRE or LURA NOPE CUM UBRE, and bearing in mind that Latin did not distinguish between 'U' and 'V', showed that it can be made to spell out the Latin for 'pulverized carbon' (*carbonum pulvere*).[119] However, remembering that the proportions given in the earlier method, which were five of carbon to five of sulphur and six of saltpetre, the translator of the letter, T. L. Davis, offers an alternative solution, R. VI. PART. V. NOV. CORVLI. V. ET, which would transform the sentence into 'However of saltpetre the formula has six parts, of young willow (charcoal)

five and five of sulphur.' These proportions would not make particularly effective gunpowder – a more effective ratio is around 15 of
saltpetre to 3 of carbon and 2 of sulphur – but it would certainly
have been good enough to produce the sort of pyrotechnic effects
that Bacon mentions. These are particularly well described in the
Opus tertium:

> From the flashing and flaming of certain igneous mixtures and
> the terror inspired by their noise wonderful consequences ensue.
> As a simple example may be mentioned: the noise and flame
> generated by the powder, known in divers places, composed of
> saltpetre, charcoal, and sulphur. When a quantity of the powder
> no bigger than a man's finger is wrapped up in a piece of parch-
> ment and ignited, it explodes with a blinding flash and a stun-
> ning noise. If a larger quantity were used, or if the case were
> made of some solid material, the explosion would of course be
> much more violent and the flash and din altogether unbearable.[120]

Bacon certainly did not invent gunpowder, nor did he really conceive
of its explosive potential (the first gun was not made until the first
half of the fourteenth century), perhaps in part because of his ineffective mix, but he was one of the first to point out that it could
be used for something more than amusement and that solid casings
would increase the effect of the blast.

Unfortunately for Bacon, in those dark years of the mid-1200s
there would have been many who would have regarded the flash
and noise and pungent smells of ignited gunpowder as magic pure
and simple. In fact, it is likely that weak forms of gunpowder and
early fireworks were part of the conjuror's stock-in-trade, used to
create startling reports and coloured flames. Credulous audiences
would be all too happy to see this as a power that originated from
magical forces – or worse, from the Devil himself. If Bacon were
in the habit of letting off gunpowder charges, it would be easy to
see how this would have attracted accusations of diabolical

collusion. You would even be able to smell traces of the Devil's favourite perfume, brimstone (sulphur), on his clothes.

Fire and brimstone notwithstanding, Bacon's view was that there was only one true source of witchcraft and magic, and that was the malign influence of anger and hatred. He describes the effect in the *Opus majus*:

> And especially must this fact be considered when men and animals become angry and have the desire to do harm and a mind of malignity. For witchcraft is reduced to this source; what force it has comes from this source, since without doubt impression then becomes stronger, because nature obeys the thoughts and the desire of the soul and she is aroused to stronger action . . .[121]

✓ Bacon is saying that there is no external magic, and that any witchcraft is the result of the evil within us. By comparison with the views of magic that were common at the time, and are even held by some people today, this is a very rational, scientific viewpoint. For Bacon there were just four causes of any object or action: God as creator and redeemer; nature (His creation); art (the creations of the created; the works of man); and finally the 'anti-art' of witchcraft, the result of our negative emotions of anger and hatred. There was no need to invoke any supernatural forces other than those of God.

✓ Despite this clear opinion set forth in his writing, Bacon's fervent interest in the sciences could have gained him a reputation as a magician even among the educated members of the council which would be responsible for his condemnation. The 'suspected novelties' were beginning to pile up. Roger Bacon had dabbled with the doubtful sciences of astrology and alchemy. He was rumoured to be a magician, no matter how hard he tried to deny it. He had railed against the accepted authorities of the day. He was a tacit supporter of Joachim of Flora. And there was even more: he treated heathens as equals.

Perhaps most of all it was Bacon's breadth of outlook that

condemned him. He not only considered the ancient Greek philosophers to have spoken words of wisdom, but went so far as to suggest that they were under divine guidance, even though they had failed to get the theological message quite right. Furthermore, he emphasized the ethical values of the Islamic writers who were widely read in his day, like al-Farabi and Avicenna, in a way that was likely to raise suspicion in even his most tolerant brethren.

For Bacon it was the big picture that mattered. He saw a magnificent whole, taking in the knowledge of the ancient Greeks, the practical philosophy and ethics of the Arabs, and the true beliefs of Christianity. His was an inclusive vision when the society of the time was set on exclusion. Bacon was no ecumenical – the concept would have been meaningless, as he had a clear picture of religious truth – but he could not see why being mistaken about religious beliefs should necessarily mean that a man's scientific ideas were faulty. His breadth of vision is likely to have been at the heart of the 'novelties' for which he was condemned.

Today, when most scientists only ever study a minute fraction of a small segment of a single branch of just one of the sciences, Bacon's holistic approach is refreshing if impractical. He believed that a man's knowledge was worthless unless it was complete in scope – that it was necessary to know *all* the sciences, whatever the sources. What's more, he believed that this broad understanding of nature was necessary not just for scientists but for theologians and artists as well. Even in Bacon's day, such a view would have been revolutionary.

◄o►

While there is never likely to be absolute proof that Bacon was imprisoned by d'Ascoli, one thing speaks out loud and clear. From the late 1270s and throughout the whole of the 1280s there is not a single piece of writing from this hugely and compulsively productive man. Silence falls. And it is hard to imagine anything that could have silenced him except the dull thud of the closing prison-cell door.

There can have been few prisons less appealing than the one at Ancona into which Bacon would have been cast. There is no hard evidence that this friary in central Italy, near the Adriatic coast, was the destination of Bacon and his fellow condemned men, but legend has it that this is where Bacon was imprisoned. Whether here or in another friary, being locked up was seen as a merciful alternative to being burned alive, the conventional method of disposing of heretics. Yet the result was to replace a short spell of terrible torture with years of hopeless pain. The prisoners would each be confined in a tiny cell, chained up. Unable to take exercise, to talk to anyone, to do anything, the only refuge for many was madness.

Most frightening of all for those condemned to this punishment was the permanent withdrawal of the sacrament. Not even in death would these poor men be allowed to take Communion. There would be no last rites. This meant dying in a state of sin, which to the simplistic medieval Christians was nothing less than a one-way ticket to hell. Despair is too light a word to describe the condition of Bacon and his fellow prisoners as year after year passed, unmarked by anything other than the cycle of light and darkness and the steady arrival of a minimal diet of water and gruel. They were already dead men.

8

Into the Light

Now these matters are understood, I shall tell of certain
marvels wrought through the agency of Art and Nature,
and will afterwards assign them to their causes and modes.
In these there is no magic whatsoever, because, as has been
said, all magical power is inferior to these works and
incompetent to accomplish them.

Roger Bacon, *De mirabile potestate artis et naturae*

One of the legends that sprang up about Roger Bacon tells how he
found a crack in the wall of his dark cell in Ancona. Through it he
is said to have passed on an education to local children who were
first attracted by his cries and later returned, fascinated by his stories
of strange beasts and other lands and the dance of the stars. Unlike
many of the Bacon stories, this one has a potential ring of truth. It
does not speak of magical powers, but of Bacon doing what he liked
to do best – communicating knowledge to the glory of God.

We know from the pride with which he described his shining
pupil John, who was entrusted with the task of delivering Bacon's
masterpiece to the pope, that Bacon enjoyed educating the young.
It isn't difficult to imagine how the need to plan his next lesson, to
assemble and structure his thoughts, could have helped to focus his
mind in those seemingly endless days. His one small hope would

have been that the next day, or the next, there would be someone there, someone to listen. It may even have been that there was no one there at all, but the very activity of preparing for a possible student was a lifeline that kept him sane.

The years passed, but eventually this informal teaching was to be supplanted by something much more tangible. In 1288 Jerome d'Ascoli became Pope Nicholas IV. His replacement as Minister General of the Franciscan Order, the Provençal churchman Raymond of Gaufredi, was a very different leader. Although not technically a spiritual himself, he was much more sympathetic to their cause and sought to achieve unity through the type of love that St Francis had preached, rather than by the agency of brutal decrees and suppression favoured by his predecessors. This agenda was to lead in 1295 to Raymond being removed from his position by the pope, but for the moment the atmosphere in the Order changed dramatically.

Around 1290, on Raymond's orders, the prisoners at Ancona were released. Tradition has it that Raymond took part in the freeing himself and wept on seeing the inhumane conditions in which these friars, innocent of everything but belief, had been kept.

Bacon being freed around 1290 fits well with the writing of his last book, *Compendium studii theologiae*, in 1292. Not only does the timing – a book appearing after a gap of many years – suggest that Bacon really had been locked away, but the tone of the writing is consistent with a man whose spirit has been bent if not broken. There is still some of the old Bacon's irritation at the theologians whom he felt had no real basis for their authority, but his writing is more tempered in tone.

Now an old man, in his seventies, Roger Bacon was ready for the final act of the play of his life. In the Bacon legend told in *The Famous Historie of Fryer Bacon*, his last years find him repentant. His proud pursuit of knowledge has brought him nothing but grief. He calls together a group of friends around a great fire he has built and tells them:

'What has all my knowledge of nature's secrets gained me? Only the loss of a much greater knowledge, the loss of divine studies that make the soul of a man blessed. I have found that my knowledge has been a heavy burden, keeping me from good thoughts.

'But I am going to take away the cause, these books, which I am going to burn in front of you.'

They all begged him to spare the books, because the information in them would be of great value to men in the future, but Bacon would not listen. He threw them all into the fire, and in those flames burned the greatest learning in the world.[122]

The mythical Roger then turns away from his magic and renounces all his worldly possessions:

Then Bacon gave away his goods, some things to poor scholars, some to other poor folk. He left nothing for himself. Then he had a cell built in the church wall and locked himself in. Bacon was to remain there until his death. He spent his time in prayer, mediation, and divine exercises, seeking by all the means at his disposal to dissuade men from the study of magic.

He lived in that cell for two years, never coming out. He was given his food and drink through a window, and at that window he would speak to those who came to him. Bacon dug his own grave with his fingernails and lay in it when he died.

This was the Life and Death of this famous Fryer, who lived most part of his life a Magician, and dyed a true Penitent Sinner and an Anchorite.[123]

But Bacon was no anchorite. He had never been a hermit who locked himself away from others. As a friar he had no goods to give away, and any repentance he might have felt was for honest sins, not for his often impatient attempts to destroy ignorance. As he lay on his hard straw pallet in the friary at Oxford, Bacon might have mused that he who had always been so certain of the benefits of science had gained little from it personally. But the goal of his work had always been to benefit Christendom, not to ease the lot of one man.

◄o►

Although he was a Franciscan, helping individuals had never been one of Bacon's strong points. Of all the sciences, medicine was the one with which he felt least comfortable. His book on the retarding of ageing does not compare with his other works, and any medical wisdom that he professed was largely a matter of passing on unfiltered the wisdom of Greek writers such as Galen. Sometimes this led him to list some of the more bizarre aspects of folk medicine among his medical remedies. For instance, he had noted in his letter *On Art and Nature* that:

> The Lady Tormery of England, while searching for a white hind, found an ointment with which the keeper of the woods anointed his whole body except the soles of his feet – and he lived three hundred years without any corruption save pains and suffering in the feet. Many of us are well aware in our own times that farmers living without the advice of medical men frequently attain the age of a hundred and sixty or thereabouts.[124]

When he kept away from his folkloric cures, Bacon was admittedly much more sound – often surprisingly so, given the crude and ineffective nature of medieval medicine. As we have already seen (pp. 130–2), he was aware of the placebo effect. He also gave advice that is remarkably similar to the recommendations of health consultants more than 700 years later:

> A real remedy against the specific corruption [of the body] might be found if a man from his youth would exercise a complete regulation of his health in all matters pertaining to food and

Early copy (14th century) of page of Bacon's works for Clement IV.

From the *On Language* section of Bacon's *Opus majus*, demonstrating accents on Hebrew characters and the use of diphthongs in Greek.

There are no contemporary pictures of Bacon and his pupil John, but this illustration from the mid–15th century shows him with an unnamed pupil.

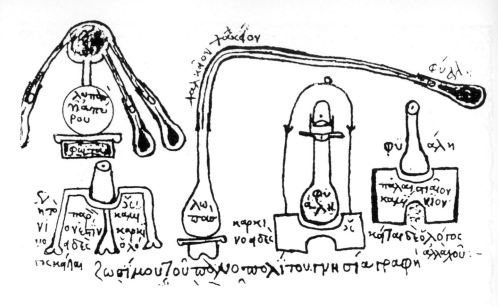

Early chemical equipment including alembics for distillation from Marcellin P.E. Berthelot's *Collection Des Anciens Alchemistes Grécs*.

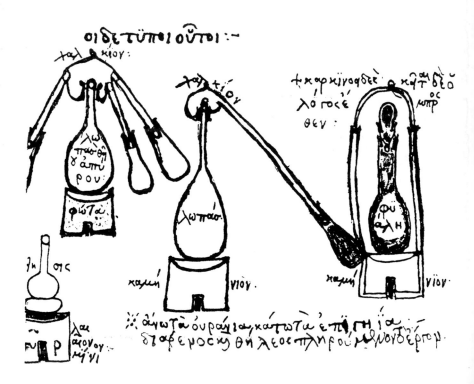

Miles and Bacon in an illustration from an early 20th
century edition of *The Famous Historie of Fryer Bacon.*

The Tower in Oxford on Folly Bridge alleged
in the 17th century to be Bacon's study.

Pages from the Voynich manuscript.

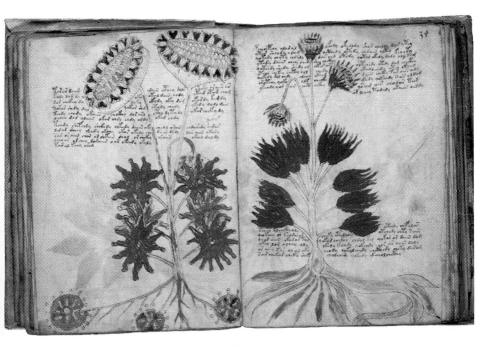

A medieval alchemical laboratory.

ROGER BACON an Inglishman.

Bacon and John Dee as members
of the Illuminati in an early 20th
century work on occultism.

D.ͬ DEE avoucheth his Stone is brought by Angelical
Ministry.

drink, sleep and waking, movement and rest, retention, air, and passions of the soul. For if anyone will observe this regimen from his birth, he will live to the utmost that is permitted by the nature which he has inherited from his parents . . . Beyond this he cannot go, for the regimen of health is not a remedy for the corruption of our ancient parents.[125]

In other words, with a good diet, appropriate amounts of sleep and exercise, and relief from stress, you are likely to get the best out of your life – exactly what too many of us now seem unwilling to acknowledge. Despite his ill treatment from his brothers, Bacon had seemed to manage well himself on this score, but now there was nothing more that food and drink or sleeping and waking could do for him.

◄○►

As we have seen, Bacon also brought astrology into the medical arena, believing that the Sun, Moon, and planets could have a direct effect on the way a person felt. Yet astrology was only one part of his study of astronomy. He seemed to enjoy the intellectual challenge of studying the universe, the complex mix of the near-theological challenge of cosmology, of speculating on the whys and wherefores of the whole of creation, and the very practical applications of the calendar and map-making.

One of the few occasions on which Bacon managed to catch out Aristotle was in astronomy. On most topics he was happy to give Aristotle the benefit of the doubt, but Aristotle had said that the stars got their light from the Sun. The Greek philosopher's reasoning was a little obtuse. He pointed out correctly that the Moon went dark when the Earth got in the way of the sunlight. It could be eclipsed only if it was lit by the Sun. But the same thing didn't happen to the stars. So how could they be lit by the Sun as well?

Aristotle argued that in principle the stars could be eclipsed, but that the Earth's shadow extended essentially only as far as Mercury. (Bear in mind that in Aristotle's model of the universe the Earth stood at the centre with the Sun, Moon, planets and stars all revolving around it, so Mercury and the Earth could never be on opposite sides of the Sun.) By the time the Earth's shadow reached the much more distant stars, he believed that it would be so small as to have no effect. Even so, Aristotle saw no reason why the stars should work differently from the Moon, and reckoned that they managed to eclipse each other 'when the lower ones fall between the Sun and the higher ones',[126] though the effect was difficult to spot.

Bacon wasn't happy with this theory as it stood. He rejected the suggestion that the stars could be like mirrors, reflecting the light of the Sun, and decided that they must give off light of their own. However, there was a flaw in his argument because, like Aristotle, he used the Moon as an example in his argument. He believed that the straight-line geometry of optics is such that the Moon would cast light only on a small part of the Earth if it shone by reflecting light from the Sun. He imagined that you would be able to see a part of the horizon that wasn't lit by the Moon if this were the case. So he argued that the Moon's light (and hence the light of the stars) was not reflected, but emitted directly from its surface.

Bacon had picked up on one of Aristotle's errors, but managed to fall into another himself when he assumed that he could gener- alize for the heavenly bodies and treat the Moon and the stars in the same way. Bacon accepted that the Moon would reflect some light, but thought that it would be scattered off to a small section of the sky. That apart, he reckoned that the light of the stars and the Moon was generated from within them, as a result of invisible forces (his species) streaming out from the Sun. That way, the Moon's radiation could still originate from the Sun, but would shine in all directions, like sunlight.

Although Bacon and his contemporaries had no idea of the sheer scale of the universe, their astronomical speculation did go beyond the motions of the Sun, Moon, and planets. It may come as a surprise that there was a medieval concept of 'universe'. In fact, the idea dates back to the ancient Greeks (and beyond, if the term is applied to any attempt to describe the world as it is perceived). Aristarchus of Samos, a contemporary of Archimedes, had been the first to suggest that the Sun, rather than the Earth, was at the centre of the universe. He also envisaged a much larger universe than had other astronomers. Archimedes commented:

> Now you are aware that 'universe' is the name given by most astronomers to the sphere whose centre is the centre of the Earth and whose radius is equal to the straight line between the centre of the Sun and centre of the Earth. This is the common account, as you have heard from astronomers.[127]

He goes on to say that Aristarchus 'brought out a book' in which he suggested that the universe was much larger than this, with the Earth revolving around the Sun and the stars lying a great distance beyond the Earth's orbit. Archimedes has to criticize the size Aristarchus allocates to the universe, because he seems to have said that the stars are as far away in proportion to the Earth's orbit as the surface of a sphere is to its centre. That doesn't make sense, and what Aristarchus really meant, suggests Archimedes, is that the ratio of the size of the Earth to its orbit is the same as the ratio of the Earth's orbit to the sphere of the stars. Some modern writers have suggested that what Aristarchus was really saying was that the distance to the stars is infinite – that he was being more literal than Archimedes credited him with.[128]

Bacon did not argue with the accepted structure of the universe, with the Earth at its centre (it would take Copernicus to overthrow that structure, hundreds of years later), but he seems to have thought it to be larger than Archimedes allowed. He also considered its shape. Archimedes presents no argument for the universe being spherical, just assuming that it is, but Bacon isn't content with an assumption. Thinking through the possible shapes the universe might have, he points out in the *Opus majus* that his ancient Greek hero, Aristotle, gave some other possibilities:

> Other figures especially suitable would be either of oval shape or those like it, or of lenticular shape and those formed like it, according to Aristotle in his book *On the Heavens and the World*. But he states that the heavens do not have a shape of this kind, yet he does not give a reason.[129]

Bacon goes on to explain what he means by 'lenticular'. These days we would say it meant than an object was lens-shaped, but Bacon goes back to the origins of both 'lenticular' and 'lens' and comments that, 'A lenticular shape is that of the vegetable called lentil.'[130]

Bacon is not worried that Aristotle gave no reason for the universe being spherical – he has one of his own. He argues that the universe could not be, for instance, 'of some angular form'[131] because when it rotated (we will come back to this assumption that it rotates) it would leave behind a vacuum and 'Nature does not endure a vacuum.'[132] He then went on to dismiss other shapes such as the lens, or 'the form of a cheese'.[133] Such shapes could be rotated safely around one axis, but there would be problems with other axes. Imagine a circular lens, held by two fingers at the lens's edge, on opposite sides of the centre. Start to rotate it around the axis between those fingers. Watch the edge of the lens: wherever it was a moment ago is now empty. If this were the universe, you would have just created a vacuum where the universe used to be.

So, argues Bacon, unless the universe is a sphere there is always the possibility of its movement creating a vacuum, an uncomfortable nothingness. Although a stationary universe, or a lens or cheese shape rotating around the short diameter, wouldn't create a vacuum, to Bacon's peculiarly medieval logic that just wasn't good enough. He believed that nature would 'not endure a vacuum nor a possibility of one forming'.[134] Such was the impossibility of vacuum that there could not be even the chance of it existing (who was to say that the universe wouldn't move a little on the wrong axis?), so the universe had to be spherical – the only shape that could rotate in any direction around its centre and not leave a vacuum. (Perhaps fortunately for Bacon, he seems not to have realized that *any* shape would cause a vacuum if it moved laterally, which would have left the universe with no shape at all.)

With the universe established to his satisfaction as spherical, Bacon went on to consider whether there could be more than one universe and whether or not the universe was infinite (Present-day cosmologists have been known to play with the idea of multiple universes as a way of explaining away some of the strange inconsistencies in the relationship between the matter that is observed in the universe and the quantities that should be out there according to the presently accepted theories.) Bacon dismissed the existence of multiple universes using the same argument he used to rule out a non-spherical universe. Two universes, a pair of spheres, together form a non-spherical shape. Once more, Bacon argues, rotation will leave behind an unacceptable vacuum. (He doesn't deal with the possibility that one universe totally encloses the other, but arguably this is just one bigger universe.)

As for the size of the universe, Bacon believed that it could not be infinite. He brought in geometry to justify this view, imagining drawing lines from the centre of the universe out to its edge, as shown in the diagram.

He starts with two lines (the large V in the diagram), starting from the same point at the centre of the universe and stretching to the edge of the immense sphere. Because the universe is spherical, these lines are each of the same length. He then adds a third line (the shorter, heavier line), parallel to the right side of the V and also heading off to the edge of the universe. Now, if the universe is infinite, he argued, the two parallel lines should be the same length (presumably because two parallel lines meet at infinity – the strict mathematical way of saying that they never meet). The two sides of the V are of identical length, but the heavy line is also the same length as the part of the dotted line from where they meet to the edge of the universe – another pair of lines going from the same point to infinity. So, argues Bacon, part of the dotted line equals the whole of the dotted line. This is an impossibility. So the edge of the universe isn't at an infinite distance at all (and, therefore, the parallel lines weren't the same length after all).

Unfortunately, Bacon had no chance of getting this right, owing to one of the many counter-intuitive aspects of the mathematics of infinity: infinity plus a bit more *is* infinity. So his attempts at a geometric proof offer no effective arguments against an infinite universe. The reality was to be much more complex and would take many hundreds of years to untangle. The current belief is that the universe *is* finite, but has no defined edge, effectively folding back onto itself, just as a circle is finite but has no beginning and no end.

◄o►

Bacon regarded the workings of the universe as one aspect of astronomy, and astrology as another. The third part, which now would be regarded as a subject in its own right, was geography. He included it in astronomy because he realized that geographical knowledge on a large scale – where are we on the Earth, how big the Earth is – is best deduced from observations of the sky.

Unlike some of his more esoteric subjects of study, Bacon's interest in geography was shared by many of his Franciscan brothers. The Franciscans were not unworldly: they were not closeted in the secluded life of a monastery like other orders. The friars saw their role to be very much part of the world, both to bring God's word to others and to increase their own understanding. St Francis had led the way by his great enthusiasm for the natural world. Franciscans not only studied natural philosophy but went out to explore this marvellous world, seeking its place in God's Creation. This quest comes through strongly in Bacon's work.

It is often stated that, according to the most commonly accepted wisdom of the time, the Earth was flat. If so, this belief was historically a retrograde step. The Greeks had argued from the time of Pythagoras, around 500 BC, that the Earth was a sphere, but the medieval world is believed by some to have rejected this view in favour of a flat disk-shaped Earth positioned at the centre of the universe, with Jerusalem at the centre of the Earth.

This flat-Earth model was based on a literal interpretation of the Bible and not on any scientific observations. This approach seems to be derived from the writings of two of the early Fathers of the Church, Lactantius, writing in the third century AD, and Cosmas in the sixth century.[135] However, it is highly doubtful that the flat-Earth theory was the norm in medieval times. Many now consider this to be a piece of propaganda introduced in the nineteenth century, perhaps in an attempt to demonstrate how the Christian Church had held back science (or, more charitably, as a result of misinterpreting the maps of the time).[136]

Bacon certainly believed the Earth to be a sphere. He used the argument of the otherwise inexplicable view of the shore as seen from a ship at sea. Bacon compared what can be seen of a distant port from the deck and from the top of the mast of a ship. If the world were flat, then the distance from the deck to the shore would be slightly shorter than the distance from the top of the mast – it's standard triangular geometry. But, he says:

We know by experience that he who is at the top of the mast can see the port more quickly than a man on the deck of the ship. Therefore it remains that something hinders the vision of the man on the deck of the ship. But there can be nothing except the swelling of the sphere of water.[137]

In other words, on a flat Earth a man on the ship's deck would make his first sighting of the port at practically the same time as a man up the mast. But if the Earth were curved, then the port would be hidden by that curvature. As the ship neared the port, the man up the mast would be high enough to see over the curve and spot the port. The practical experience of sailors showed that this was true – the view from the mast was better.

From the work of the last great Greek natural philosopher Ptolemy and later Arab commentators, Bacon thought that the Earth's radius was 5,230 kilometres and he calculated the circumference as three and one-seventh times the diameter. This very rough approximation to π (pi) seems to have been for convenience of calculation. In the third century BC Archimedes had pinned down the value to between 3.14103 and 3.14271,[138] and though Bacon might not have had access to his work, it is unlikely that Bacon had available no value better than 22/7 (3.14286). The modern value (correct to five decimal places, like the values above) is 3.14159.

As was typical of him, Bacon put the concept of the curvature of the Earth to a very practical purpose. In the *Opus majus* he suggests that it should be possible to head west from Spain and arrive at India.[139] This is the section that was lifted almost verbatim by Cardinal Pierre d'Ailly, and was to inspire the voyages of exploration undertaken by Christopher Columbus. When Columbus was planning his journey, one of his sources of inspiration was d'Ailly's book *Imago mundi*, which featured the passage taken from Bacon. That Columbus took his copy of this book seriously is obvious from the 900-plus notes he made in its margins. Columbus quoted d'Ailly, and hence Bacon, in a letter he wrote from the *Hispaniola* to

Ferdinand V and Isabella of Castille, the sponsors of his expeditions. It would be an exaggeration to say that Columbus would not have set sail had he not read Bacon's words, but it is obvious that they played their part.

At the heart of Bacon's unusually modern slant on geography was mapping. The approach he took explains why he made no real distinction between geography and astronomy. Like Aristotle before him, Bacon imagined three axes at right angles, shooting out from the globe of the Earth and reaching to the heavens. He followed these axes into the Earth to meet at its centre: 'we must imagine that the Earth is spherical and [the three axes] will pass through the centre of the Earth, intersecting each other at the point at right angles'.[140] Bacon argues that accurate mapping of the Earth's surface was achievable by collating and comparing astronomical sightings made from a particular point on the surface. His idea was that by fixing heavenly reference points above the poles and four points on the equator separated by 90°, that the relative locations of other spots on the world could be calculated by noting the angle to those reference points.

Bacon was also a very strong supporter of the use of latitude and longitude in the development of maps. This came originally from Ptolemy's *Geography*, but was not popular in the West in Bacon's time. It was not until the end of the fifteenth century that the system became widely adopted.

In the thirteenth century maps were artistic, conceptual affairs with no great correspondence to reality. Look, for example, at the intricate medieval *mappa mundi*, the great map at Hereford Cathedral. The maps were oriented to the east, to Jerusalem, then held to be the centre of the world. (The very word 'oriented' originally meant 'facing east', from the practice of aligning churches and maps in this way.) By comparison, Bacon's map that accompanied the *Opus majus* (now sadly lost, but we can reconstruct it conceptually) was much sparser. Like a modern map, it had north at the top and consisted of a series of red circles representing the positions of cities. Although this map, like all maps, was a flat, two-dimensional representation, the positions were calculated from a knowledge of latitude and longitude and projected from a three-dimensional sphere onto the two-dimensional page. If such map projections had become widely available in Bacon's time, the great European voyages of exploration might have begun much earlier.

Bacon's geography was not limited to mapping, though. He faithfully recorded as many as he could of the travellers' tales that were common at the time, mixing historical myth and hot news. Two particularly valuable sources were the remarkable Franciscan explorers and emissaries Johannes Carpini and William of Rubruck.

Johannes de Plano Carpini had been a companion of St Francis of Assisi – he was one of the twelve founder members of the Franciscans. He was already in his sixties when Pope Innocent IV sent him on a mission from Lyons in France. The pope was concerned about rumours of a Mongol army building in the east in readiness for an invasion of Europe. Carpini was part fact-finder, part diplomat. When he and his companion reached Genghis Khan's court at Karakorum (in present-day Mongolia), he had already been travelling for fifteen months. They arrived in time for the enthroning of Genghis's eldest son, Kuyuk, who sent them back to the pope with a marvellously dismissive letter – it was the Khan's right to please himself on the matter of invasion and no business of the pope's.

It took Carpini another year to get back to Lyons, where he was able to pass on his news and compose a detailed account of his journey. This was the end of his travels – as a reward, he was appointed Archbishop of Antivari in Dalmatia. He died in 1252, which makes it unlikely that Bacon ever met him. His successor, though, was much more a contemporary of Bacon's, and they do seem to have met.

William of Rubruck, thought to have been born in a village in French Flanders, had an even more chequered personal history than Bacon. A second expedition to the Mongols in 1248 had failed, eliciting an even more dismissive letter from Kuyuk's mother. The French king, Louis IX, had heard a rumour that one of the Tartar chieftains, Sartak, son of Batu, had been baptized a Christian and thought it worth trying diplomacy one more time. William of Rubruck was the new, though informal, emissary.

In Karakorum William attended a great congress of faiths, convened by the Kahn to discuss and compare Christianity, Islam, and Buddhism. Apart from a report on the congress, William also brought back with him much information on the area. When he returned to Europe he was in popular demand, and it is likely to have been on a visit to Paris that Bacon came across him (though it isn't beyond the bounds of belief that William's lecture tour took in Europe's second and third greatest universities in England). Bacon comments that he had studied William's book diligently and that he had conferred with its author.

William was obviously a good storyteller with an eye for detail, and in the *Opus majus* Bacon makes clever use of his graphic reports to emphasize the importance of having eyewitness accounts rather than relying on hearsay. He also paints a dramatic picture of the political geography of the time. (See Appendix II to get a flavour of the 'On Geography' section of the *Opus majus*.)

It is interesting to compare Bacon's narrative-based geography with that of his Parisian rival Albertus Magnus. Albertus also wrote on geography, in a book called *De natura locorum* ('On the Nature of Places'), but this was very much a dry list of locations and features, lacking the human touch that Bacon introduced. Both scholars emphasized the importance of geography in understanding the world, but Albertus' picture is more theoretically based, whereas Bacon goes further into the political and even theological implications of his description. Where Albertus presents data, Bacon gives information (data plus interpretation), the starting-point of knowledge.

Geographical knowledge, Bacon argued, could be developed to three ends. The first was to build an understanding of the infinite heavens. The second was to become familiar with the places and the physical geography mentioned in the Bible; this was considered particularly important as there were often spiritual or allegorical implications of a place or feature that would be lost without appropriate geographical knowledge. The third reason for gaining geographical knowledge was to understand history and predict where any threats to Christianity would come from. Bacon's geography, as with all his other sciences, was intended as a practical tool of the Church and the state.

Although Bacon's geographical work often depended on pulling together the experience of others, and it was not his strongest subject, there is no doubt that his contribution to the science was profound. Armando Cortesão, the respected Portuguese historian of map-making, comments that Bacon's work was 'exceptionally significant' for his focus on measuring, his estimates of distances, and his drawing of a map, which was 'the first known to have been drawn on a projection since the time of Ptolemy'.[141]

―◄o►―

In Bacon's time much of the natural world was a mystery, and rumour and fiction often took on the guise of reality, especially in accounts of exotic locations. While Bacon was always enthusiastic to test theory by experiment, some of his comments on the natural world are clearly limited to second-hand reports. When you consider the complex and remarkable truths behind much of the biological world, it's not too surprising that Bacon, when talking about how some animals can influence physical things at a distance, comments:

> . . . as for instance the Basilisk kills by sight alone, that the wolf makes a man hoarse if he sees him first, and that the hyena does not permit a dog to bark if he comes within its shadow . . . Aristotle tells in the book *De vegetabilibus* that female palm trees

mature ripe fruit through the odour of the males; and mares in
certain countries are fertilized by the smell of horses . . .[142]

These fanciful descriptions are best considered in the context of
Bacon's understanding of the operation of force at a distance (see
page 63). Nowadays we have such a clear mental separation of the
different aspects of science that it's easy to forget just how remarkable action at a distance is – magnetism and gravity, for example.
It is not unreasonable that the medieval mind should ponder biological examples of remote action. Perhaps Bacon should have been
suspicious, given that he had never personally observed any of these
phenomena, but he was happy to accept that some of them were
very rare.

Also, his was a time when some of the bizarre wonders of the
animal world were beginning to arrive on English shores. The first
elephant to reach the country, a present to King Henry from Louis
IX, was housed in the Tower of London in Bacon's lifetime. Imagine
the awe that such a creature must have struck in a populace that
had never before seen an animal bigger than a horse or a cow.

Some creatures, though, were never going to be seen. It is no
surprise that Bacon tells us he has not seen a basilisk, a creature
also known as a cockatrice, as this mythical beast was supposed to
be born from a cockerel's egg. Bacon would have been aware, though,
of the instructions for breeding a medieval test-tube basilisk that
were later written down by the physician and occultist Paracelsus:

The basilisk is produced and grows from the chief impurity of
a woman, namely from menstrual blood. So, too, from the blood
of semen. If it is placed in a glass receptacle and allowed to
putrefy with horse dung, from that putrefaction is a basilisk
produced. But who would be so bold as to wish to produce it,
even to take it and at once kill it, unless he had first clothed and
protected himself with mirrors? I would persuade no one to do
so, and wish to advise everyone to be cautious.[143]

Paracelsus (a rather easier title to handle than his proper name, Phillipus Aureolus Theophrastus Bombastus von Hohenheim) lived more than two centuries after Bacon's death, but the natural history of the fabulous basilisk had not changed much, and neither had the mechanisms that were suggested for dispatching the creature. Mirrors would kill the basilisk as they had the gorgon, by reflecting its deadly gaze back upon itself. As far as we can tell from his writings, Bacon took the same line as Paracelsus and believed that attempting to create a basilisk was simply not worth the risk. But the fatally powerful creature to which he gave life was no mythical beast, but science itself.

◄o►

The fifteenth-century Warwickshire historian John Rous tells us, 'The noble doctor Roger Bacon was buried at Grey Friars in Oxford AD 1292 on the feast of St Barnabas the Apostle',[144] which would make his burial date 11 June. According to one of Rous's contemporaries, the historian John Twyne, after Bacon's death the friars fastened all his works with long nails to the shelves of their library (or in some versions of the story to the walls of the church) and left them to rot.[145] This dramatic picture still appears all too often as historical fact. A recent article in a respectable history magazine told how Bacon's fellow friars gathered in the library to tear the vellum pages from his manuscripts and nail them to the library shelves, leaving his writing to fade away to nothing.[146] But Twyne's story was more a metaphorical description of the way Bacon's writing was handled than a literal account. Bacon's books were banned for a number of years, but his legacy, the *Opus majus* and its companion volumes, would continue to speak for him long after his death.

Roger Bacon did not live long after regaining his freedom. For as long as fourteen years he had been locked away, unable to contribute anything. Yet the legacy of his first forty years of work, culminating in his books for the pope, makes up for those missing years. Bacon's three great works weave their way through the fields of science, geography, languages, philosophy, and beyond. This breadth of coverage is no accident. Bacon believed that the only way really to understand and underpin the twin essentials of moral philosophy and theology – the 'sciences' of the nature of man and God – was to be versed in all the knowledge available.

Even in the thirteenth century, in those formative days of academic life, many scholars would raise an eyebrow at anyone who attempted such a holistic view. Yet, in the end, Bacon's grand vision was to triumph. Not only would his works inspire a host of advances in different areas of knowledge, but they would also give birth to what is arguably the single most important development in human history. But before the genius of Roger Bacon was recognized, it would have to penetrate a smokescreen that persisted for centuries, with legend distorting his memory like fairground mirrors.

9

The Smokescreen

Although Nature is powerful and marvellous, using Art to
make use of Nature is more powerful still, as we see in
many instances. Indeed, whatever is beyond the operation of
Nature or of Art is not human or is a fiction and the doing
of fraudulent persons.

Roger Bacon, *De mirabile potestate artis et naturae*

After his death, Bacon's life and work became obscured by a smokescreen of legend and myth. In less than a hundred years a man
who was passionate about the potential usefulness of science had
become a fairytale character.

In 1385 the Dalmatian physician Peter of Trou wrote about the
antics of a 'Friar Roger, called Bachon'.[147] The amazing friar that
Peter describes was capable of conjuring a bridge out of thin air
to span a river, and possessed two amazing mirrors in his Oxford
cell, one by which a candle could be lit at any hour of day or night,
and the other giving a view onto any part of the world. Needless
to say, this was a magical spyglass beyond the imaginings of the
real Roger Bacon.

By the sixteenth century this early tale and other stories had solid-
ified into the lively, earthy collection of romances that makes up *The
Famous Historie of Fryer Bacon*.[148] Soon afterwards, Bacon's adventures

were brought to life for the public in a popular play based on the *Historie* entitled *The Honourable History of Friar Bacon and Friar Bungay*, by Robert Greene,[149] a largely forgotten contemporary of William Shakespeare. Greene's Bacon was a Faustian figure – in fact for a long time *The Honourable History* was thought to be an opportunist copy of Christopher Marlowe's popular play *The Tragical History of Dr Faustus*, dashed off in an attempt to hitch a ride on the Faustus bandwagon. Marlowe himself was not above a little plagiarism, using as his source the Faust legend that had built up around the fifteenth-century German scholar and magician Johann Faust.

The real Faust was born in Württemberg around 1480. He went to university, but found the easy life of fortune-telling and conjuring more attractive than his studies and began to travel from town to town, making money wherever and however he could. To boost his reputation he openly boasted that he had sold his soul to the Devil, a claim that Martin Luther took seriously enough to brand him a master of demonic powers. Other, more worldly observers thought that Faust was an opportunist charlatan, but nonetheless a dangerous man to have around. He was thrown out of the city of Ingolstadt in 1528. The municipal records note that 'A certain man who called himself Dr Johann Faust of Heidelberg was told to spend his penny elsewhere, and he pledged himself not to take vengeance on or to make fools of the authorities for this order.'[150] After his death, Faust's reputation started a legend that spread throughout Europe.

Marlowe's *Dr Faustus* tells of a man obsessed with power. In exchange for his soul he gains knowledge and influence, but by the end of the story he repents of his actions, even though he is too late to be saved from damnation. It now seems that Greene's play could be slightly older that Marlowe's. *The Honourable History of Friar Bacon* was first published in 1594 and had been performed a couple of years earlier. It is thought to have been written in 1589, as Greene received his MA from Oxford in 1588 (his second MA, following the award of a masters at Cambridge in 1583), and the play is thought to be a tribute to one of the great names associated with his university. Marlowe's *Dr Faustus* was probably written in about 1592, the year Greene died; the earliest traceable copies date from 1604. The chances are that *The Honourable History* was independently written. If there was any plagiarism, it's more likely to have been Greene influencing Marlowe than the other way around.

Greene is probably best remembered now for his vitriolic attack on his better-paid contemporary, Shakespeare. In his rather bizarrely titled *Groatsworth of Wit Bought with a Million of Repentance*, he wrote:

> For there is an upstart crow, beautified with our feathers, that with his tiger's heart wrapped in a player's hide, supposes he is as well able to bumbast [bombast] out a blank verse as the best of you; and being an absolute *Johannes fac totum*, is in his own conceit the only Shake-scene in a country.[151]

The term *Johannes fac totum* is an early version of 'Jack of all trades', picking up on Shakespeare's ability to combine the roles of producer, actor, and playwright. Greene's intended audience was other playwrights, probably including Marlowe, whom he wished to persuade not to write for Shakespeare's company.

Greene's play makes even more of the magical aspects of the Bacon legend than does *The Famous Historie*, which inconsistently wanders between ascribing Bacon's feats to magic and to natural philosophy. In both fictional versions Bacon suffers as a result of his excessive pride. In fact, despite his own recent academic achievement, Greene seems to have had significant doubts about the wisdom of academics. In his *Farewell to Folly* he wrote that a philosopher 'by long staring at the stars forgets the globe at his feet'.[152]

Bacon's taste for magic is made clear when he first appears in the play, though initially it is cloaked in a Latin conversation he holds with his assistant Miles:

BACON: Miles, where are you?
MILES: Hic, sum, dostissime et reverendissime doctor.
BACON: Attulisti nos libros meos de necromantia?
MILES: Ecce quam bonum et quam jocundum, habitares libros
in unum.[153]

This Miles also features in the *Famous Historie*, in which he appears
as an idiot servant and foil to Bacon's genius. In the play he has
been upgraded to a subsizar, a poor student who paid for his board
and tuition by acting as a servant (as Isaac Newton would seventy
years later), which explains the breaking out into Latin, even if the
meaning (Here I am, learned and reverend doctor – Have you
brought us my books on necromancy? – Lo, how good and pleasant
it is to dwell together among books!) was probably lost on most of
the audience. Even fewer of them would have picked up Greene's
play on words in Miles's second remark, which is a quote from
Psalm 133 (verse 1) with 'books' substituted for 'brothers'.

Greene is also not above using Bacon's magic to curry favour
with royalty. Bacon's final speech in the play, addressed to Henry
III, describes a future that benefits extraordinarily well from hind-
sight, predicting as it does the coming of Queen Elizabeth (the play
was probably written just after England's victory over the Spanish
Armada).

HENRY: Why, Bacon, what strange event shall happen to this
land?
Or what shall grow from Edward and his queen?
BACON: I find by deep prescience of mine art,
Which once I temper'd in my secret cell,
That here where Brute* did build his Troynovant†
From forth the royal garden of a king

---

* Brute: Brutus, the legendary king of the Britains.
† Troynovant: New Troy.

Shall flourish out so rich and fair a bud
Whose brightness shall deface proud Phoebus's flower,
And over-shadow Albion with her leaves.
Till then Mars shall be master of the field,
But then the stormy threats of war shall cease.
The horse shall stamp as careless of the pike;
Drums shall be turn'd to timbrels of delight;
With wealthy favours plenty shall enrich
The strond* that gladdened wand'ring Brute to see,
And peace from heaven shall harbour in these leaves
That gorgeous beautifies this matchless flower.
Apollo's hellitropian [sic] then shall stoop,
And Venus' hyacinth shall vail† her top;
Juno shall shut her gillyflowers up,
And Pallas' bay shall bash‡ her brightest green;
Ceres' carnation, in consort with those,
Shall stoop and wonder at Diana's rose.§[154]

Both in the play and in the collection of stories that make up *The Famous Historie,* Bacon is frequently embroiled with one Friar Bungay, also a magician. As far as we can tell, the association is purely fictional, perhaps to take advantage of the alliterative combination of 'Bacon' and 'Bungay'. There was a real Friar Bungay, apparently born in the small Sussex town of that name, who rose to the powerful position of Provincial Minister of the Franciscan Order in England in 1271; but there is no reason to think that Bacon and Bungay were ever close colleagues, and there is no record of Bungay having had any interest in science or magic.

In the *Historie* it is usually Bacon's role to rescue Bungay from the consequences of his conjuring or to protect him from an attack by

---

* Strand: strand, i.e. beach.
† Vail: lower.
‡ Bash: remove.
§ Diana's rose: Elizabeth's Tudor rose.

a black magician. The legendary Bungay seemed particularly good at getting himself into trouble. But in the story that was to become associated most closely with Bacon, Bungay acts as a medieval Dr Watson to Bacon's Sherlock Holmes, assisting the great man in his work. This was the construction of a new form of defence:

> Friar Bacon, reading one day of the many conquests of England, thought how he might keep it safe against future conquests, and so make himself famous for posterity. After great study he found that the best way to do this was to make a head of brass, and if he could make this head speak (and hear it when it spoke) then he might be able to wall all England about with brass.[155]

It is typical of the Bacon of the *Historie* that his prime concern should be to add to his fame – though to be fair, he had a patriotic motive as well. Bacon brings in Bungay to be his assistant:

> To this purpose he got one Friar Bungay to assist him, who was a great scholar and magician (but not to be compared with Friar Bacon). These two with great study and pains so framed a head of brass, that in the inward parts thereof were all things as in a natural man's head . . .[156]

How Bacon and Bungay proceed to animate the awesome head is described graphically by the Victorian writer Thomas Frost in his 1876 book *The Lives of the Conjurors*. He tells how between them the friars constructed the brazen head but could not get it to speak. In desperation, they called on Satan to help them. With classic diabolical duplicity, he gave them the means to get what they wanted but made it almost impossible for them to succeed. They had to hear the head speak for themselves, and it might pronounce at any time in the next month – the Devil said that, 'the time of the month or day he knew not'.[157] Frost takes up the story:

The friars dismissed the fiend and returned to their laboratory, where they prepared the needful decoction and watched its effects night and day for three weeks. [Because the friars were] then overpowered by somnolence, Bacon's servant, Miles, was set to watch the brazen head with strict instructions to call the two friars in the event of any articulate sounds from it.

Miles tried to keep awake by singing, but he did not succeed; and when he was awakened by hearing the head pronounce the words 'Time was,' he thought such a brief utterance was too insignificant for notice, and went to sleep again. Presently the words 'Time is' issued from the brazen lips; but Miles thought the remark as unworthy of attention as that which had preceded it. Then came the final utterance, 'Time is past!' upon which lightning flashed and thunder rolled, and the brazen head fell upon the floor and was broken to pieces. The friars rushed in at the noise, and Bacon, in his rage at the disaster, would have severely chastised the negligent Miles, if his brother Franciscan had not restrained him.[58]

In fact, Frost strays a little from the story in the *Historie*. There, Miles sang three decidedly risqué songs (reproduced in the *Historie* word for word) to pass the time, and had no problem with falling asleep – he simply heard the apparently trivial words the head uttered and thought them insufficiently important to bring to the attention of his master. Also, according to the *Historie*, despite Bungay's attempts to protect him, Bacon struck Miles dumb for a whole month as punishment.

The story of the brass head is delightful, but as with the majority of the *Historie* there is little correspondence with Bacon's real life. Still, this bizarre story illustrates perfectly the mix of awe and disdain with which Bacon was regarded for the hundreds of years before translations of his works began to appear and the reality of his genius became more widely known. He was considered a charlatan, a deceiver who nonetheless had magical abilities. He was labelled both a fraud and a dangerous manipulator of power.

But the story of Bacon and the brazen head was a transplant, grafted onto the worryingly omniscient Roger to put him in his place. The head of brass first appeared not in stories of the thirteenth-century friar but in much earlier Arab legend, which itself could have been inspired by the Greek legend of Talus, the living man of brass created to guard Crete.

When the story of the talking brass head first reached Europe, long before Bacon was born, it was associated with another man of dangerous ideas, the French cleric Gerbert of Aurillac. By the time this scholarly abbot became Pope Sylvester II in 999, he had already gained the reputation of being a black magician that seemed to attach itself to anyone with scientific leanings. Gerbert and the brass head come together in one of the little anecdotes used by William of Malmesbury, a monk at the abbey there, to liven up his histories. He tells us that Gerbert imbued the head with its magical powers by casting it using 'a certain inspection of the stars when the planets were about to begin their courses'.[159] It was inevitable that the likes of Gerbert and Bacon should have been seen as necromancers. These were men who had no qualms about investigating the mysterious workings of nature. Not only did they write books, they also described marvellous devices and drew strange diagrams that looked like magical symbols.

Anyone who delved into the workings of nature was regarded with suspicion at a time when the study of natural philosophy was only just beginning to creep back into Europe. Western scientific knowledge was being extracted largely from the work of the Greek philosophers, who from 500 BC had begun to speculate on the nature of the universe. With the fall of Greek civilization, what knowledge there had been was lost, or at least mislaid. The Arabs began to discover the remnants of Greek libraries, and set about a painstaking reconstruction of what had been known, to which they added their own insights, but it was only when Christian scholars brought this Greek–Arab amalgam into Latin-speaking

Europe that the study of nature began to find acceptance – and then only among the cognoscenti. For the common people it was all still a mystery – and Gerbert, Bacon, and others were branded as sorcerers.

By the time Bacon was studying in Paris, the legend of the head had transferred itself from Gerbert to another figure. It was now said to be the creation of the Bavarian Albertus Magnus, Bacon's only rival as the greatest scientific genius of the period. Albertus was a formidable encyclopedist of science, writing on as many subjects as Bacon did, and though he did not have Bacon's fundamental grasp of the importance of the scientific method, he did make the telling remark in his *De miner* that 'The aim of natural science is not simply to accept the statements of others, but to investigate the causes that are at work in nature.'[160]

Albertus continued to be held in respect on the Continent, but in England it was Bacon's name that stuck in the popular mind, and by Tudor times the head of brass had become firmly established as Friar Bacon's property. Even though the tale of the head is clearly fictional, such was the strength of the legend that it came to influence reality. Two Oxford colleges have in the past claimed Bacon as an alumnus – Merton and Brasenose. However, as we saw in Chapter 1, the collegiate structure was not in existence when Bacon first went up to university. Although there was probably some overlap between the existence of Merton, founded in 1264, and Bacon's second stay in Oxford, the first few years of Merton's existence were dedicated to educating the sons of Walter of Merton's seven very productive sisters. That hardly made it a likely destination for Bacon immediately after he had written the *Opus majus*, and by the time the college had taken on a wider function, he was probably already locked up.

The Brasenose story has even less going for it than Merton's, though the college has to be admired for the sheer cheek of its attempt to claim Roger for its own. Brasenose didn't open until 1509, more than 200 years after Bacon's death. But by then the brass head legend would have been well established, and it could well have been that the 'brasenose' of the name, a brass nose placed over the gatehouse of the college, was believed to be a remnant from the explosion of that famous brass head. This was probably why Roger Greene, in his play, chose to make Brasenose Bacon's home (despite the obvious anachronism). He has Bacon say to some visitors, 'Why flock you thus to Bacon's secret cell / A friar newly stall'd in Brazen-nose.'[161]

Historical facts did not stop the Oxford colleges from later cashing in on the Bacon legend. As late as the seventeenth century, the Oxford historian Anthony Wood observed that there was a 'tower with a gate and common passage underneath' that was known to be 'Fryer Bacon, his study'.[162] Wood wasn't sure how true this was, but he thought that Bacon quite possibly used the tower for astronomical observations, as it was easy to reach from the Oxford convent by a backstreet, crossing a stream called the Trillmill.

In the collection of engravings known as Gough's prints at Oxford's Bodleian Library there is an illustration alleged to be the tower that housed Bacon's study. It is an impressive two-storey structure with a single sturdy chimney and two banks of rectangular windows that seem to give a view onto the bell tower of Christ Church college. The positioning of the buildings suggests that it was Merton College that was attempting to rake in some cash through an association with Bacon. That the tower existed seems very likely, but any connection it had with the real Roger Bacon is nothing more than wishful thinking.

◄○►

From the pages of the *Historie* we get a rich if spurious picture of the mythical Bacon. His wisdom was known throughout the land, making him the obvious man to call in when the wealthy, the royal, and the famous had urgent problems that needed solving – a mystical troubleshooter. Although his powers seemed to verge on the diabolical – and at least once, when constructing the brass head, he called on the Devil for help – he still managed to outwit Satan when a poor man mistakenly sold his soul to wipe out his debts. This imaginary Bacon comes across as a proud, self-centred man, not above adding to his own riches and fond of playing a trick on those he met, particularly on his servant Miles, to make a point.

This picture of Bacon as a self-seeking magician tainted his reputation for many years. In 1659 one of Bacon's most approachable works, his letter 'On Art and Nature', was translated into English. The translator, known only as T. M., warns the reader of how Bacon's image had been tarnished by legend:

A Prejudicate [i.e. prejudiced] eye much lessens the noblenesse of the Subject. Bacon's name may bring at first an inconvenience to the Book, but Bacon's ingenuity will recompensc it ere he be solidly read.[163]

In other words, the name of Roger Bacon might initially put you off, but don't let prejudice get in the way, because you will be rewarded for sticking with the story.

This as an Apology is the usher to his other Workes, which may happily breathe a more free Air hereafter, when once the World sees how clear he was, from loving Negromancy.[164]

T. M. was hoping that, once it became obvious to the reader that Bacon was not a magician (a necromancer), it would encourage the reading of his other works. With a certain Protestant enthusiasm, T. M. goes on to blame papist thinking for confusing science with heresy:

Twas the Popes smoak which made the eyes of that Age so sore, as they could not discern any open hearted and clear headed soul from an heretical Phantasme. The silly Fryers envying his too prying head, by their craft had almost got it off his shoulders.[165]

After some further reflections on the value of Bacon's work, T. M. concludes with the hope that whoever he is addressing will read the book and make his or her own opinion.

By now, Bacon had all but disappeared behind the flamboyant personality of his fictional counterpart. It was not until Victorian times that more of his books were translated and people came to see just how great a debt was owed to this remarkable friar.

◄o►

The immediate result of the rediscovery and redemption of Roger Bacon was a misunderstanding. As more and more of his work was uncovered he came to be hailed as a Victorian scientist, 700 years ahead of his time. In his breadth of interests and his emphasis on the need for experiment he was identified with the giants of the Victorian scientific revolution, and transformed into the type of romantic hero that only the Victorians could create. Once again he was being made into a fantastical figure, this time one endowed with near-psychic foresight. It would come as no surprise if it had been suggested that he *was* a nineteenth-century man who had made use of H. G. Wells's time machine to take Victorian science back to the thirteenth century. This is nicely summed up by the nineteenth-century French writer Émile Charles, who penned the first biography that was an attempt to find the historical rather than the legendary Bacon: 'The monk of Oxford has paid with his repose and with his liberty for the privilege of being in advance of his time.'[166] It was this picture of Bacon, the man ahead of his time, that made the mysterious manuscript purchased by a rare book dealer so intriguing.

In the early months of 1912, Wilfred Voynich, an American dealer in antique books, bought a strange manuscript that had been found in an Italian villa near Frascati. It was said to contain the secrets of nature, but its author had taken much care to conceal this dangerous knowledge from prying eyes. More than two hundred heavily illustrated pages were filled with a dense, incomprehensible script which no one had yet deciphered, accompanied by enigmatic sketches and diagrams. In its time this remarkable book may have been the property of the astrologer John Dee and it certainly found its way into the hands of the Holy Roman Emperor Rudolph II. The author was said to be Roger Bacon.

Nine years after Voynich's purchase, the manuscript was to cause an international sensation. The man responsible was William Newbold, Professor of Intellectual and Moral Philosophy at the University of Pennsylvania. After making a careful study of the Voynich manuscript's complex script he had seen a pattern, not in the characters themselves but in minute markings above the strange lettering. Newbold announced not only that could he confirm that the secret document was the work of Roger Bacon, but that its contents seemed to blow apart the conventional idea of what was known in Bacon's time.

As Newbold's work on the manuscript progressed, he found confirmation of Bacon's authorship. But the revelations that were to amaze the world were that the text accompanying some of the less clear diagrams identified them as depicting distant objects in space and the microscopic features of sperm. These remarkable observations seemed to prove that Bacon had built telescopes and microscopes hundreds of years before they were believed to have been invented.

Newbold needed to confirm that Bacon had written the Voynich manuscript because, despite a long history of its association with Bacon, its author was not explicitly identified. Rudolf II certainly believed that it was Bacon who had written the manuscript when the emperor purchased the book in 1586 for the sizeable fee of 600 gold ducats, but that was simply because he had been told so. It was for the frisson of secrecy that he paid such a royal fee. The book looked – still looks – as if it contained a wealth of scientific and magical secrets. And Bacon had always stressed that it was vital to keep the secrets of science hidden from the common herd. Here was documentary evidence of how Bacon maintained secrecy.

The emperor had been told that the manuscript must be Bacon's work because it appeared to be cryptically autographed by Bacon. On the last page are three lines of text in a different hand from the rest of the book. They seem to provide an incomplete key to the code used in the main text. Although this key itself is enciphered, it uses a simple form of code already well known in the thirteenth century, so in theory this addition could have been Bacon's work. It seemed, on decoding, that the first few words read 'To me, Roger Bacon' – though to discover this the reader would also have to unscramble an anagram. The man who brought this inscription to the emperor's attention is said to be the same man who had sold it to him, a man who believed Bacon to be much more than the caricature figure of the legend. That man was John Dee.

Dee was the personification of much that legend had built up Bacon to be. An occultist and alchemist, he was royal astrologer to Queen Elizabeth I. Despite escaping a prosecution for sorcery in 1553, he was constantly held in suspicion by the common people, and eventually much of his extensive library (more than 4,000 books) was destroyed in a fire that was intended to burn Dee alive for his witchcraft. Like Bacon, Dee had wide-ranging interests, arguably sometimes inspired by Bacon. He applied mathematics to geography, improving the navigational techniques that were used at the time. He provided a preface for a translation of Euclid into English, and was active in theatre and the arts. But unlike Bacon, Dee had a very real dark side.

Where Bacon was dismissive of magic and magicians, there is no doubt that Dee revelled in the power that is conferred by a claim to manipulate nature by magical means. With his companion Edward Kelley, very much the Bungay to Dee's Friar Bacon, he was said to have conjured up all manner of spirits. Like Bacon in Peter of Trou's stories, Dee was said to possess a magic mirror in which Kelley could see distant events take place. Dee, it was said, single-handedly defeated the Spanish Armada's invasion plan by summoning up bad weather. It's hard to believe that he would ever have denied this feat.

Dee also claimed to be able to communicate with angels by using a special alphabet that he had devised. He has been credited with the founding of the Rosicrucian Order,[167] supposedly a Protestant equivalent to the Jesuits but in fact a secret organization with an inclination towards the occult. It is telling that when Shakespeare wanted a model for Prospero, the powerful but amoral sorcerer in *The Tempest*, he used Dee. He is also said to have inspired the character of the mad King Lear.

This Elizabethan occultist developed a passion for Roger Bacon (who would have been horrified by much that Dee did). Dee's library contained the largest known collection of Bacon's works, many of which survived the fire. In his preface to Henry Billingsley's translation of Euclid's *Elements*, Dee says of Bacon that he was 'the flower of whose worthy fame can never dye nor wither'.[168] It is obvious that Dee drew heavily on Bacon's work. The closest Dee came to pure science was in his *Propadeumata aphoristica* ('Preliminary Aphoristic Teachings'), of which Benjamin Wooley remarks in his 2001 biography of Dee, 'This became the basis of Dee's natural philosophy, and in several ways anticipates Newton's groundbreaking *Principia mathematica...*'[169] In *Propadeumata*, Dee puts forward his theory that everything in the universe gives off rays of a force which then influence other bodies — nothing more than Roger Bacon's species.

It even seems that Dee went so far as to claim to be related to Bacon. In a pamphlet on the reformation of the calendar addressed to Queen Elizabeth in 1582, he took the opportunity both to praise his hero and to try to establish a connection with him:

> None has done it more earnestly, neither with better reason and skill, than hath a subject of this British Sceptre Royal done, named as some think David Dee of Radik, but otherwise . . . called Roger Bacon.[170]

While it's true that Bacon had argued strongly for calendar reform, Dee's enthusiasm to claim Bacon as an ancestor seems to have overcome his sense of reality – there is no evidence anywhere that Bacon changed his name in this fashion. Any relationship was in Dee's mind alone. It would not have been surprising, then, if Dee himself, to develop the pedigree of the Voynich manuscript, had added the three lines that seemed to link it to Bacon.

This is something that cannot be proved. Little is certain with this manuscript, even the matter of Dee's involvement. A letter attached to the manuscript, written by Prague scientist Johannes Marcus Marci and dated 1665, tells us that the book was sold to Rudolf for 600 ducats. We also know that in 1586, when Dee was in contact with Rudolf, Dee records having 630 ducats, an unusually large sum as he was not well off at the time. Other circumstantial evidence has pointed to Dee's ownership, though some scholars continue to doubt it.[171] But whether or not Dee owned or tampered with the document, the contents remained a total mystery until Professor Newbold's sensational translation.[172]

–◄o►–

Newbold basked briefly in the glory of his discovery, but very soon the critics descended upon him. The method Newbold had used to decipher the manuscript was complex and open to misuse. He claimed that the characters in the inscriptions themselves were meaningless, there only to mislead the reader. The message, he thought, lay hidden in almost invisible markings above the strange letters. These markings, he suggested, were similar to a shorthand used by the Greeks. But that wasn't the end of the mystery. To decode the text, Newbold had to use double-character combinations – assuming that two marks in the manuscript made up a single letter of writing – and then apply anagrams, jumbling up groups of characters to make appropriate words. In the hands of his critics, this led to the destruction of Newbold's credibility. They were blistering in their criticism of the Pennsylvania professor's approach, condemning his whole structure as imaginary, and objecting that the use of anagrams meant that almost any meaning could be extracted from a text of this length.

It is certainly true that within Newbold's 'translation' there was much that sat uncomfortably with Bacon's time and seemed to suggest wishful thinking on the professor's part. For example, Bacon appeared to call the members of the Franciscan Order 'monks', a description that would not have been made at a time when the distinction between monks and friars was a recent introduction and very clear. Other apparent historical references to Bacon's life could simply not be true. Any fit with the historical facts of the period was superficial and collapsed when the detail was examined. It seemed that Professor Newbold had used his imagination to augment the text.

Since Newbold's abortive attempts, the closest there has been to a translation of the Voynich manuscript has come from the acknowledged expert on it, Robert S. Brumbaugh.[173] Brumbaugh managed to establish a sensible structure behind the encoding of the titles of the illustrations, if not of the main text. Unfortunately the technique that seems to have been used to produce the text is numerological, each letter having been converted into a single-digit number before being translated into another character. This process inevitably means that it is hard to decode, as a single number could represent any of several different letters. Brumbaugh's work, together with a closer examination of the style of the manuscript, has proved that Bacon's connection with it is fictional.

Also, the age of the manuscript itself argues against any link. Although the physical materials used in the manuscript could have been thirteenth-century, little else shows any sign of being contemporary with Bacon. The style of the book – or rather the collection of five different books that it appears to be – is much more like that of the early sixteenth century, particularly in the botanical illustrations. Some of these – confirmed by Brumbaugh's translated captions – include a sunflower and a capsicum pepper, both of which were unknown in Europe until Columbus brought them back to Spain in 1493.

Apart from Brumbaugh's publication, there have been a string of books and papers on the Voynich manuscript, most notably Mary D'Imperio's *The Voynich Manuscript: An Elegant Enigma*.[174] For the future, perhaps the best hope of cracking the mysterious manuscript may lie in using the statistical techniques developed for the Human Genome Project to search for structures and patterns in the text.[175] Modern Voynich enthusiasts are also producing a high definition computer-based copy of the work to replace the hazy microfilm that Voynich historians have had to work from in the past. However, it seems that what appeared at first to be a new window onto Roger Bacon's work is just as much fantasy as the more obviously grotesque mythological tales that appear in the *Historie*. It's not that the Voynich manuscript itself is a fraud, but any link with Bacon lies in the imagination, quite possibly the fevered imagination of John Dee.

By the time the Voynich manuscript had been proved not to be Bacon's work, the backlash against the maudlin Victorian image had struck. Retribution was swift and totally out of proportion to the original error. A new band of twentieth-century Bacon scholars tore into his Victorian image, denouncing it as just as much a myth as the mountebank magician of the *Historie*. They showed quite rightly that Bacon's views were anything but Victorian. Not surprisingly he was, particularly in his writings on the significance of theology, a man of his own time.

But these rampant historians were so eager to disprove Bacon's precognizance that they dismissed his real, incredible achievements. A typical example comes in the first volume of *The History of the University of Oxford*. In the otherwise excellent section on medieval science, J. A. Weisheipl writes:

But Bacon exerted little or no influence on his contemporaries or successors. It was left to a later age to mythologize him as a 'modern scientist' before his time, a genius misunderstood and persecuted by his unenlightened contemporaries, a precursor of our age of technology and scientific progress.[176]

Unfortunately, as is often the case with a backlash, the reaction overlooks the point. Bacon *was* of his time. He did subscribe to many of the views commonly held in the thirteenth century. But this does not stop him from being one of the most remarkable figures of all time, someone who brought into being the agent of change that would transform the modern world. Weisheipl is right in one respect, though: Bacon wasn't a 'modern scientist'. He was much more.

10

Magister

> He, therefore, who wishes to rejoice without doubt in regard
> to the truths underlying phenomena must know how to
> devote himself to experiment. For authors write many
> statements, and people believe them through reasoning
> which they formulate without experience. Their reasoning
> is wholly false.
>
> Roger Bacon, *Opus majus*

All the clues have been presented. The *dramatis personae* have played out their roles. We are in the final act of the detective story and it is time for the denouement. We now know *who* Roger Bacon was, but *what* was he? What effect has his life and work had on the modern world?

We have seen how individual aspects of Bacon's work have influenced the future. From Pierre d'Ailly's extracts from the *Opus majus* that would help inspire the voyages of Christopher Columbus, to his precise optical diagrams which were reproduced and enthused over by the seventeenth-century German scientist Johannes Combach,[177] time and again Bacon's work was a source of inspiration. Yet even if every one of his individual contributions had been forgotten, there would still be a unique legacy for the modern world. With four fundamental concepts, four intellectual building blocks, he made possible what we now take for granted. With these concepts, Roger Bacon was to invent science.

We ought at this stage to review our terminology. When Bacon uses the words that are (reasonably enough) translated as 'mathematics' and 'science', *mathematica* and *scientia*, he did not have exactly the same thing in mind as we have today. His mathematics includes geometry and number, but also astronomy and music. As for science, for Bacon that too implies a broader coverage than it does now.

In the *Communia naturalium*, Bacon says that natural science (*naturalia*) deals with those things where there is a principle of motion and rest – for example, minerals, plants, and animals.[178] He also includes the study of the heavens, though he makes this a special case, as the heavens are never at rest. In *Opus majus* he refers to seven 'special sciences': perspective (optics), astronomy, weights, alchemy, agriculture, medicine, and the science of experiment.[179]

It seems, then, that the topics we would now think of as the physical and biological sciences come under Bacon's *scientia* umbrella. He also includes moral philosophy as a science, and by this he appears to mean the study of how men behave – what we might now label anthropology, with a bit of philosophy and theology thrown in. And theology itself, from Bacon's viewpoint, certainly was a science. To the medieval mindset of certainty it was no less a study of reality than any natural science. That aside, though, he comments that all other sciences are 'concerned with the actions of art [technology] and nature'.[180]

◄○►

The first block in Bacon's four-part concept of science, the foundation stone, was the relation of science to mathematics. We now accept without question that scientific breakthroughs are underpinned by mathematics, yet even three centuries later, in the time of Roger's Elizabethan namesake Francis Bacon, there was a clear division between science and mathematics. Francis has since been given disproportionate credit for developing the scientific method. The name they had in common has been enough often to hide Roger from modern view. Yet though Francis had reasonable claim to be a scientist, and formulated a more complete version of the scientific method, he had little enthusiasm for mathematics. Where Roger Bacon took the modern view of science as built on a foundation of mathematics, Francis Bacon considered mathematics as a useful but hardly essential method of clarification.[181]

Roger himself was no mathematician. He did not advance knowledge of mathematics. His relative weakness in the subject is exemplified by a throwaway line in which he thought he was demonstrating that even his great hero Aristotle occasionally got things wrong. He comments in the *Opus majus*:

> . . . nor is it surprising, since [Aristotle] confesses that he did not know everything. For he confesses that he was ignorant in regard to the squaring of the circle, a problem clearly understood in these days . . .[182]

This problem certainly wasn't 'clearly understood' in Bacon's day – it simply isn't possible to solve it. Unless Bacon meant that the insoluble nature of the problem was clearly understood (unlikely from his wording), he had been fooled by some of the more extravagant mathematical claims of his time.

Squaring the circle is one of those problems that seem to work out in the mind, but can never be solved in practice. The idea is to construct a square with exactly the same area as a particular circle. This apparently simple puzzle so fascinated the ancient Greeks that they even had a word, τετραγονιζειν, for someone who spent his time attempting to solve it.

Thought of visually, squaring the circle seems a perfectly easy thing to do – which is probably why Bacon was convinced that this problem had already been solved. Imagine a square made of stretchy material. Start with a square a little less in area than the circle and gradually increase it in size, maintaining it as a square. At some point, surely, you must pass through the same area as that of the circle? For that matter, take a circle made of flexible material and bend it into the shape of a square. Problem solved? Unfortunately, the mathematics is not as simple as that – such a visual approach gives the impression of showing that the circle can be squared, but not the exact proof that mathematics requires.

The area of the circle is related to the number π, which has the property that its decimal places never fall into a regular pattern. Correct to the first few decimal places, $\pi = 3.1415926535898932$ . . . – it never settles down into any regular, repeating pattern. And, unlike some irrational numbers (those that can't be represented by a ratio), such as $\sqrt{2}$, π can't be made the result of any normal equation: the only way to pin it down is to write it as the sum of an infinitely long series of terms. These facts took a long time to establish. It wasn't until 1768 that the Swiss mathematician Johann Lambert showed that π was irrational, and as late as 1882 that the German Carl Lindemann proved it had no value that could be defined as the root of a polynomial equation, and hence that squaring the circle was impossible.

Bacon's mistake doesn't lessen the importance of his stance on mathematics. It is quite possible to recognize the significance of something without being an expert on it. In stressing mathematics as a fundamental requirement for the study of nature, Bacon was entirely correct. And his assessment was far ahead of his time.

That the crucial importance of mathematics to science is a surprisingly recent realization is obvious not just from Francis Bacon's attitude. The like of Roger's support for mathematics would not be seen again during the next 400 years. The mathematician John Wallis, writing to his colleague the great Gottfried Wilhelm Leibniz towards the end of the seventeenth century, commented:

> Those who in the present century (following Galileo) joined mathematics to natural philosophy have advanced physics to an

enormous extent. This was also being attempted by Roger Bacon (a great man in a dark century) four hundred years ago (and more).[183]

In this rare acknowledgement of Roger Bacon by name before his rediscovery by the Victorians, Wallis highlights just how far ahead of his time Bacon could sometimes be.

Bacon makes a big thing of mathematics, and not only to emphasize its importance. He had to defend mathematics, to fight against those who would label it the work of magicians. As we have seen, the obscure legacy of deterministic astrologers was also known as mathematics. Bacon's struggle was partly to emphasize how much could be built on a mathematical foundation, partly to separate the legitimate mathematics from the hokum. While he was firmly convinced of the real scientific basis for some astrology, he felt there was a need to separate it from the chicanery and magical dabbling that surrounded it. It was this 'mathematics' that Bacon was keen to divorce from the real thing. His awareness of the significance of mathematics to science shines through in the *Opus majus*:

> He who is ignorant of mathematics cannot know the other sciences and the things of this world . . . Moreover, what is worse, men who are ignorant of mathematics do not perceive their ignorance, and therefore seek no remedy. While, on the other hand, knowledge of this science prepares the mind and elevates it to a sure knowledge of all things, so that if it perceives the roots of wisdom which surround this science and applies these roots to an inquiry into other sciences and things, then it will be able to know all things in sequence without doubt or error, and in ease and power.[184]

It wasn't that other thirteenth-century scholars ignored mathematics – after all, the *quadrivium*, the second element of the late medieval curriculum, was in effect mathematically based, consisting, as we have seen, of arithmetic, geometry, astronomy, and music. But these subjects were treated in isolation. Bacon's vision included a simple structure for the sciences that was quite alien to his time.

Bacon felt that there was a hierarchy of relationships which had to be grasped if one was to understand all of science. The basic natural sciences (effectively physics) were built on the foundation of mathematics. From these came alchemy (chemistry). Out of this was born agriculture (biology) and on that was constructed medicine. The same structure, with each step becoming more practical and less fundamental, still defines the relationships of the sciences today. Yet again, Bacon had captured an essential aspect of science that was to escape his contemporaries and subsequent generations of natural philosophers.

◄○►

With mathematics solidly established as a foundation, Bacon piled on the second of his building blocks. Here he ran into some trouble. In the modern world, we all have a tendency to reject sources of information, however good, if they don't fit with our own world view. We don't want what we are hearing to be true, so we don't listen. We have convinced ourselves that there is a pattern that we don't want to break. We simply haven't time to check all sources, and in an age of information overload we have rely on instinct to select those we can trust. We may have heard unsubstantiated rumours about a source, and so ignore it. Or we choose to avoid a source regarded as politically incorrect. In Bacon's time, rather than political correctness the problem was more likely to be religious correctness.

For many of Bacon's contemporaries anything outside the Judaeo-Christian tradition was heretical and dangerous. It didn't matter how good the science was – if the source wasn't Christian, then the argument could not be trusted. Although exceptions were made for much Classical wisdom, as soon as an author got too near the knuckle his work would be ignored – as for example when Aristotle's works on natural philosophy were banned in Paris. Bacon had the much bolder vision of the whole of history feeding into the final Christian truth. That is why he welcomed the knowledge of the dangerously Islamic writings in Arabic whereas others treated it with suspicion.

Of course, this is not to say that Bacon didn't have a religious agenda. A devout Christian, he believed that the Church had largely rejected the sciences (and even Aristotelian philosophy) because of an unfortunate assumption that equated much of science with the despised magic. His aim in promoting science was to support moral philosophy and theology – the twin pillars of mankind and God.

With this aim in mind, Bacon, ever the practical man, wasn't concerned about the source or original context of a piece of knowledge – if it was valid and useful it ought to be incorporated into our understanding of the world. His lack of prejudgement, his openness to take information from any source, was the second great building block in his construction of science. When Francis Bacon put forward his own description of the scientific method in 1620, he would emphasize the importance of abandoning prejudices and preconceived ideas, which he referred to as idols.[185]

Even so, students of nature have time and again selected only from information that conformed with their established beliefs – and as soon as they did so, they ceased to be true scientists. Of course, suppressing your belief structure isn't easy. Even today, scientists who have Bacon's openness to the possibility of totally new ways of looking at nature, and would put them to the test rather than mock them, can be considered cranks. Professor Brian Josephson won the Nobel Prize for Physics in 1973 for his work on superconductor junctions. Now he directs the Mind–Matter Unification Project of the Theory of Condensed Matter Group at Cambridge University's Cavendish Laboratory. In a direct echo of Bacon, Josephson is scathing of colleagues who:

start off with an opinion that a belief is wrong and create an argument to justify this opinion. The arguments spread by word of mouth and are never updated with contrary information that may subsequently arrive, thus becoming the 'correct position' to take. It is perilous to say anything that indicates doubt about whether this position is in fact correct (though a certain proportion of scientists look more closely and can see the cracks in the official position). This effectively prevents any work in the areas concerned being published in the major journals where they will be seen by others.[186]

When I pointed out the similarities between his own and Bacon's philosophy, Josephson was surprised, unaware of the details of his distant predecessor's work, though he pointed out that the Royal Society's motto *Nullius in verba*, roughly 'Take nothing on word alone', dated back to the Roman poet Horace. But if Bacon were alive today, he could have written Josephson's attack on closed minds.

◄○►

The third requirement for effective science is communication. The urge to share your scientific results and insights is part of what makes a scientist. Modern science relies for its effectiveness on free access to published research.

Bacon was in no sense original in his enthusiasm to share scientific information. While I would argue that the Greek philosophers were not scientists as they did not conform to all my criteria, many of them committed their ideas to writing and discussed them widely. Yet it would be hard to find a figure in history who went to more effort than Bacon to communicate his ideas – even going to the extent of breaking the rules of his order to get the *Opus majus* to the pope. It is interesting to compare his approach with Leonardo da Vinci, who has also been called the first scientist.[187]

Leonardo had many of the characteristics of a scientist, but seemed almost to go out of his way not to communicate his find-ings, making notes in ways that were designed to prevent others interpreting them. This does not detract from the importance of Leonardo's genius, but does make it doubtful that he could be called a scientist. Bacon communicated as if he were driven to do so.

◄○►

So, Bacon had in place mathematics as a foundation, an openness to consider information without bias, and an understanding of the need to communicate. He now added one last building block, the true essential that would turn natural philosophy into science. That final component was experiment.

Natural philosophy had traditionally relied on listening to the arguments of other philosophers, disputing them, and finally agreeing on an accepted theory. Once an individual became regarded as an authority it would be tantamount to sacrilege to question his ideas. After that, all that was allowed was to make commentaries on the original.

This tradition of reliance on authority continued not only to Bacon's time but persisted through the Renaissance. Even in the 1660s, Isaac Newton was regarded as unusual in rejecting the authority of the Classical philosophers and starting from scratch with his own ideas. Before Newton's time, making a challenge could be life-threatening. Yet without fighting the cloying weight of authority it was almost impossible to make significant progress. And progress cannot be made without discarding outdated notions, however dearly they were once held.

The tension between the word of authority and deduction from experiment was very obvious at the end of the sixteenth century, when Galileo attempted to challenge Aristotle's views on gravity. The Greek philosopher had opined that the speed at which different objects fell varied with their weight. A heavy object like a stone would fall much faster than a light object like a feather. And the heavier the stone, the faster it would fall.

Even though two millennia had passed since Aristotle made his pronouncement, the weight of his authority was such that no one felt it necessary to test his gravitational theory. Galileo was prepared to take on that challenge. According to a well-known story, he carried two cannonballs, one ball much larger than the other, up to the parapet of the leaning campanile in the cathedral square in Pisa. From this precarious position he dropped the two cannon-balls. An associate at the bottom of the tower was able to observe that both landed together. The time they took to fall was not influenced by their weight.

There is some doubt about whether these events took place. The only source we have for it is Vincenzo Viviani, one of Galileo's assis-tants, who wrote down his master's reminiscences when Galileo was an old man.[188] It seems slightly suspicious: Galileo was never one to hold back on self-publicity, yet there is no evidence that he ever mentioned the experiment himself. However, what is beyond doubt is that Galileo believed objects of different weight to fall at the same rate, and that he had backed up this theory with experiment, even if he did not use the dramatic stage of the Leaning Tower. What we do know, strangely, is that the tower was the setting in 1612 for an experimental attempt to prove Galileo wrong. One of the profes-sors of Pisa University dropped items off the Leaning Tower that had different weights. According to his timings, they did not hit the ground at exactly the same time. Galileo responded with relish:

> Aristotle says that a ball of 100 pounds falling from a height of 100 cubits hits the ground before a one pound ball has fallen one cubit. I say they arrive at the same time. You find, on making the test, that the larger ball beats the smaller one by two inches. Now, behind those two inches you want to hide Aristotle's 99 cubits, and speaking only of my tiny error, remain silent about his enormous mistake.[189]

Galileo was saying that a ball of 100 pounds would fall 100 cubits (a cubit is the length from the elbow to the tip of the middle finger) in the same time as a ball of one pound would fall 100 cubits. As he later found to his cost when he declared his support for the theory that the Sun is at the centre of the solar system, Galileo had taken the dangerous step of putting experimental evidence above the voice of authority. It was a brave move, but anything but original. It was, in fact, simply a reiteration of Bacon's insistence on the necessity of experiment.

It would be ridiculous to suggest that Bacon invented the concept of experimentation itself, which must go back to the Stone Age at least. But he stood out from his predecessors and the other philosophers of his time in making experimental science an essential part of understanding nature, and in defining the scientific method as a formal scientific discipline.

Right at the start of the section of the *Opus majus* that deals with experimental science, Bacon weighs in and delivers a body blow to the practice of basing scientific knowledge on argument, a procedure that had reigned unchallenged since the time of the Greeks:

> There are two modes of acquiring knowledge, namely by reasoning and experience. Reasoning draws a conclusion . . . but does not make the conclusion certain, nor does it remove doubt so that the mind may be confident it has reached the truth, unless the mind discovers [the conclusion] by the path of experience.[190]

He goes on to make it clear that this 'experience' isn't the normal, casual experience of life, but that scientific truths are arrived at only by consciously setting out to achieve a specific goal:

> He therefore who wishes to rejoice without doubt in regard to the truths underlying phenomena must know how to devote himself to experiment.[191]

Since Bacon's day we have come to consider this experimental approach the natural basis for pretty much all of science. But before Bacon there was only natural philosophy – theorizing about the causes and mechanisms of nature with no reference to practical experiment. Again, we have to be careful about terminology. Bacon's idea of experiment was much looser than a modern scientist would accept. Yet he was so convinced that it was necessary to go beyond the unthinking acceptance of authority as a source of knowledge and to look instead to the practical that he devoted a whole section of the *Opus majus* to arguing for this approach, something that has been referred to as 'peculiarly Baconian'.[192]

—◄o►—

Bacon has not received the recognition he deserves for this remarkable development because of two blows to his credibility. The first came from the namesake we have already met, Sir Francis Bacon.[193] This flamboyant figure was best known in his day as a politician. He was born in the Strand in London in 1561. After his time at Cambridge University, he was to spend a good thirty years in Parliament, becoming an MP at the age of twenty-three. He was never greatly popular with Elizabeth I, perhaps because he wrote her letters giving her advice. No doubt the advice was good, but Elizabeth was not particularly amused. With the accession of James in 1603, though, Francis soared into favour.

Bacon's suggestions on the union of England and Scotland that the Scottish King of England, James I, was attempting to forge went down well with the king. When he also suggested measures to deal with Roman Catholics who were objecting to the imposition of a Protestant state, he won himself a knighthood within months. Four years later he was awarded the important parliamentary post of Solicitor General. In 1618, he was made Lord Chancellor with the title Lord Verulam (from the Roman name of the city of St Albans). In 1621 Bacon was given yet another title,

Viscount St Albans. Although a later bribery scandal excluded him from Parliament, he continued to be influential in his writing until his death in 1626.

The Elizabethan Bacon's greatest claim to fame, however, is not his statesmanship or his political flexibility, but the book he wrote in 1620, the *Novum organum, or indications respecting the interpretation of nature*. This has proved a central work in the development of the modern scientific method. From this single volume we can see why Roger Bacon was eclipsed for so long. The *Novum organum* argued the case for a new way of investigating nature. Francis pointed to the tendency to depend too much on common everyday notions and generalization from axioms. Instead, he said, there should be proper, systematic recording of observations. However, instead of collecting observations and deducing 'laws' from common ground as had been the usual practice until then, Francis Bacon argued for a method of induction that also made use of negatives to eliminate the possibilities that weren't true.

As a simple example of the difference between positive and negative argument, you cannot prove that a sheep is a dog by arguing that dogs have four legs – by that token, since a sheep also has four legs then it must be a dog. But by using the legs criterion you can prove that a spider *isn't* a dog, since the spider has eight legs as opposed to the dog's four. It is often much easier to prove that something isn't true than to prove that it is, an observation that Francis put at the heart of his new scientific method.

While Francis Bacon's work was genuinely valuable (and went significantly further than Roger Bacon's), it managed to push out of sight the principles that Roger Bacon had espoused, so that for a long time when the name 'Bacon' and the term 'scientific method' were combined it was always Francis who was thought of. All too often this is still the case today.

—◄○►—

As we have seen, when Roger Bacon's work was rediscovered in the nineteenth century it was fêted and he was described as a genius. Soon, though, there was another challenge to his standing, an attempt to belittle his contribution. Almost everything Bacon wrote was dismissed as having been copied from others, and if he was given any credit it was merely as an effective encyclopedist. This denigration was even applied to his approach to experimental science, using a clever argument that Bacon himself, that master of the complaint about bad translations, would have been impressed by. Remarkably, the Bacon critics claimed that he had never written about experimental science at all.

This theory is summed up well by the historian of science Pierre Duhem, who wrote in the early years of the twentieth century that Bacon had simply replaced the Classical method of reasoning with the use of experience, recording whatever observers claimed to have experienced.[194] If this was all that Bacon meant, Duhem argued, then he showed no grasp whatsoever of the experimental method, and was little more than a collector of old wives' tales. The *Opus majus*, according to Duhem's argument, is less of a scientific master-piece and more a medieval equivalent of *Old Moore's Almanac*.

At first glance this is a wild claim. There is a large section of the *Opus majus* clearly labelled '*Scientia experimentalis*'. However, as we have seen, there is a need to be careful with terminology. It is not always enough to assume that a Latin word that looks like an English one will have the same meaning. And the Bacon sceptics pointed out that this *scientia experimentalis* could just as well mean 'the science of experience' as 'experimental science'.[195]

This is more than philological quibbling. It could have been that Bacon was arguing for exactly the approach that Francis Bacon had shown to be worthless when he complained about 'depending too much on common everyday notions'.[196] And certainly Roger Bacon was guilty of this in passing on stories of cockatrices, Amazon women, and other marvels without anything resembling a proof. But on reading his words it becomes clear, unless you are determined to come out with a negative result, that there was much more than this to his experimental science.

It is true that Bacon was no great experimenter himself, though he did conduct more experiments than some critics would acknowledge. In the *Opus majus*, when describing the motion of the stars, he comments:

> So, moreover, Ptolemy in the fifth book of the *Optics* teaches us to note the same fact, and Alhazen also in his seventh book, and I have noted it in instruments, and it is an assured fact.[197]

Light and optics was the one area where Bacon was prepared to get his hands dirty and experiment. The reason is obvious if you consider his fundamental theory (see Chapter 4): he believed that at the heart all physics was a process of radiation – his propagation of species. As light was a special case of species that could be observed, it was the natural subject for him to experiment with.

Where Bacon did not experiment himself he relied on someone else's results, just as a modern scientist will build on work reported in the published papers of other scientists around the world. Even in Bacon's time, where the body of scientific knowledge was much more limited, it would not have been practical for everyone to take everything back to first principles every time. This is not to say that everyone else's word is to be taken as absolute truth, and Bacon never suggested this – quite the reverse. The fact remains that his experimental science was just that.

Bacon gives us a clear example of what he means by experimental science which refutes any suggestion that he is merely referring to recording everyday experience. He presents in detail a study of the rainbow and how experimental science can contribute. He describes using prisms and other shapes of glass to generate small rainbows. He explains how measurements can be made to show how the rainbow functions: the experimenter measures the angular distance of the Sun above the horizon to find the angle at which the rainbow effect cuts out –42°. This is no reflection of mere experience. Here is Bacon commenting on the method:

> The experimenter further tries to find out whether the bow is caused by incident rays or by reflection, and whether it is an image of the Sun, as was assumed in the statements made on perspective [optics], and whether there are real colours in the cloud itself. He must also enquire about the variety and cause of its shape; since a statement was made above merely in regard to the size of its form, namely that sometimes it is a complete circle, and sometimes the larger portion, and sometimes the smaller. But to understand these matters we must employ definite experiments.[198]

What is happening here, as Bacon points out, is that his experimental science can be used to test hypotheses of the other sciences. This is more than simply recounting tales of experience. He says that experimental science

> investigates by experiment the notable conclusions of all those [other] sciences. For the other sciences know how to discover their principles by experiments, but their conclusions are reached by reasoning drawn from the principles discovered. But if they should have a particular and complete experience of their conclusions, they must have it with the aid of this noble science.[199]

In other words, where reasoning has been used to reach conclusions, experiment can (and should) be used to test the validity of those conclusions. What's more, he states very specifically that theoretical knowledge could not and should not be the only route to progress. Experience yields new instruments and experiments provide new data. Bacon's involvement with Peter Peregrinus brought him (admittedly as a theoretician) to the forefront of practical experimental science.

We should also bear in mind that in the *Opus majus, Opus minus,* and *Opus tertium* Bacon was providing a hurried proposal for a real compendium of science. No one could reasonably expect him to have established a perfect experimental basis for all his concepts in a proposal. One reason for making the proposal it was to elicit the funding and resources to enable experiments to be carried out. But Bacon's catastrophic downfall meant that this would never be possible.

Finally, and most significantly, we should remember that Bacon was primarily a theoretician. The all too common misconception held about him is that if he had truly invented experimental science, he must himself have been an experimental scientist. But no one should claim this. Devising the *concept* of experimental science is after all a theoretical, rather than a practical achievement. Like all the good theoreticians who followed him, Bacon recognized the value of experiments, but that didn't mean that he had to undertake them himself.

As a theoretician, though, Bacon put too much trust in the purported experiments of other natural philosophers, leading him to pass on mistakes and being belittled as a consequence. He has been criticized, for example, for his description of the force of attraction in twigs:

> Cut a branch (or twig) of hazel in two; separate the two ends, and you will soon feel the two isolated parts stretching themselves out to approach one another; you will perceive the effort that they make.[200]

Nonetheless he is careful, as ever, to ascribe what happens to natural causes:

> This is a very wonderful thing. For this reason magicians perform this experiment, repeating different incantations, and they believe that this phenomenon is caused by virtue of the incantations. I

have disregarded the incantations and have discovered the wonderful action of nature, which is similar to that of the magnet on iron.[201]

There is no doubt that the experiment was flawed – twigs do not attract each other in this way – and it is likely that Bacon was merely passing on the word of others. However, his detractors also fall into the same trap. I would be very surprised if any of the twentieth-century historians of science who mocked Bacon for believing in this phenomenon had themselves carried out the experiment – they too were relying on the experience of others. Most importantly, though, as the nineteenth-century biographer Émile Charles points out quite correctly, the significant thing here is not the result but the method. Whether Bacon actually undertook the experiment or took someone else's word for it, it was only in the execution that he was faulty, not in the experimental theory.

Bacon was all too aware of the dangers of error. In the very first part of the *Opus majus*, before he touches on any other aspect of science, he goes through four different ways in which one can fall into error, each as valid today as it was in Bacon's time. They are submission to a faulty authority, relying on custom, following the vagaries of popular prejudice, and being unaware of your own limitations (or being determined to hide them) – in his words, 'concealing ignorance behind an ostentatious display of cleverness'.[202] There is also an inverted version of this last form of error. When we don't have knowledge, it is all too tempting to criticize others in an attempt to distract from our own ignorance. Bacon gives a particularly vivid, if not exactly politically correct example of this last type of error:

> Matters of which we are ignorant, where we cannot make a display of our knowledge, we slight, find fault with, abuse, and bring to naught, that we may not seem ignorant of any matter, glossing over our ignorance like a woman with her finery and meretricious colouring, a foul remedy.[203]

Those who have criticized Bacon for too easily taking information on trust point out that he falls victim to one of his own errors. Yet that's hardly surprising under the circumstances. As Bacon explains to the pope at the start of the *Opus majus*, 'The subjects in question are weighty and unusual, they stand in need of the grace and favour accorded to human frailty.'[204] There were going to be mistakes, Bacon was saying, especially given the immense speed with which Bacon had had to assemble his huge work.

Being aware of the causes of error might not have been enough to prevent Bacon from making mistakes, but it is ridiculous to suggest that he was therefore not a scientist. There are few great scientists, however self-centred, who would be prepared to swear on their life that they have never made a mistake. Einstein made his self-confessed 'greatest mistake' in devising the cosmological constant, a fudge factor he incorporated into his equations describing the state of the universe, to fix an error that he *assumed* was present. Richard Feynman, one of the greatest physicists of the twentieth century (in fact one of the greatest scientists ever), notably commented, 'To develop working ideas efficiently, I try to fail as fast as I can.'[205]

◄○►

Bacon's four building blocks – a basis of mathematics, an openness of mind, the desire to communicate, and the fundamental contribution of experiment – made his methodology the direct forerunner of every subsequent work of science. He actually had every reason *not* to develop this independent scientific approach. Accepting the word of authority was orthodoxy at all levels of medieval society. It threaded through Bacon's life at the university. It was at the heart of the life of the Franciscans and other orders. And it was an unquestioned absolute in the theology of his age. Yet time after time, Bacon showed that he would not fall into line, would not take the easy course.

In many of his writings, Bacon rails against the spurious authority of many contemporary teachers. Although he makes much use himself of the views of classical writers like Aristotle, he also makes it very plain that even such supreme figures could make mistakes. Instead of unthinking belief he advocates testing theories – even the theories of authorities – by experience and experiment. Also, for Bacon there is no point in arbitrary knowledge for its own sake: always there is the requirement of utility.

No one before Bacon combined an insistence on the fundamental need for testing the statements of authority with the single-mindedness to maintain this viewpoint despite the consequences. The ancient Greek philosophers had themselves challenged the accepted wisdom of their mythology, but their approach was always based on pure argument without the objective input from experimental testing. Figures such as Albertus Magnus and Robert Grosseteste may have had scientific minds that could equal or even better Bacon, but they were not able to throw off the shackles of convention and belief in authority and take the revolutionary step that Bacon took.

Bacon's hero of practical science, Peter Peregrinus, might have made much use of experiment, but it was down to Bacon to extract the meat of what Peter was doing and make it into a principle. In his only extant work, the short *De magnete*, Peter remarks on the importance of the use and 'carefulness' by the scientist of 'his own hands'. [206] Whether, as some have suggested, Bacon influenced Peter in this respect, or Peter sent Bacon off in the right direction (as seems more likely from the way Bacon writes about his colleague), the fact remains that Peter could never have begun the revolution that Bacon was to be responsible for. For Peter Peregrinus it was enough to experiment and to know the results – Bacon had the urge to make universal science available to mankind.

I have set out to show two things: that Bacon was a scientist, and that he was the first. He was not much of an experimenter, as we have seen, but he did buy equipment for experiment (part of his £2,000 expenditure), he described himself as undertaking experiments, and it is widely accepted that the optical work in the *Opus majus* and elsewhere seems to be based on original experiment.[207] In the end, though, as the example of Einstein clearly illustrates, you do not need to do experiments to be a scientist. Equally, it might be argued, Bacon wasn't a very good scientist – he too often took at face value information he was given by others. But it would be frankly surprising if he had been too good at it. No one is amazed that the Wright brothers weren't outstanding aviators – the remarkable thing is that they got off the ground at all. Being first often goes hand in hand with only just making it. Bacon does survive my four tests – he stressed the importance of mathematics, he did not dismiss data through prejudice, he communicated his findings, and he was convinced of the essential contribution of experiment. For me, then, Bacon *was* a scientist.

Was he the first, though? That can never be proved conclusively. This was a time when science was emerging from natural philosophy. Arguments could be made for awarding the title of first scientist to one of the Arab philosophers such as Alhazen, or to Bacon's contemporaries Albertus Magnus or Robert Grosseteste. Yet I believe that Bacon was the first to clearly fulfil the requirements I have imposed.

It took time for Bacon's small flame to take a hold. For many years the fire was damped down by tradition. But by the seventeenth century it had become a blaze that was to forge and temper every aspect of the modern world. Bacon's gift to us, like the gift of fire in ancient mythology, has proved a mixed blessing. By losing our dependence on authority we may have ushered in a world of scientific wonders, but we have also replaced the comfort of certainty with the discomfort of doubt. Even so, the balance seems to be in favour of the scientific revolution. Any view of the past that sees it as anything other than brutish and unpleasant is decidedly rose-tinted. The life expectancy of the common person in the Western world has doubled since Bacon's day so that now many more of us live to Bacon's ripe old age and beyond. We can make more of our life, and we have much more opportunity for enjoyment and discovery. And though in the short term there was a loss of a spiritual anchor when scientific rationalism attempted to take over from religion, in the longer term religion has proved robust enough to survive the scientific revolution.

Historian John Bridges describes Bacon as 'thirsting for reality in a barren land infested with metaphysical mirage'.[208] Bacon's invention of science was a wellspring that transformed that barren land. Roger Bacon, that pernickety friar, that pedantic but glorious writer, that most remarkable of men, was indeed the first scientist.

Notes and References

Where no author is indicated, the reference is to one of Roger Bacon's works.

1   Powicke, *The Oxford History of England*.
2   Easton, *Roger Bacon and His Search for Universal Science*.
3   Hackett, *Roger Bacon and the Sciences*.
4   *Opus majus*, Part 4, First distinction, Chapter I.
5   Scott, *The Mathematical Work of John Wallis*.
6   Ewing Duncan, *The Calendar*.
7   Quoted in Bridges, *The Life and Works of Roger Bacon*.
8   Quoted in Bridges, *The Life and Works of Roger Bacon*.
9   Thorndike, *A History of Magic and Experimental Science*.
10 Easton, *Roger Bacon and His Search for Universal Science*.
11 Quoted in *De mirabile*.
12 Rous, *Historia regum angliae*; Easton, *Roger Bacon and His Search for Universal Science*.
13 *Opus majus*, Part 5, First distinction, Chapter I.
14 *Opus tertium*.
15 Platt, *Medieval England*.
16 Platt, *Medieval England*.
17 Rous, *Historia regum angliae*.
18 *The Famous Historie of Fryer Bacon*.
19 Easton, *Roger Bacon and His Search for Universal Science*.
20 Quoted in Catto, *History of the University of Oxford*.
21 Catto, *History of the University of Oxford*.
22 Geoffrey of Monmouth, *History of the Kings of Britain*.
23 Catto, *History of the University of Oxford*.
24 Catto, *History of the University of Oxford*.

25   Quoted in Catto, *History of the University of Oxford*.

26   Paris, *Historia major*.

27   Quoted in Easton, *Roger Bacon and His Search for Universal Science*.

28   Easton, *Roger Bacon and His Search for Universal Science*.

29   *De retardandis*.

30   *De retardandis*, Dedication.

31   E.g. Easton, *Roger Bacon and His Search for Universal Science*.

32   *Opus tertium*.

33   *Opus tertium*.

34   Easton, *Roger Bacon and His Search for Universal Science*.

35   *Opus tertium*.

36   Platt, *Medieval England*.

37   Easton, *Roger Bacon and His Search for Universal Science*.

38   *De mirabile* (except where indicated, all subsequent quotes in this chapter are from *De mirabile*).

39   Clarke, 'Extra-terrestrial relays'.

40   Ronan, 'Leonard and Thomas Digges'.

41   *Opus tertium*, referred to in Westacott, *Roger Bacon in Life and Legend* and Hackett, *Roger Bacon and the Sciences*.

42   *Opus majus*, Part 5, Last distinction, Chapter IV.

43   *Compendium studii philosophiae*.

44   Most of the information on the early years of the Order is drawn from Moorman, *History of the Franciscan Order*.

45   Catto, *History of the University of Oxford*.

46   Most of the information on Grosseteste is from Southern, *Robert Grosseteste*.

47   Grosseteste, *De luce*.

48   *Opus majus*, Part 5, First distinction, Chapter I.

49   *Opus majus*, Part 5, First distinction, Chapter I.

50   *Opus majus*, Part 5, First distinction, Chapter I.

51   Itard, *Les Livres arithmétique d'Euclide*.

52   For further information on Alhazen see Clegg, *Light Years*.

53   *Opus majus*, Part 5, Seventh distinction, Chapter IV.

54 Burnet, *Exploring Plato's Dialogues.*

55 *Opus majus*, Part 5, Second distinction, Chapter I.

56 *Opus majus*, Part 5, First distinction, Chapter II.

57 *Opus majus*, Part 5, Second distinction, Chapter I.

58 *Opus majus*, Part 5, Third distinction, Chapter VII.

59 *De multiplicatione specierum.*

60 Details of al-Kindi's life are taken from Atiyeh, *Al-Kindi.*

61 Alkindus (al-Kindi), *De aspectibus.*

62 *De speculis comburentibus.*

63 Huygens, *Traité de la lumière.*

64 *Opus majus*, Part 4, Fourth distinction, Chapter IX.

65 *Opus majus*, Part 4, First distinction, Chapter III.

66 *Opus majus*, non-chaptered section, near end.

67 *Opus majus*, non-chaptered section, near end.

68 Paris, *Chronicles of Matthew Paris.*

69 *Opus majus*, Part 4, non-chaptered section, near end.

70 *Compendium studii theologiae.*

71 Gasquet, 'Unpublished fragment'.

72 Easton, *Roger Bacon and His Search for Universal Science.*

73 Information on Bonaventura is taken from the *Catholic Encyclopaedia.*

74 Quoted in Easton, *Roger Bacon and His Search for Universal Science.*

75 Platt, *Medieval England.*

76 *Opus majus*, Part 4, non-chaptered section, calendar part (except where indicated, all subsequent quotes in this chapter are from this part of the *Opus majus*).

77 Ewing Duncan, *The Calendar.*

78 Details of de Foulques's life and work may be found in the *Catholic Encyclopaedia.*

79 Gasquet, 'Unpublished fragment'.

80 Gasquet, 'Unpublished fragment'.

81 Quoted in Easton, *Roger Bacon and His Search for Universal Science.*

82 Letter from Pope Clement IV, Vatican Archive.

83 *Opus tertium.*

84 *Opus majus*, Part 1, Chapter I.

85 *De multiplicatione specierum.*

86 Easton, *Roger Bacon and His Search for Universal Science.*

87 *Opus tertium.*

88 *Opus majus*, Part 3, Chapter I.

89 *Opus majus*, Part 3, Chapter XI.

90 *Opus majus*, Part 3, Chapter XII.

91 Hackett, *Roger Bacon and the Sciences.*

92 Nicholas Damascenus, *De Plantis.*

93 *Opus majus*, Part 3, Chapter I.

94 *Opus majus*, Part 3, Chapter I.

95 *Opus majus*, Part 3, Chapter VI.

96 *Opus majus*, Part 1, Chapter X.

97 Easton, *Roger Bacon and His Search for Universal Science.*

98 *Opus minus.*

99 *Opus tertium.*

100 Euclid, *Preclarissimus liber elementorum.*

101 *Opus tertium.*

102 *Compendium studii philosophiae.*

103 *Opus majus*, Part 2, Chapter I.

104 St Augustine, *The Confessions.*

105 Quoted in Andrew Dickson White, *Warfare of Science with Theology.*

106 Quoted in Dodson, 'Fryar Roger called Bachon'.

107 *Opus majus*, Part 2, Chapter VII.

108 Hackett, *Roger Bacon and the Sciences.*

109 *Opus majus*, Part 4, non-chaptered section, on astronomy.

110 Westacott, *Roger Bacon in Life and Legend.*

111 *De mirabile* (except where indicated, all subsequent quotes in this chapter are from *De mirabile*).

112 *Opus majus*, Part 4, Fourth distinction, Chapter VII.

113 Quoted in Woolley, *The Queen's Conjuror.*

114   *Opus majus*, Part 4, non-chaptered section, on magic.

115   *Opus majus*, Part 4, non-chaptered section, on magic.

116   *Opus majus*, Part 1, Chapter IV, quoting pseudo-Aristotle, *Secretum secretorum*.

117   *De mirabile* (Bacon attributes this to Aristotle in *Noctium atticarum de collatione sapientium*).

118   Little, *Roger Bacon Essays*.

119   Kopp, *Geschichte der Chemie*, quoted in *De mirabile*.

120   *Opus tertium*.

121   *Opus majus*, no chapter ref.

122   *The Famous Historie of Fryer Bacon*.

123   *The Famous Historie of Fryer Bacon*.

124   *De mirabile*.

125   *De mirabile*.

126   Quoted in *Opus majus*, Part 4, Fourth distinction, Chapter I.

127   Archimedes, *The Sand-reckoner*.

128   Thomas Little Heath, *Aristarchus of Samos*.

129   *Opus majus*, Part 4, Fourth distinction, Chapter X.

130   *Opus majus*, Part 4, Fourth distinction, Chapter X.

131   *Opus majus*, Part 4, Fourth distinction, Chapter X.

132   *Opus majus*, Part 4, Fourth distinction, Chapter X.

133   *Opus majus*, Part 4, Fourth distinction, Chapter X.

134   *Opus majus*, Part 4, Fourth distinction, Chapter X.

135   Russell, *Inventing the Flat Earth*.

136   Russell, *Inventing the Flat Earth*.

137   *Opus majus*, Part 4, Fourth distinction, Chapter X.

138   Calinger, *Classics of Mathematics*.

139   *Opus majus*, Part 4, non-chaptered section.

140   *Opus majus*, Part 4, non-chaptered section, on geography.

141   Hackett, *Roger Bacon and the Sciences*.

142   *De mirabile*.

143   Waite, *The Lives of Alchemistical Philosophers*.

144   Rous, *Historia regum angliae*.

145   Royal MS 126, folio 152.

146 Dodson, 'Fryar Roger called Bachon'.
147 Quoted in Little, 'Roger Bacon'.
148 *The Famous Historie of Fryer Bacon.*
149 Greene, *Friar Bacon and Friar Bungay.*
150 Ingolstadt Municipal Records, 17 June 1528.
151 Greene, *Groatsworth of Wit*, quoted in the *Oxford Dictionary of Quotations.*
152 Greene, *Farewell to Folly*, quoted in Greene, *Friar Bacon and Friar Bungay*, Introduction.
153 Greene, *Friar Bacon and Friar Bungay.*
154 Greene, *Friar Bacon and Friar Bungay.*
155 *The Famous Historie of Fryer Bacon.*
156 *The Famous Historie of Fryer Bacon.*
157 *The Famous Historie of Fryer Bacon.*
158 Frost, *The Lives of the Conjurors.*
159 William of Malmesbury, untitled, trans. 'Dr Giles' (Bohn's Antiquarian Library), quoted in Westacott, *Roger Bacon in Life and Legend.*
160 Albertus Magnus, *De miner.*, lib. II, tr. ii, I; quoted in the *Catholic Encyclopedia.*
161 Greene, *Friar Bacon and Friar Bungay.*
162 Wood, *Antiquities of the City of Oxford.*
163 'T. M.', *Frier Bacon.*
164 'T. M.', *Frier Bacon.*
165 'T. M.', *Frier Bacon.*
166 Charles, *Roger Bacon.*
167 Woolley, *The Queen's Conjuror.*
168 Quoted in Bridges, *The Life and Works of Roger Bacon.*
169 Woolley, *The Queen's Conjuror.*
170 Quoted in Bridges, *The Life and Works of Roger Bacon.*
171 Woolley, *The Queen's Conjuror.*
172 Newbold, *The Cipher of Roger Bacon.*

173   Brumbaugh, *The Most Mysterious Manuscript.*
174   D'Imperio, *The Voynich Manuscript: An Elegant Enigma.*
175   Zandonella, *Book of Riddles.*
176   Catto, *History of the University of Oxford.*
177   Bridges, *The Life and Works of Roger Bacon.*
178   Hackett, *Roger Bacon and the Sciences.*
179   Hackett, *Roger Bacon and the Sciences.*
180   *Opus majus*, Part 7, First part [sic].
181   Francis Bacon, *Works of Francis Bacon.*
182   *Opus majus*, Part 1, Chapter VI.
183   Scott, *The Mathematical Work of John Wallis.*
184   *Opus majus*, Part 4, First distinction, Chapter I.
185   Francis Bacon, *Novum organum.*
186   Josephson, Review of *Voodoo Science.*
187   Michael White, *Leonardo.*
188   Viviani, *Racconto istorico della vita di Galileo.*
189   Quoted in Gribbin and Gribbin, *Galileo.*
190   *Opus majus*, Part 6, Chapter I.
191   *Opus majus*, Part 6, Chapter I.
192   Hackett, *Roger Bacon and the Sciences.*
193   For more on Francis Bacon, see Zagorin, *Francis Bacon.*
194   Duhem, *Essays.*
195   Hackett, *Roger Bacon and the Sciences.*
196   Francis Bacon, *Novum organum.*
197   *Opus majus*, Part 4, Fourth distinction, Chapter II.
198   *Opus majus*, Part 6, Chapter VII.
199   *Opus majus*, Part 6, Chapter II.
200   *Opus majus*, Part 6, Third prerogative.
201   *Opus majus*, Part 1, Chapter IX.
202   *Opus majus*, Part 1, Chapter I.
203   *Opus majus*, Part 1, Chapter IX.
204   *Opus majus*, Part 1, Chapter I.
205   Feynman, *Surely You're Joking.*
206   Libri, *Histoire des sciences.*

207 Hackett, *Roger Bacon and the Sciences.*
208 Bridges, *The Life and Works of Roger Bacon.*

Bibliography

The first part of the bibliography lists books which are recommended for further information on the life and works of Roger Bacon and the historical background. Most of these are cited in the notes; other sources cited there are listed in the second part of the bibliography.

Recommended Reading

James Blish, *Doctor Mirabilis* (Arrow, 1976). A historical novel based on Bacon's life by this under-rated science-fiction author. An excellent attempt to get into the mind of Bacon.

John H. Bridges, *The Life and Works of Roger Bacon* (Williams & Northgate, 1914). A rather old-fashioned but mostly sound trip through Bacon's life and work.

Robert S. Brumbaugh, *The Most Mysterious Manuscript: The Voynich 'Roger Bacon' Cipher Manuscript* (Carbondale, 1978). Although this book provides good evidence that the Voynich manuscript was not Bacon's, it is still a fascinating set of long articles on attempts to decode and provide a history for the Voynich manuscript.

J. I. Catto (ed.), *The History of the University of Oxford, Volume I: The Early Oxford Schools* (Oxford University Press, 1984). Fascinating both for its background on the foundation of the university and for its section on medieval science from an Oxford viewpoint.

Brian Clegg, *Light Years* (Piatkus, 2001). An exploration of the history of humanity's fascination with light. Puts Bacon's contribution into place in the larger understanding of this remarkable topic.

Stewart C. Easton, *Roger Bacon and His Search for a Universal Science*

(Blackwell, 1952). A scholarly attempt to piece together a biography of Bacon and to understand his driving urge to build a picture of a universal science. Intentionally ignores legend.

David Ewing Duncan, *The Calendar* (Fourth Estate, 1998). A very readable history of the calendar from its origins to the present day.

The Famous Historie of Fryer Bacon (Banton Press, 1992). This is a reprint of an 1828 edition of the *Historie* with an introduction from that period, when serious interest in Bacon was starting to re-emerge. Although there is no historical accuracy about the *Historie*, it is a fascinating insight into the legendary aspects of Bacon.

Robert Greene, *Friar Bacon and Friar Bungay* (Edward Arnold, 1964). This play from a contemporary of Shakespeare's, strongly based on *The Famous Historie*, was partly responsible for Bacon's lasting legendary form as a mountebank magician.

Jeremiah Hackett (ed.), *Roger Bacon and the Sciences* (E. J. Brill, 1997). A collection of articles on the different sciences covered by Bacon – a more modern version of the *Roger Bacon Essays (see below)*. Suffers a little from a lack of overall view and definitely influenced by the twentieth-century swing against Bacon's originality, but a valuable source.

David Lindberg, *Roger Bacon and the Origins of Perspectiva in the Middle Ages* (Clarendon Press, 1996). Lindberg's scholarly work gives much valuable information on the role of Bacon's work in the early understanding of optics.

A. G. Little (ed.), *Roger Bacon Essays: Essays contributed by various writers on the occasion of the commemoration of the seventh centenary of his birth* (Oxford University Press, 1914). The first significant collection of essays on Bacon's contribution to science (the anniversary assumes 1214 for the year of Bacon's birth). It mixes echoes of the Victorians' claim to Bacon as their own with twentieth-century cynicism.

H. Stanley Redgrove, *Roger Bacon* (Holmes, 1995). Little more than a pamphlet, but offers some interesting insights into Bacon's historical importance and philosophy.

Lynn Thorndike, *A History of Magic and Experimental Science*, Vols. 1

and 2 (Columbia University Press, 1923). A massive analysis of the interaction between magic and science. Thorndike was one of the strongest exponents of the theory that Bacon was little more than an encyclopedist.

E. Westacott, *Roger Bacon in Life and Legend* (Banton Press, 1993). Although this is a reprint of an edition first published in the 1950s, it has the feel of a much older text. It provides interesting summaries of other works, but perpetuates some of the 'facts' about Bacon now generally regarded as suspicious.

Benjamin Woolley, *The Queen's Conjuror* (HarperCollins, 2001). A very readable biography of John Dee, who became Roger Bacon's greatest follower in Tudor times. Very limited references to Bacon, but useful for Dee's background.

Other Sources

Alkindus (al-Kindi), *De aspectibus*. A published translation is included in 'Alkindi, Tideus und Pseudo-Euklid. Drei optische Werke', *Abhandlungen zur Geschichte der mathematischen Wissenschaften*, Vol. 26/3 (1912).

Archimedes, *The Sand-reckoner*, trans. T. L. Heath (Dover, 2002).

George N. Atiyeh, *Al-Kindi, The Philosopher of the Arabs* (Kazi Publications, 1977).

St Augustine, *The Confessions*, trans. Henry Chadwick (Oxford Paperbacks, 1998).

Francis Bacon, *Novum organum; or, indications respecting the interpretation of nature* (Open Court Publishing, 1994).

Francis Bacon, *The Works of Francis Bacon*, ed. James Spedding *et al.* (Longman, 1857–74).

Roger Bacon, *Compendium studii philosophiae*, in *Fr. Rogeri Bacon opera quædam hactenus inedita*, ed. J. S. Brewer (London, 1859).

Roger Bacon, *De mirabile potestate artis et naturae*, trans. Tenney L. Davis (Kessinger, 1940).

Roger Bacon, *De multiplicatione specierum*, in *Roger Bacon's Philosophy of Nature*, trans. & ed. David C. Lindberg (St Augustine's Press, 1998).

Roger Bacon, *De retardandis accidentium senectutis: cum aliis opusculis de rebus medicinalibus*, ed. A. G. Little & E. Withington (Clarendon Press, 1928).

Roger Bacon, *De speculis comburentibus*, in *Roger Bacon's Philosophy of Nature*, trans. & ed. David C. Lindberg (St Augustine's Press, 1998).

Roger Bacon, *Opus majus*, trans. Robert Belle Burke (Kessinger, 1998).

Roger Bacon, *Opus minus*, in *Fr. Rogeri Bacon opera quædam hactenus inedita*, ed. J. S. Brewer (London, 1859).

Roger Bacon, *Part of the* Opus tertium *of Roger Bacon, including a fragment now printed here for the first time*, ed. A. G. Little (British Society of Franciscan Studies, 1912).

John Burnet, *Exploring Plato's Dialogues* (Internet Applications Laboratory at the University of Evansville, 1998).

Ronald Calinger (ed.), *Classics of Mathematics* (Moore Publishing Company, 1982).

Catholic Encyclopaedia (Robert Appleton, 1907).

Émile Charles, *Roger Bacon: Sa vie, ses ouvrages, ses doctrines* (Paris, 1861).

Arthur C. Clarke, 'Extra-terrestrial relays: Can rocket stations give world-wide radio coverage?' *Wireless World*, October 1945.

Nicholas Damascenus, *De plantis*, trans. H. J. Drossaart-Lulofs and E. L. J. Poortman (Amsterdam, 1989).

Mary E. D'Imperio, *The Voynich Manuscript – An Elegant Enigma* (Aegean Park Press, 1978).

Dianna L. Dodson, 'Fryar Roger called Bachon', *British Heritage Magazine*, May/June 1999.

Pierre Duhem, *Essays in the History and Philosophy of Science*, trans. Roger Ariew and Peter Barker (Hackett, 1996).

Euclid, *Preclarissimus liber elementorum*, trans. Adelard of Bath, 1482. A published edition of Euclid is T. L. Heath (trans.), *The Thirteen*

Books of Euclid's Elements (Cambridge University Press, 1956).

Richard P. Feynman, *'Surely You're Joking, Mr Feynman!': Adventures of a Curious Character* (Vintage, 1992).

Thomas Frost, *The Lives of the Conjurors* (London, 1876).

F. A. Gasquet, 'An unpublished fragment of a work by Roger Bacon', *English Historical Review*, Vol. 12 (1897).

Geoffrey of Monmouth, *A History of the Kings of Britain*, trans. Sebastian Evans (Dent, 1941).

Robert Greene, *Groatsworth of Wit Bought with a Million of Repentance*, quoted in *Oxford Dictionary of Quotations* (Oxford University Press, 1979).

John and Mary Gribbin, *Galileo in 90 Minutes* (Constable, 1997).

Robert Grosseteste, *De luce*, trans. Julian Lock (Canterbury Press, 1996).

T. L. Heath, *Aristarchus of Samos* (Oxford University Press, 1913).

Christiaan Huygens, *Traité de la lumière* (1679). An English edition is *Treatise on Light*, 'rendered into English' by Silvanus P. Thompson (Macmillan, 1912; reprinted Dover, 1962).

J. Itard, *Les Livres arithmétique d'Euclide* (Paris, 1962).

Brian Josephson, Review of *Voodoo Science* by Robert Park, *The Times Higher Education Supplement*, 1 December 2000.

Hermann Kopp, *Geschichte der Chemie*, Vol. 3 (Braunschweig, 1845).

Guillaume Libri, *Histoire des sciences mathématiques en Italie* (Renouard, 1838).

A. G. Little, 'Roger Bacon', *Proceedings of the British Academy*, Vol. 14 (1928).

John Moorman, *A History of the Franciscan Order* (Oxford University Press, 1997).

William Romaine Newbold, *The Cipher of Roger Bacon* (University of Pennsylvania Press, 1928).

Oxford Dictionary of Quotations, 3rd edition (Oxford University Press, 1979).

Matthew Paris, *Chronicles of Matthew Paris*, trans. Richard Vaughan (Sutton Publishing, 1986).

Matthew Paris, *Historia major.* A published edition is *Matthew Paris's English history: from the year 1235 to 1273*, translated from the Latin by J. A. Giles (H. G. Bohn, 1852–4).

Colin Platt, *Medieval England: A Social History and Archaeology from the Conquest to 1600 AD* (Routledge, 1978).

Sir Maurice Powicke, *Oxford History of England, Vol. 4: The Thirteenth Century* (Clarendon Press, 1953).

Colin Ronan, 'Leonard and Thomas Digges: Inventors of the telescope', *Endeavour*, Vol. 16 (1992).

John Rous, *Joannis Rossi antiquarii warwicensis historia regum angliae*, ed. Thomas Hearne (Oxford, 1716). Microfilm reprint by Woodbridge, CT Research Publications, Inc. (1986).

Jeffrey Burton Russell, *Inventing the Flat Earth* (Praeger Paperback, 1997).

J. F. Scott, *The Mathematical Work of John Wallis* (Taylor & Francis, 1938).

Richard Southern, *Robert Grosseteste: The growth of an English Mind in Medieval Europe* (Clarendon Press, 1992).

'T. M.', *Frier Bacon His Discovery of the Miracles of Art, Nature and Magick, faithfully translated out of Dr. Dee's own copy by T. M and never before in English* (London, 1659).

Vincenzo Viviani, *Racconto istorico della vita di Galileo* ('Historical Account of the Life of Galileo') (1717).

Arthur Edward Waite, *The Lives of Alchemistical Philosophers* (John Watkins, 1955).

Andrew Dickson White, *A History of the Warfare of Science with Theology in Christendom* (D. Appleton, 1896).

Michael White, *Leonardo: The First Scientist* (Abacus, 2001).

Anthony Wood, *A Survey of the Antiquities of the City of Oxford* (Clarendon Press, 1889).

Peres Zagorin, *Francis Bacon* (Princeton University Press, 2000).

Catherine Zandonella, 'Book of Riddles – Are we on the brink of decoding the most mysterious document in the world?' *New Scientist*, 11 November 2001.

Bacon's Books

The published works of Roger Bacon amount to some 22 volumes plus assorted smaller pieces, though there is always a degree of argument over the exact number of the books that were actually written by Bacon himself. It's not always possible to be sure even by title, as the names given to books at the time were not fixed, but were rather a brief description of their content. Bacon himself refers to one of his books by at least three different titles. This list is not complete, but where possible includes details of translations, as all Bacon's work was written in Latin. Many of Bacon's books have still not been translated into English. Included are some of the editions, mostly in Latin, that have been printed. Books followed by (?) have been ascribed to Bacon, but his authorship of them has been questioned.

Datable Works

De retardandis senectutis accedentibus et de sensibus conservandis ('The Cure of Old Age and the Preservation of Youth'). May be an early work, *c.*1240. Bacon was very much ahead of his time in his emphasis on diet and hygiene, though the remedies are less impressive. Latin edition: Little and Withington (1928 – see Bibliography).

De mirabile potestate artis et naturae ('On the Marvellous Power of Magic and Nature'). *c.*1250. A long letter, possibly written to William of Auvergne or John of Basingstoke, in which Bacon draws a clear distinction between the way magic may work by suggestion and the realities of natural science. Also contains some very cryptic references to the formula for gunpowder. Among many editions are Latin: Paris (1542), Oxford (1594), Hamburg (1618), Zetzner (1659), Magnet (1702); English: 'T. M.' (1659), Tenney L. Davis (*c*.1920, reprinted 1940 by Kessinger – see Bibliography).

Commentary on Aristotle's De sensu et sensato. *c*.1250.

De multiplicatione specierum ('On the Propagation of Force'). Late 1250s. At least 24 manuscript copies exist, of which more than half ascribe this book to Roger Bacon in a contemporary hand. The earliest, written in Oxford, dates from 1280–1300. According to David C. Lindberg in his annotated translation, Bacon refers to a treatise, probably this one, variously as *Tractatus de generatione et multiplicatione et corruptione et actione de specierum*, *Tractus de radiis*, *Tractatus de speciebus*, *Tractatus specierum*, and *Tractatus specierum rerum activarum*. According to Bacon's *Opus tertium*, he sent the pope this treatise in two different versions, and had begun but not completed a third. Among known editions are Latin: Combach (1614), Jebb (1733), Bridges (1897); Latin/first English translation: Lindberg (1983 – see Bibliography).

Communia naturalium. Early 1260s.

Computus naturalium. A treatise on the calendar, written *c*.1263.

Opus Majus ('Great Work'). *c*.1266. The first of the series of three manuscripts produced in response to Pope Clement IV's request. Wide-ranging, covering error, philosophy, mathematics (including astrology, astronomy, the calendar, and music), optics, experimental science, and natural philosophy. Autographed manuscript in Vatican library. We know that the Vatican library held manuscripts shortly after it was written (because it was referred to by Witelo, who died *c*.1275), and in the fifteenth century, as there is a library lending record for the philosopher Pico della Mirandola. Various other manuscript copies, including one known to have been in John Dee's collection (now in Oxford's Bodleian Library). Latin editions: Combach (partial, 1614), Jebb (1733), Bridges (1900); first English translation: Robert Belle Burke, Professor of Latin at the University of Pennsylvania (1928, reprinted 1998 by Kessinger – see Bibliography).

Opus Minus ('Lesser Work'). *c.*1267. Latin edition: Brewer (1859 – see Bibliography).

Opus Tertium ('Third Work'). *c.*1267. Latin editions: Brewer (partial, 1859), Little (partial, 1912 – see Bibliography).

De speculis comburentibus ('On Burning Glasses'). 1260s–1270s. Four extant manuscripts, the earliest from around 1350 – only one is ascribed to Bacon, but David C. Lindberg in his annotated translation points out that, both stylistically and in subject matter, this attribution seems valid. Latin edition: Combach (1614); Latin/first English translation: Lindberg (1983 see Bibliography).

*Compendium studii philosophiae. c.*1273. Perhaps intended as an introduction to the never-to-be-written *Scriptum principale*, this contains strong criticism of the Franciscan and Dominican Orders, the papal court, and secular authorities. Single partial manuscript remains. Latin edition: Brewer (partial, 1859).

Compendium studii theologiae. His last work, written in the early 1290s. Latin edition: Rashdall (1911).

Undated Works

Breviloqium alkimiae (?) ('Short discussion of alchemy').

De balneis. Sadly no longer extant, a book on baths, written at the request of a friend.

Gasquet fragment. An unpublished but important fragment of Bacon's writing, described by historian F. A. Gasquet (see Bibliography). Probably the covering letter finally used for the *Opus majus.*

Greek Grammar. Latin edition: Cambridge University Press (1902).

Hebrew Grammar. Latin edition (partial): Cambridge University Press (1902).

Metaphysica.

Quaestiones. On assorted subjects. Effectively lecture notes in the form of questions and responses. Probably but not definitely

Bacon's. Appears to date from his time in Paris, as he comments 'If I could touch the Seine with my palm' in one of them. Contained in a huge single manuscript in Amiens, simply identified as number 406.

Radix mundi (?) ('Root of the World').

Scriptum Principale. Bacon's planned but never-written masterpiece, his encyclopedia of all natural science.

Secretum secretorum cum glossis et notulis Fratris Rogeri. Bacon's edition of the pseudo-Aristotelian 'Secret of Secrets'.

Speculum alchemiae (?) ('The Mirror of Alchemy').

Tractatus expositorius enigmatum alchemiae ('Treatise on the Obscurity of Alchemy').

Appendix I

Extract from *The Famous Historie of Fryer Bacon*

The legend of Roger Bacon had continued to grow during the three centuries between his death and the publication in the sixteenth century of the little book that is the *Historie*. The title page of the earliest known edition tells us that it is 'very pleasant and delightful to read' and that the copies were 'printed at London by E. A. for Francis Grove and are to be sold at his shop, at the upper end of Snow-Hill against the Saracen's Head'.

Bacon's legendary role is demonstrated beautifully in this story from the *Historie* (the paragraphing is mine).

How the king sent for Fryer Bacon, and of the wonderful things he shewed the king and queene

The king being in Oxfordshire, at a Noblemans house, was very desirous to see this famous fryer, for he had heard many times of his wondrous things that he had done by his art: therefore hee sent one for him to desire him to come to the court. Fryer Bacon kindly thanked the king by the messenger and said, that he was at the kings service, and would suddenly attend him: but sir, saith he (to the gentleman) I pray make you haste, or else I shall be two houres before you at court.

For all your learning (answered the gentleman) I can hardly believe this, for schollers, old-men and travellers, may lye by authority.

To strengthen your beliefe (said Fryer Bacon) I could presently shew you the last wench that you lay withall, but I will not at this time.

One is as true as the other (said the gentleman) and I would laugh to see either.

You shall see them both within these four houres, quoth the fryer, and therefore make what haste you can.

I will prevent that by my speed (said the gentleman) and with that rid his way: but he rode out of his way, as it should seem; for he had but five miles to ride, and yet was he better than three houres a riding them; so that Fryer Bacon by his art was with the king before he came.

The king kindly welcommed him, and said that hee long time had desired to see him; for he had as yet not heard of his life. Fryer Bacon answered him that fame had belide him, and given him that report that his poore studies had never deserved, for hee beleeved that art had many sonnes more excellent than himselfe was. The king commended him for his modesty, and told him, that nothing could become a wise man lesse than boasting: but yet withall he requested him now to be no niggard of his knowledge, but to shew his queene and him some of his skill.

I were worthy of neither art or knowledge (quoth Fryer Bacon), should I deny your majestie this small request: I pray seat yourselves, and you shall see presently what my poore skill can performe: the king, queene, and nobles sate them all down. They having done so, the fryer waved his wand, and presently was heard such excellent musicke that they were all amazed, for they all said they had never heard the like.

This is, said the fryer, to delight the sense of hearing, I will delight all your other sences ere you depart hence: so waving his wand againe, there was lowder musicke heard, and presently five dancers entred, the first like a court-laundresse, the second like a footman, the third like an usurer, the fourth like a prodigall, the fifth like a foole: these did divers excellent changes, so that they gave content to all the beholders, and having done their dance, they all vanished away in their order as they came in.

Thus feasted he two of their sences; then waved he his wand againe, and there was another kind of musicke heard, and whilest it was playing, there was sodainly before them a table richly covered in all sorts of delicates: then desired he the king and queene to taste of some certaine rare fruits that were on the table, which they and the nobles present did, and were very highly pleased with the taste; they being satisfied, all vanished away on the sodaine.

Then waved he his wand againe, and sodainly there was such a smell, as if all the rich perfumes of the whole world had bin there prepared in the best manner that art could set them out: whilst hee feasted thus their smelling, he waved his wand againe and there came divers nations in sundry habits (as Russians, Polanders, Indians, Armenians) all bringing sundry kinds of furres, such as their countries yielded: all which they presented to the king and queene: these furres were so soft in the touch, that they highly pleased all those who handled them. Then after some odde fantasticke dances (after their countrey manner) they vanished away: then asked Fryer Bacon the king's majesty, if that hee desired any more of his skill?

The king answered that hee was fully satisfied for that time and that hee onely now thought of something that hee might bestow on him, that might partly satisfie the kindnesse that hee had received. Fryer Bacon said, that hee desired nothing so much as this majesties love, and if that he might be assured of that, hee would thinke himselfe happy in it:

For that (said the king) be thou ever sure of it, in token of which receive this jewell, and withall gave him a costly jewell from his necke.

The fryer did with great reverence thanke his majestie, and said: as your majesties vassall you shall ever finde me ready to do you service, your time of neede shall find it both beneficiall and delightfull. But amongst all these gentlemen, I see not the man that your grace did send for me by, sure he hath lost his way, or else met with some sport that detaines him so long, I promised to be here before him, and all this noble assembly can witnesse I am as good as my word: I heare him coming.

With that entered the gentleman all bedurted (for hee had rid through ditches, quagmires, plashes and waters, that hee was in a most pittifull case) he seeing the fryer there looked full angerly, and bid a poxe on all his devils, for they had led him out of his way, and almost drowned him.

Be not angry sir (said Fryer Bacon) here is an old friend of yours that hath more cause: for she hath tarried these three houres for you (with that hee pulled up the hangings, and behinde them stood a kitchen-mayde with a basting-ladle in her hand) now am I as good as my word with you: for I promised to helpe you to your sweetheart, how do you like this?

So ill, answered the gentleman, that I will be revenged of you.

Threaten not (said Fryer Bacon) least I do you more shame, and doe you take heed how you give schollers the lye againe: but because I know not how well you are stored with money at this time, I will bear your wenches charges home: with that she vanished away:

The king, queene, and all the company laughed to see with what shame this gentleman indured the sight of his greasie sweetheart, but the gentleman went away discontented. This done Fryer Bacon tooke his leave of the King and Queene, and received from them divers gifts (as well as thankes) for his art he shewed them.

Appendix II

Extracts from the *Opus majus*

The *Opus Majus*, Bacon's greatest extant work, is a huge book of over half a million words. These two extracts, from the 1928 translation by Robert Belle Burke, are included here to show how Bacon presented his material and to indicate his broad knowledge of scientific subjects. Some of the paragraph breaks are mine, as Bacon tended to write extremely long paragraphs.

On Geography

Bacon's geography, which he categorizes as part of mathematics, goes much further than his excellent grasp of using latitude and longitude to fix location and to project the spherical world onto a flat map. As this extract shows, he was also interested in the peoples of the places he mapped and in their social and political structures. This is not surprising, given Bacon's very utilitarian view of science – it was of obvious benefit to traders, politicians, and the Church to know just who and what they would be dealing with in a foreign land.

Beyond Russia to the north is the Hyperborean race, so named from the great mountains called Hyperborean. This race, owing to the healthfulness of the climate, lives in the woods, a race long-lived to a degree that they disdain death, of excellent habits, quiet and peaceful, harming no one and molested by no other nation. But others flee to this race as to a refuge. How it is possible for this region to be very temperate, I explained previously in treating of the characteristics of the localities of the world. Thus we have before us the notable northern regions in Europe.

The rites of these races are of different kinds. For the Pruseni, Curlandi, Livonii, Estonii, Semi-Galli, and Lencovi are pagans. The Alani no longer exist, because the Tartars invaded that country and drove the Cumani to Hungary. The Cumani are pagans, so likewise were the Alani, but they have been destroyed. The Rusceni are Christians, but schismatics following the Greek rite, but they do not speak the Greek tongue but the Sclavonian, which is one of the tongues spoken in many regions. For it is the language of Russia, Poland, Bohemia, and of many other nations.

The Tartars inhabit the land of the Alani or Cumani from the Danube almost to the remotest parts of the east; and the other nations bordering on them to the north and south have they subjugated for the most part. For some tribes are in the mountains in very well-protected places which they are unable to conquer, although these tribes are their neighbours, because they are unconquerable.

The Tanais River flows down from the very lofty Riphaen mountains in the north. At the end of Russia and Alania, where congregate merchants and others who have come from Hungary, Cassaria, Poland, and Russia, there is a village, where the river Tanais is crossed by boat. The Tanais at that place is about the width of the Seine in Paris. Beyond that river is upper Albania as far as yet another great river called Ethilia, four times larger than the Seine, and one of the larger rivers of the world, swelling in summer like the Nile. To the north the river is distant from the Tanais ten days' march, but toward the south they are far apart. For the Tanais falls into the Pontic Sea, and the Ethilia into the Caspian, and with many other rivers forms this sea. These rivers flow from Persia and from other localities. For the Pontic Sea, according to Pliny, is distant 380 miles from the Caspian.

In this land dwelt the Cumani, but the Tartars destroyed them all, just as they did on the other side of the Tanais as

far as the Danube as has been stated. The Tartars have countless herds of cattle and dwell in tents, having neither houses
nor fortified places except very rarely. One chief with his army
and his herds roams between the rivers, as, for example, between
the Danube and the Tanais, and a second chief between the
Tanais and the Ethilia, and so on eastward, because they have
always been divided by the pastures and the waters. From
January they begin to travel to the northern parts within the
rivers until August, and then they return toward the south on
account of the cold in winter. Toward the north the Ethilia is
distant from the province of Cassaria one month and three
days as the Tartars ride.

This land of the Tartars has between the Tanais and the
Ethilia certain tribes to the north. First is the Arumphean tribe
near the Riphaean mountains, which is similar in all respects
to the Hyperboreans. These two tribes are near the pole in
the north; but not so far north beyond the Tanais there is first
a tribe called Moxel, subject to the Tartars. They are still
purely pagan without law; they have no city but inhabit huts
in the forests. Their chief and many of them were slain in
Poland by the Poles, Alemanni, and Bohemians. For the Tartars
led them to war with the Poles. They strongly favour the Poles
and the Germans, still hoping to be freed by them from the
Tartar yoke.

If a trader comes among them he must give to the master
of the first house in which he is entertained his expenses
for the whole time he expects to remain there. For this is
the custom of that region. Next to these eastward is a tribe
called Merduim, subject to the Tartars. They are Saracens,
following the laws of Mahomet. After these comes the
Ethilia, a river before mentioned, which flows down from
greater Bulgaria, a land of which mention will be made
later.

To the south of this land of the Tartars beyond the Pontic

Sea are the Hiberi and the Georgians. In Georgia there is a metropolitan city called Thephelis, in which the preaching friars have a house. Beyond toward the east is the land of the Corasimini, but they have been destroyed by the Tartars. In these localities the Amazons used to dwell in ancient times, according to Pliny and the astronomer Ethicus. For the Amazons, as Ethicus states, were women leading a great army collected from women and without men. The Amazons, calling men to them at certain times of year, conceived; but they slew the male children when born, reserving the females, whose right breasts they cut off by art of surgery in their youth, that they might not be hindered by their breasts in shooting arrows.

On the Rainbow and the Experimental Method

Bearing in mind that the *Opus majus* was just a *persuasio* – a sales tool to encourage the pope to fund the real masterwork – this example goes into a surprising amount of detail, certainly requiring the level of understanding of an amateur astronomer. Clement IV must have had a sufficient interest in science to cope with this, or at least Bacon must have assumed he had. This is an example of Bacon both demonstrating his scientific method and presenting some original work – his theory of the rainbow was in advance of that of his inspiration, Robert Grosseteste, and the figure of 42° is a good approximation to measured values.

Since, moreover, we find colours and various figures similar to the phenomena in the air, namely, of the iris, corona, and streak, we are encouraged and greatly stimulated to grasp the truth in these phenomena that occur in the heavens. Further, let the experimenter take the required instrument and look through the openings in the instrument and find the altitude of the Sun over the horizon, and keeping the instrument immovable, let him turn in the opposite direction and look through the openings of the instrument until he sees the summit of the bow, and let him note the altitude of the rainbow above the horizon; and he will find that the higher the Sun's altitude is, the lower is that of the bow, and conversely. By this means he knows that the rainbow is always opposite the Sun, and that one line passes through the centre of the Sun, and through the centre of the observer's eye, and the centre of the circle of which the bow is an arc to the Sun's nadir, which is the point in the heavens opposite the centre of the Sun. As the extremity of this line toward the Sun is elevated above the horizon, the other is depressed, which passes through the centre of the bow, and conversely; just like the rule at the back of the astrolabe, one of whose ends is depressed as the other is elevated. The trained experimenter can test until he discovers the opposed altitude of the rainbow and of the Sun, namely, that beyond which there can be no appearance of the rainbow. He must then give his attention to the calculation of the altitude of the circles.

We must bear in mind that the horizon is a circle, and that at its centre an axis is raised to the starry heavens to the zenith of the observer's head, and let a circle pass through that point and through two parts of the horizon, as, for example, if we desire, through east and west, and let it pass beneath the Earth to the point opposite the zenith overhead. This circle is the circle of the altitude of the fixed star, and it passes through its body, for when the star rises above the horizon, we say that it ascends according to the degrees of that circle until it reaches the line of the meridian. Then the star is at its greatest altitude, and this circle intersects the horizon at right angles; and they divide each other into equal parts, and each is a great circle of the sphere. The altitude, then, of a fixed star above the horizon is the arc of this circle intercepted between the star and the limit of the horizon. But the altitude of Saturn and of the other planets must not be reckoned on a circle intersecting the horizon, but on a smaller and concentric circle, because the circle passing through the body of Saturn or of another lower planet does not pass through the extremity of the axis of the horizon, but through another point, lower in the axis, which is a point beneath the zenith overhead, and therefore this circle does not pass through the limits of the horizon, which is the circle *ab*, but through the circle concentric with it, through the circle *cd* [Bacon included a diagram of two concentric circles, the outer one labelled *ab* (*a* at the 'north pole' and *b* at the 'south pole') and the inner circle *cd*], and this circle of the altitude of Saturn passes through the body of Saturn, which in this circle is elevated above the horizon and depressed beneath it.

Moreover, the circle of Jupiter passes through a smaller concentric circle and through a point lower in the axis, beneath the zenith overhead, and similarly with regard to the other planets; so that the lower a body is, so much smaller a circle does it have passing through a lower point in the axis of the horizon, and intersecting a smaller circle concentric with the horizon. Although the statement made above is in accordance with the actual fact, yet in ordinary speech we do not distinguish those points in the axis from the zenith overhead, nor the circles equidistant from the horizon do we distinguish from the horizon itself, but we call them all horizons. We also reckon the circles of altitude all equal and regard them as passing through the zenith overhead, although they are unequal. And although for clearness I thus placed them all in the same surface, and because this can happen, yet in many cases it happens that they are in different surfaces and intersect one another in many ways.

Further, we must also consider that the visual ray is equidistant from the horizon and the circles concentric with it, and that therefore the arc of the circle of the altitude which is between the horizon and the visual ray must be noted, which is in accordance with the amount of elevation of the body of observer. But the altitude commonly taken of an object is said to be the arc of the circle of the altitude intercepted between the elevated object and the horizon, yet, strictly speaking, if the altitude of an object is taken, it is the arc of the circle of the altitude between the object and the visual ray; because the eye is not at the centre of the horizon, but is above the centre in the axis of the horizon; and therefore objects that are in the air and in the Moon are considered according to an altitude of this kind. For they have a difference in aspect because they are near the Earth, but the Sun and the other remoter bodies are not affected in this way, owing to their greater distance. For the amount of elevation of the observer has no sensible difference in regard to the remoteness of those bodies, but it bears a considerable relationship to those that are visible in the air, like comets and rainbows. From these statements, then, it is evident that the altitude of the rainbow, taken strictly, is the arc of its circle of altitude intercepted between the summit of the bow and the visual ray parallel to the horizon, which must be known because of what follows.

The experimenter, therefore, taking the altitude of the Sun and of the rainbow above the horizon, will find that the final altitude at which the rainbow can appear above the horizon is 42 degrees, and this is the maximum elevation of the rainbow. This elevation contains the arc between the summit of the bow and the visual ray, and this is its altitude, strictly speaking, although besides this there is the arc, which is between the ray and the limit of the horizon, through which the circle of the altitude of the bow passes. And the rainbow reaches this maximum elevation when the Sun is on the horizon, namely at sunrise or sunset; and also when it is near sunrise and sunset below the horizon, not up to the end of the evening twilight, nor up to the beginning of the morning twilight, but near sunrise and sunset, as has been said.

Then if moisture is ready in advance higher in the clouds, the gibbosity of the rainbow will appear, although the Sun is too far below the horizon, since his rays can reach vapours near the horizon. The experimenter, moreover, knows how to make the test, because when the Sun is at an altitude of 42 degrees the rainbow does not appear in the sky, expect that a small part of its blue gibbosity can appear near the horizon, if moisture is already present there. When the Sun rises higher, the rainbow can nowhere appear. Therefore Aristotle and Seneca state that in summer in the heat of the day the rainbow does not appear. The reason for this is because at the latitude of Paris the altitude of the Sun at noon of the equinox is 41 degrees and 12 minutes, the Sun at that time being at almost such an altitude that the rainbow cannot appear, and therefore a little later it must be elevated so much higher that at noon it is more than 42 degrees on the circle of altitude above the horizon, and therefore in the heat of the summer the rainbow does not occur at noon until the Sun descends to an altitude of less than 42 degrees.

Index